TWENTIETH-CENTURY ARTISTS ON ART

TWENTIETH-CENTURY ARTISTS ON ART

EDITED BY DORE ASHTON

PANTHEON BOOKS · NEW YORK

All rights reserved under International and Pan-American Copyright Conventions. Published in the United States by Pantheon Books, a division of Random House, Inc., New York, and simultaneously in Canada by Random House of Canada Limited, Toronto.

Ashton, Dore.
    Twentieth-century artists on art

    Bibliography: p.
Includes index.
    1. Art, Modern—20th century.   2. Artists—
Psychology.   3. Artists—Biography.   I. Title.
N6490.A79   1985   709'.04   84-22676
ISBN 0-394-52276-1
ISBN 0-394-73489-0 (pbk.)

Since this copyright page cannot accommodate all permissions acknowledgements for both pictures and text, they appear along with the Source List on pages 272–287.

BOOK DESIGN BY GINA DAVIS

Manufactured in the United States of America

FIRST EDITION

CONTENTS

FOREWORD

When Robert Goldwater and Marco Treves edited *Artists on Art*, they were obliged to limit their edition to artists born no later than 1890, remarking that "the younger men deserve another book." This, I hope, is the other book, although like my predecessors, I must lament the restrictions of space.

No one knows exactly how many artists there are in the twentieth century. The *Oxford Companion to Modern Art* mentions more than four thousand artists of note, and another four thousand could probably have been added. My task has been to select artists who are known to many people in many countries and to try to find their characteristic recorded thoughts. If not all notable artists are here, there are various reasons. Some artists have remained resolutely mute about their work (I think for example of the noted figure painter Balthus). Others have been so laconic that nothing could be wrested from various articles or studies of their life's work. Still others have suffered from a tendency to unintelligibility. Given these circumstances, some omissions must be counted as necessary.

I have not been as strict as Goldwater and Treves about birth dates, and I have included artists born up to the end of the Second World War, but on the whole, this anthology is intended to cover artists who are firmly established in the exhibiting world.

I have mostly omitted artists who are represented in the Goldwater and Treves anthology, but I have included a preliminary section with statements by modern masters made after the earlier anthology was edited. After much searching, I had to reluctantly omit artists of the Orient, whose statements are rarely translated into Western languages (and when they are, are badly translated). I especially regret the absence of vigorous contemporary Japanese artists and hope they will understand.

Concerning classification: Many modern artists have moved about considerably in their lifetimes and it is difficult to place them in terms of nationality. I have tried to simplify matters by categorizing them in the countries where they spent the major part of their working life.

All translations in the book are mine unless otherwise noted.

I wish to thank everyone who graciously consented to give permissions, and to thank particularly Clive Phillpot, Director of the Library of the Museum of Modern Art in New York, and his staff; and Geurt Imanse, Director of the Library of the Stedelijk Museum in Amsterdam, for their invaluable help.

EARLY
MODERN
MASTERS
IN STATE-
MENTS
AFTER 1940

PABLO PICASSO *Portrait of Igor Stravinsky.*
1920. Pencil on gray paper. 24⅜ x 19⅛".

PABLO PICASSO

(1881–1973)

Son of a painter, José Ruiz Blasco, Picasso took his mother's name—Picasso—around the time of his first exploratory visit to Paris in 1900. After two more visits, the Barcelona-trained painter settled in Paris in 1904. There he quickly became the center of a lively band of poets and painters, among them Max Jacob and Guillaume Apollinaire, intent on establishing an antitraditional aesthetic. Picasso's shifts in style—from the muted nostalgia of his figure paintings during the so-called Blue Period; to the figure studies inspired by his perusal of both archaic and primitive cultures, known as the Rose Period; to his invention of a pictorial language, together with Georges Braque, known as Cubism—were attentively followed by other artists in Paris during the years 1904–1914. The interruption of the First World War led Picasso to Rome to design costumes and sets for the Ballets Russes managed by Diaghilev. He participated for a time in a revival of classicism during the early 1920s, and in the late 1920s showed an interest in Surrealism. In the 1930s, he returned to Cubist principles for his great mural protest against Franco's Fascist insurrection, Guernica *(1937). After the Second World War, Picasso settled in the South of France, where he produced innumerable sculptures, ceramics, paintings, drawings, etchings, lithographs, and linoleum-block prints. His fecundity left an indelible mark on the entire evolution of twentieth-century art.*

No doubt, it is useful for an artist to know all the forms of art which have preceded or which accompany his. That is a sign of strength if it is a question of looking for a stimulus or recognizing mistakes he must avoid. But he must be very careful not to look for models. As soon as one artist takes another as model, he is lost. There is no other point of departure than reality. Why should I copy this owl, this sea urchin? Why should I try to imitate nature? I might just as well try to trace a perfect circle. What I have to do is utilize as best I can the ideas which objects suggest to me, connect, fuse, and color in my way the shadows they cast within me, illumine them from the inside. And since of necessity my vision is quite different from that of the next man, my painting will interpret things in an entirely different manner even though it makes use of the same elements.   *[c. 1948]*

The secret of many of my deformations—which many people do not understand—is that there is an interaction, an intereffect between the lines in a painting: one line attracts the other and at the point of maximum attraction the lines curve in toward the attracting point and form is altered.

This change through attraction, that's what the collector never sees and will never understand in a painting. And often one does a painting really for a corner of the canvas that no one looks at.

One does a whole painting for one peach and people think just the opposite—that that particular peach is but a detail.   *[c. 1954]*

I consider a work of art as the product of calculations, calculations that are frequently unknown to the author himself. It is exactly like the carrier pigeon, calculating his return to the loft. The calculation that precedes intelligence. Since then we have invented the compass, and radar, which enable even fools to return to their starting point. . . . Or else we must suppose, as Rimbaud said, that it is the other self inside us who calculates.
                                                               [c. 1955]

Braque always said that the only thing that counts, in painting, is the intention, and it's true. What counts is what one wants to do, and not what one does. That's what's important. In Cubism, in the end what was important is what one *wanted* to do, the intention one had. And *that* one cannot paint.   *[c. 1963]*

Something holy, that's it. It's a word something like that we should be able to use, but people would take it in the wrong way. You ought to be able to say that a painting is as it is, with its capacity to move us, because it is as though it were touched by God. But people would think it a sham. And yet that is what's nearest to the truth.

You can search for a thousand years, and you will find nothing. Everything can be explained scientifically today. Except *that*. You can go to the moon or walk under the sea, or anything else you like, but painting remains painting because it eludes such investigation. It remains there like a question. And it alone gives the answer.   *[c. 1963]*

What I find horrible nowadays is that people are always trying to find a personality for themselves. Nobody bothers about what you might call a painter's ideal . . . the kind that's always existed (I say ideal because that's what comes nearest to it). No. They couldn't care less about that.

All they're trying to do is to make the world a present of their personality. It's horrible.

Besides, if you're trying to find something, it means you haven't got it. And if you find it simply by looking for it, that means it's false.

For my part, I can't do anything else but what I am doing.   *[c. 1965]*

HENRI MATISSE

(1869–1954)

After a classical education, Matisse became a law clerk, but soon abandoned the law, in 1891, to study art in Paris with the unconventional teacher Gustave Moreau. He admired the work of Gauguin, Van Gogh, and Cézanne and, toward 1901, began to heighten his colors. By 1905, when he and his friends caused a sensation with their brilliantly colored paintings at the Salon d'Automne, earning from critics the unflattering title of "Fauves" (or wild beasts), Matisse was already considered a leader in the avant-garde. In 1908 his "Notes of a Painter" clearly delineated his view of his role as a draftsman and colorist. It was widely cited in Europe and Russia and established Matisse as a major influence. From this time until his death, he remained one of the major figures in European painting. Matisse was also celebrated as one of the century's most accomplished sculptors. Moreover, in designing the Chapel of the Rosary (1950–1951) in Vence, France, he developed a decorative scheme of sublime unity, using murals, stained-glass windows, and tiles. His last works were composed of pasted cut-outs made from papers he colored himself (he said he cut into color directly, using his scissors as a sculptor used his chisel).

I can say nothing of my feeling about space which is not already expressed in my paintings. Nothing could be clearer than what you can see on this wall: this young woman whom I painted thirty years ago . . . this "bouquet of flowers" . . . this "sleeping woman" which date from these last few years, and behind you, this definitive plan of a stained-glass window made of colored paper cut-outs.

From *Bonheur de Vivre*—I was thirty-five then—to this cut-out—I am eighty-two—I have not changed; not in the way my friends mean who want to compliment me, no matter what, on my good health, but because all this time I have looked for the same things, which I have perhaps realized by different means.

I had no other ambition when I made the Chapel. In a very restricted space—the breadth is five meters—I wanted to inscribe, as I had done so far in paintings of fifty centimeters or one meter, a spiritual space; that is, a space whose dimensions are not limited even by the existence of the objects represented.

You must not say that I re-created space starting from the object when I "discovered" the latter: I never left the object. The object is not interesting in itself. It's the environment which creates the object. Thus I have worked all my life before the same objects which continued to give me the force of reality by engaging my spirit toward everything that these objects had gone through for me and with me. A glass of water with a flower is different from a glass of water and a lemon. The object is an actor: a good actor can have a part in ten different plays; an object can play a different role in ten different pictures. The object is not taken alone, it evokes an ensemble of elements. You reminded me of the table I painted isolated in a garden? . . . Well, it was representative of a whole open-air atmosphere in which I had lived.

The object must act powerfully on the imagination; the artist's feeling expressing itself through the object must make the object worthy of interest: it says only what it is made to say.

On a painted surface I render space to the sense of sight: I make of it a color limited by a drawing. When I use paint, I have a feeling of quantity-surface of color which is necessary to me, and I modify its contour in order to determine my feeling clearly in a definitive way. (Let's call the first action "to paint" and the second "to draw.") In my case, to paint and to draw are one. I choose my quantity of colored surface and I make it conform to my feeling of the drawing, like the sculptor molds clay by modifying the ball which he first made and afterward elicits his feeling from it.

Look at this stained-glass window again: here is a dugong—an easily recognizable fish, it is in the Larousse—and, above, a sea animal in the form of algae. Around are begonias.

This Chinese soldier on the mantelpiece is expressed by a color whose shape determines its degree of effectiveness.

This fellow [the artist turns it between his fingers]—who is turquoise and aubergine as no soldier has ever been—would be destroyed if he were dressed in colors taken from material reality. To invented colors whose "drawing" determines the contours is added the artist's feeling to perfect the object's meaning. Everything here is necessary. This brown spot, which represents the ground on which one imagines the figure, gives the turquoise and aubergine an atmospheric existence which their intensity could make them lose.

The painter chooses his color in the intensity and depth which suit him, as the musician chooses the timbre and intensity of his instruments. Color does not command drawing, it harmonizes with it.

"Vermilion doesn't do everything . . . " said Othon F[riesz] with bitterness. Neither must color simply "clothe" the form: it must constitute it.

You ask me if my cut-outs are an end of my researches? . . . My researches don't seem to me to be limited yet. The cut-out is what I have now found the simplest and most direct way to express myself. One must study an object a long time to know what its sign is. Yet in a composition the object becomes a new sign which helps to maintain the force of the whole. In a word, each work of art is a collection of signs invented during the picture's execution to suit the needs of their position. Taken out of the composition for which they were created, these signs have no further use.

This is why I have never tried to play chess although it was suggested to me by friends who thought they knew me well. I told them: "I can't play with signs that never change. This bishop, this king, this queen, this castle mean nothing to me. But if you were to put little figures which look like so-and-so or such a one, people whose life we know, then I could play; but still inventing a meaning for each pawn in the course of each game."

Thus the sign for which I forge an image has no value if it doesn't harmonize with other signs, which I must determine in the course of my invention and which are completely peculiar to it. The sign is determined at the moment I use it and for the object of which it must form a part. For this reason I cannot determine in advance signs which never change, and which would be like writing: that would paralyze the freedom of my invention.

There is no separation between my old pictures and my cut-outs, except that with greater completeness and abstraction, I have attained a form filtered to its essentials and of the object which I used to present in the complexity of its space, I have preserved the sign which suffices and which is necessary to make the object exist in its own form and in the totality for which I conceived it.

I have always sought to be understood and, while I was taken to task by critics or colleagues, I thought they were right, assuming I had not been clear enough to be understood. This assumption allowed me to work my whole life without hatred and even without bitterness toward criticism, regardless of its source. I counted solely on the clarity of expression of my work to gain my ends. Hatred, rancor, and the spirit of vengeance are useless baggage to the artist. His road is difficult enough for him to cleanse his soul of everything which could make it more so.   *[1951]*

JOAN MIRÓ (in collaboration with
the potter Artigas)   *Femme et Oiseau.*
1962. Ceramic. 126 x 23⅝ x 18″.

JOAN MIRÓ

(1893–1983)

*Miró studied in his native Barcelona, and the paintings in his first one-man show in
1918 reflected his interest in Catalan rural life. In 1919 he visited Paris and was
for a while influenced by his friend Picasso's Cubism. However, when he settled in
Paris in the early 1920s, he shifted to the Surrealist group. Miró's imagination was
released by his exposure to the Surrealist idea of a creative unconscious, and for the
rest of his life he strived to remain true to an intuitive or unconscious impulse. His
fantasy led him to combine both abstract and figurative signs in paintings, sculptures,
prints, and drawings throughout his career. Like other twentieth-century masters,
Miró explored many media and worked on large commissions, including murals for
Harvard University and two large ceramic walls for the UNESCO building in
Paris.*

The spectacle of the sky overwhelms me. I'm overwhelmed when I see, in an immense sky, the crescent of the moon, or the sun. There are, in my pictures, tiny forms in huge empty spaces. Empty spaces, empty horizons, empty plains—everything which is bare has always greatly impressed me.

When I began, the painters who made a strong impression on me were Van Gogh, Cézanne, the Douanier Rousseau. When I loved the Douanier Rousseau, I already loved popular art. The older I grow, the greater importance this art has for me. A hayfork well carved by a peasant is very important to me.

Immobility strikes me. This bottle, this glass, a big stone on a deserted beach—these are motionless things, but they set loose great movements in my mind. I don't feel this with a human being who changes place all the time in an idiotic way. People who go bathing on a beach and who move about touch me much less than the immobility of a pebble. (Motionless things become grand, much grander than moving things.) Immobility makes me think of great spaces in which movements take place which do not stop at a given moment, movements which have no end. It is, as Kant said, the immediate irruption of the infinite in the finite. A pebble which is a finite and motionless object suggests to me not only movements, but movements without end. This is translated, in my canvases, by forms resembling sparks flying out of the frame as out of a volcano.

As there is no horizon line nor indication of depth, they are displaced in depth. They are displaced also in plane, because a color or a line leads fatally to a displacement of the angle of vision. Inside the large forms, small forms move.

What I am seeking, in fact, is a motionless movement, something equivalent to what is called the eloquence of silence, or what St. John of the Cross meant by the words, I believe, of dumb music.

I begin my pictures under the effect of a shock which I feel and which makes me escape from reality. The cause of this shock may be a tiny thread sticking out of the canvas, a drop of water falling, this print made by my finger on the shining surface of this table.

In any case, I need a point of departure, even if it's only a speck of dust or a flash of light. This form begets a series of things, one thing giving birth to another thing.

And so a bit of thread can set a world in motion. I start from something considered dead and arrive at a world. And when I put a title to it, it becomes even more alive.

In a picture, it should be possible to discover new things every time you see it. But you can look at a picture for a week together and never think of it again. You can also look at a picture for a second and think of it all your life. For me, a picture should be like sparks. It must dazzle like the beauty

of a woman or a poem. It must have radiance, it must be like those stones
which Pyrenean shepherds use to light their pipes.

I feel the need of attaining the maximum of intensity with the minimum of
means. It is this which has led me to give my painting a character of even
greater bareness.

My tendency towards bareness and simplification has been practiced in
three fields: modeling, colors, and the figuration of the personages.

In 1935, in my pictures, space and forms were still modeled. There was
still chiaroscuro in my painting. But, little by little, all that has gone. Round
about 1940, modeling and chiaroscuro were completely eliminated.

A modeled form is less striking than one which is not. Modeling prevents
shock and limits movement to the visual depth. Without modeling or chiaroscuro depth is limitless: movement can stretch to infinity.

Little by little, I've reached the stage of using only a small number of
forms and colors. It's not the first time that painting has been done with a
very narrow range of colors. The frescoes of the tenth century are painted
like this. For me, they are magnificent things.   *[1958]*

P I E T   M O N D R I A N

(1872–1944)

*Mondrian began his career as a landscape painter after obtaining academic training
in Amsterdam. Toward 1908, he began to lighten his palette and work in a neo-
Impressionist manner until, in 1911, he took a studio in Paris and began a serious
study of Cubism. Mondrian's approach to Cubist principles soon led him far from
figurative allusion. By 1914, when he returned to Holland, he had already reduced
landscape motifs to their geometric essentials. In 1917 he wrote his aesthetic credo,
calling his new style Neoplasticism, and with Theo van Doesburg founded the de Stijl
group. Mondrian's austere white canvases, with their vertical and horizontal lines
and sparing use of primary colors, were important to the burgeoning schools of
nonobjective artists, and were also influential in the fields of architecture and modern
design. In 1938 Mondrian moved from Paris, where he had been living since 1919,
to London, and in 1940 he settled in New York. There, he opened a new chapter in
his theoretical exploration of line and color, composing works reflecting the urban
rhythm of New York and its contemporary jazz.*

Not everyone realizes that in all plastic art, even in the most naturalistic
work, the natural form and color are always, to some extent, transformed.
Actually while this may not be directly perceived, the tension of line and

form as well as the intensity of color are always increased. Plastic experience demonstrates that the natural appearance of things is not to be established in its essential realism, but must be transformed in order to evoke aesthetic sensation.

In the course of centuries, the culture of plastic art has taught us that this transformation is actually the beginning of the abstraction of natural vision, which in modern times manifests itself as abstract art. Although abstract art has developed through the abstraction of the natural aspect, nevertheless in its present evolution it is more concrete because it makes use of pure form and pure color.

Consciousness of the necessity of abstraction in plastic art was developed slowly. Originally it was practiced intuitively. Only after centuries of increasing transformation of the natural aspect, more apparent abstraction emerged, until finally plastic art was freed from the particular characteristics of subject and object. This liberation is of the greatest importance. For plastic art reveals that particular characteristics veil the pure expression of form, color, and relationships. In plastic art, form and color are the essential expressive means. Their properties and mutual relationships determine the general expression of a work. Abstraction not only establishes form and color more objectively but also reveals their properties more clearly. Thus we can see that the abstraction of form and color merely "modifies" a work of art, but that abstract art, even as naturalistic art, must create the general expression by means of the composition. Through the composition and other plastic factors, it is possible for a naturalistic work of art to have a more universal expression than a work of abstract art which is lacking in the proper use of these factors.

We come to see that the principal problem in plastic art is not to avoid the representation of objects, but to be as objective as possible. The name *nonobjective* art must have been created with a view to the object, that is in another order of ideas. Plastic art reveals that the principal expression of a work of art is dependent on our subjective vision, which offers the major obstacle to objective representation of reality. Objective vision—as far as possible—is the principal claim of all plastic art. If objective vision were possible, it would give us a true image of reality.

For centuries, our vision has been increasingly enlarged through the development of life, science, and technology. Consequently it has become possible to see more objectively. However, intuitively, plastic art has always aimed at the universal expression of reality. All plastic art establishes this expression through a dynamic movement of forms and colors. But abstract art, in opposition to naturalistic art, can do this more clearly and in conformity with modern times. It must be stated, however, that the judgment of a work of art depends on the individual vision of it. What may be clear for some one may appear vague to another. This fact explains the existence of different tendencies in the same epoch. Abstract art manifests clearly the conception and feelings which give birth to a work of art as well as the laws which dictate its creation. Consequently, it is evident that in modern times it has become possible to study and analyze these laws more exactly.

If we study the culture of plastic art during the course of centuries, we come to see that abstract art is a product of that culture. It becomes apparent that modern art, while coinciding with all modern progress, has developed out of the art of the past through practice and experience. We see the culture of plastic art as *consistently progressive;* changes in tendencies follow one another in logical succession. Periods of progress and periods of regression or standstill produce an increasing development of expression toward a more direct representation of the essential content of plastic art. The periods of regression and standstill act as negative factors in the course of the general progress of plastic art. *[1941]*

Reality manifests itself as constant and objective—independent of us, but as changeable in space and time. Consequently, its reflection in us contains both properties.

Mixed up in our mind, these *properties are confused* and we do not have a proper image of reality.

This fact explains the multiple conceptions, and, in art, the so different expressions.

The purer the artists' "mirror" is, the more true reality reflects in it.

Overseeing the historical culture of art, we must conclude that the mirror only slowly is purified. Time producing this purifying shows a gradual more constant and objective image of reality. *[c. 1943]*

FERNAND LÉGER

(1881–1955)

Born in Normandy, Léger was apprenticed to an architect in Caen from 1887 to 1889 and worked as a draftsman in Paris until 1903, when he decided to study painting. By 1909 he was experimenting with the compositional principles of Cubism, although he preferred curvilinear configurations to the angular forms of Braque and Picasso. After being gassed during the First World War, Léger returned to Paris, became associated with the purist ideals put forward by the architect Le Corbusier, and for a time painted machinelike images in rudimentary colors. Leger's interest in social ideals soon brought him to deal with the human figure in an urban environment, in a vigorous style that incorporated the tubular forms, condensed spaces, and monumental scale of his earlier period. He spent the Second World War in the United States, where he taught and where he painted groups of cyclists, and then returned to France. Léger's powerful imagery and his use of bright, flat colors strongly influenced both graphic designers and fine artists in the United States and Europe.

The feat of superbly imitating a muscle, as Michelangelo did, or a face, as Raphael did, created neither progress nor a hierarchy in art. Because these artists of the sixteenth century imitated human forms, they were not superior to the artists of the high periods of Egyptian, Chaldean, Indochinese, Roman, and Gothic art who interpreted and stylized form but did not imitate it.

On the contrary, art consists of inventing and not copying. The Italian Renaissance is a period of artistic decadence. Those men, devoid of their predecessors' inventiveness, thought they were stronger as imitators—that is false. Art must be free in its inventiveness, it must raise us above too much reality. This is its goal, whether it is poetry or painting.

The plastic life, the picture, is made up of harmonious relationships among volumes, lines, and colors. These are the three forces that must govern works of art. If, in organizing these three essential elements harmoniously, one finds that objects, elements of reality, can enter into the composition, it may be better and may give the work more richness. But they must be subordinated to the three essential elements mentioned above.

Modern work thus takes a point of view directly opposed to academic work. Academic work puts the subject first and relegates pictorial values to a secondary level, if there is room.

For us others, it is the opposite. Every canvas, even if nonrepresentational, that depends on harmonious relationships of the three forces—color, volume, and line—is a work of art.

I repeat, if the object can be included without shattering the governing structure, the canvas is enriched.

Sometimes these relationships are merely decorative when they are abstract. But if *objects* figure in the composition—free objects with a genuine plastic value—pictures result that have as much variety and profundity as any with an imitative subject.   *[1950]*

1900-1920

AUSTRIA

OSKAR KOKOSCHKA

(1886–1980)

During his student years (1904–1909) Kokoschka was strongly influenced by Gustav Klimt's Art Nouveau symbolism. But a violent Expressionist impetus was revealed in two plays he wrote that scandalized Vienna in 1909, sending him off first to Switzerland and then to Germany, where Herwarth Walden, the avant-garde writer and art dealer, welcomed him to the Sturm group of artists and poets. Kokoschka's portraits were exceptionally vivid, capturing the psychological character of his sitters. In later years Kokoschka painted landscapes and views of cities in a more tender but still Expressionist manner.

How do I define a work of art? It is not an asset in the stock-exchange sense, but a man's timid attempt to repeat the miracle that the simplest peasant girl is capable of at any time, that of magically producing life out of nothing.

[1936]

"Man know thyself," the device of ancient Greek philosophy, has guided the European whenever he proved himself mature enough to realize that this, the power of reasoning, was all he had received from the hands of the gods. The loss of free will to determine our own fate has led us into a dead end where we have no choice. We have to fit ourselves into the artificial master-plan of mechanical society in order to escape *bellum omnium contra omnes* or the Third Total War.

[1947]

I myself see no cause to retrace my steps. I shall not weary of testifying by the means given to me by nature and expressed in my art, in which only vision is fundamental, not theories. I consider myself responsible, not to society, which dictates fashion and taste suited to its environment and its period, but to youth, to the coming generations, which are left stranded in a blitzed world, unaware of the soul trembling in awe before the mystery of life. I dread the future, when the growth of the inner life will be more and more hampered by a too speedy adaption to a mechanically conceived environment, when all human industry is to be directed to fit in with the blueprints. . . . For the growth of the inner life can never be brought into any scientific formula, whatever the technician and the scientist of the soul may try. The life of the soul is expressed by man in his art. . . . The mystery of the soul is like that of a closed door. When you open it, you see something which was not there before.

[1948]

The difference between experience and all desiccated theory is that, so to speak, the this-worldly embraces the other-worldly: A moment, in the Beyond, reappears as infinity. The torpor of human impulses is a necessary background to the divine shaft of light, as silence is broken by a cry or as dull habit is swept away by the unexpected and unpredicted.   *[1953]*

Let us be clear to begin with that I am content with the world as it is and must be, and would not change it for the moon. Even a successful moon landing would not, I feel sure, make much difference to our world. Only experience can shake a man out of his lethargy, as it shows that life generally turns out contrary to plan.   *[1961]*

EGON SCHIELE

(1890–1918)

Schiele's early work was strongly marked by his admiration for the great Austrian master Gustav Klimt, whose remarkable draftsmanship Schiele studied closely. By the time he was in his mid-twenties, however, Schiele had come forward with a distinctive drawing style of his own, and had called attention to himself through the extremely erotic character of his work. A term in prison for alleged pornographic practices sobered and embittered the young artist, whose last works were somber and magnificent portraits. He died of influenza during the epidemic that ravaged Europe immediately after the First World War.

I have become aware: earth breathes, smells, listens, feels in all its little parts; it adds to itself, couples itself, falls to pieces, and finds itself, enjoys what life is, and seeks the logical philosophy of all, all in all; days and years of all transitoriness, as far as one wishes and is able to think, as far as the spirit of beings is with great contents; through our air, our light, [the earth] has become something or many things, even to creators who are necessary, and has partially perished, consumed in itself, back into itself again, and begins the smaller or greater cycle, everything that I want to call divine germinates anew and brings [forth] and creates, out of the power which few see, a creature.

The transitoriness of the material is determined in the sense of an existence; a sure becoming and passing away, a coming; life, in which concept one should understand the endless disintegration which, however, can be kept in life through organic means, yes, [life] can become retroactive, far back, so that it, by these means, can give no complete death.

There was, is, and will be the old or the new primal spirit, which wants, which out of something, out of unions, out of interminglings, must bring

EGON SCHIELE *Seated Girl with Clasped/Hands*. 1918. Charcoal on paper. 18⅛ x 11¾".

forth, must create; the real great Mother of all, of everything similar but still separate, who wills, and so was, is, and will be the wish always out of these our eternal means, to be able to create the most manifold human beings, animals, plants, living creatures in general, as soon as the physics is present, just so soon does the common will of the world exist.

I possess the immediate means within myself that can [portray by drawing], in order to record, to wish to fathom, to invent, to discover, with means within myself, which already have the great power to kindle themselves, to burn themselves up and to shine like a thought out of the eternal light, and to glow into the darkest eternities of our little world, which consists of only so few elements.

All disguises for us are, anyway, for naught, since they conceal us, instead of having the urge to interweave with other organs.

When I see myself completely, I shall have to see myself, and will have to know what I want, not only what goes on within myself, but also how far I have the ability to see what means are mine, out of what puzzling substances I am made, out of how much of the more, what I recognize, what I have so far recognized within myself.

I see myself evaporate and breathe forth stronger and stronger; the oscillations of my astral light become swifter, sharper, simpler, and like a great recognition of the world.

So I bring forth out of myself always more, always something further, in endlessly brighter shining, as far as love, which is everything, enriches me in this way and leads me to this to which I am instinctively drawn; which I want to tear into myself, so that I may create again a new thing which I, in spite of myself, have perceived.

My existence, my decay, transposed to enduring values, must bring, sooner or later, my strength to other strongly or more strongly developed beings, like a believing revelation of religion.

The farthest away will notice me, the more distant ones will look at me, and my negative ones [unbelievers in him] will live by my hypnosis!

I am so rich that I must give myself away.   *[1911]*

CZECHOSLOVAKIA

F R A N T I Š E K   K U P K A

(1871–1957)

Trained in his native Czechoslovakia by artists and aestheticians with a strong interest in spiritual symbolism, Kupka's earliest essays in pure, abstract art around 1912 were attempts to render the state of his soul in terms equivalent to music. Although he was associated in Paris with the group Section d'Or, Kupka's emphasis on spiritual analogues in painting brought him closer to the parallel philosophy of Wassily Kandinsky, and is an evolution of ideas nurtured in Czechoslovakia, Austria, and Russia rather than in France, where he worked for almost half a century.

CREATION—THE BASIC PROBLEM IN PAINTING

Once you realize that it is impossible to capture the character of the various manifestations of nature by pictorial means, and that an interpretation based on imagination is equally erroneous, you will not find yourself facing a gaping void as you might have feared.

The art of painting is essentially that of making an appeal to read the various *combinations* of plastic signs and light and color values. Evidence given about a theme or the communication of an observation only becomes art through the subjective form bestowed on natural phenomena by the artist.

The creative ability of an artist is manifested only if he succeeds in transforming natural phenomena into "another reality." This part of the creative process conceived as an independent element, if conscious and developed, hints at the possibility of *creating* a painting. It can thus charm or move the onlooker without disturbing the organic color of natural phenomena.   *[1921]*

MARCEL DUCHAMP

(1887–1968)

Both Cubism and Futurism were assimilated by Duchamp before his definitive leap into the role of challenger to all conventions in 1913, the year his Nude Descending the Staircase *made a sensation in New York's Armory Show. As he relates in the talk excerpted below, which he gave at the Museum of Modern Art in New York in 1961, he wished to prevent art from becoming a habit-forming drug, and he wished to "carry the mind of the spectator toward other regions more verbal." Duchamp's battle with sheer visual aestheticism, inaugurated during his Dada period, has funded many small movements within modern art. It has also opened the way both to artists who wished to emphasize the role of intellect in the making of modern art, and to those who wished to demolish convention, making use of wit and humor. Willem de Kooning called him "a one-man movement." Duchamp's influence has remained steady in the United States, where he settled in 1915.*

In 1913 I had the happy idea to fasten a bicycle wheel to a kitchen stool and watch it turn.

A few months later I bought a cheap reproduction of a winter evening landscape, which I called *Pharmacy* after adding two small dots, one red and one yellow, in the horizon.

In New York in 1915 I bought at a hardware store a snow shovel on which I wrote "in advance of the broken arm."

It was around that time that the word "readymade" came to mind to designate this form of manifestation.

A point which I want very much to establish is that the choice of these "readymades" was never dictated by aesthetic delectation.

This choice was based on a reaction of visual indifference with at the same time a total absence of good or bad taste . . . in fact a complete anaesthesia.

One important characteristic was the short sentence which I occasionally inscribed on the "readymade."

That sentence instead of describing the object like a title was meant to carry the mind of the spectator toward other regions more verbal.

Sometimes I would add a graphic detail of presentation which, in order to satisfy my craving for alliterations, would be called "readymade aided."

At another time wanting to expose the basic antinomy between art and readymades I imagined a "reciprocal readymade": Use a Rembrandt as an ironing board!

I realized very soon the danger of repeating indiscriminately this form of expression and decided to limit the production of "readymades" to a small number yearly. I was aware at that time that, for the spectator even more than for the artist, art is a habit forming drug and I wanted to protect my "readymades" against such contamination.

Another aspect of the "readymade" is its lack of uniqueness . . . the replica of a "readymade" delivering the same message; in fact nearly every one of the "readymades" existing today is not an original in the conventional sense.

A final remark to this egomaniac's discourse:

Since the tubes of paint used by the artist are manufactured and ready-made products we must conclude that all the paintings in the world are "readymades aided" and also works of assemblage.   *[1961]*

J A C Q U E S   L I P C H I T Z

(1891–1973)

As Lipchitz points out in the following excerpt from his autobiography, little Cubist sculpture besides Picasso's own had been produced when Lipchitz adopted the idiom during the First World War. Only Henri Laurens and Alexander Archipenko had attempted to adapt the notion of intersecting planes visible in Cubist painting to the less tractable medium of sculpture. Lipchitz's success in opening his volumes quite possibly led the way to the work in later decades by Henry Moore and Barbara Hepworth.

There is one thing I would like to emphasize in relation to my move from the curvilinear style to a more geometric style and then to Cubism. At this time, late in 1913, I had seen little sculpture that could be considered purely Cubist. In fact, not very much existed, with the exception, perhaps, of one or two experiments that Picasso made in translating collage into three dimensions. I was really acquainted with Cubism only in terms of the paintings of Picasso, Braque, Juan Gris, and others. Thus, I had to work toward Cubism in sculpture entirely on my own; and perhaps the greatest revelation that led me in this direction was the importance of light for sculpture. I suddenly discovered that volume in sculpture is created by light and shadow. Volume is light. In a smoothly rounded or curvilinear sculpture the light washes over the surface and may even diminish or destroy the sense of volume, the sense of the third dimension. When the forms of the sculpture are angular, when the surface is broken by deep interpenetrations and contrasts, light can work to bring out the truly sculptural qualities. As I said, this was a tremendous revelation and it has affected my attitude toward sculpture ever since. At various times, I have experimented with smoothly rounded forms, but I always find myself returning to angularity, inter-penetration, and contrasts of geometric shapes. . . .

I have never believed that African primitive art had much real influence in the development of Cubism. Certainly Picasso, Braque, and others, in-cluding myself, saw and were intrigued by examples of primitive art in the Ethnological Museum; and Picasso and Braque, particularly in their proto-Cubist paintings, used some details from primitive art, as in the masklike heads in the *Demoiselles d'Avignon*. But the greatest source for Cubism was unquestionably in the late works of Cézanne; you can see immediately the relationship between these works and the first pre-Cubist paintings of Braque and Picasso. . . .

I remember in 1915, when I was deeply involved in Cubist sculpture but was still in many ways not certain of what I was doing, I had a visit from the writer Jules Romains, and he asked me what I was trying to do. I answered, "I would like to make an art as pure as a crystal." And he answered in a slightly mocking way, "What do you know about crystals?" At first I was upset by this remark and his attitude, but then, as I began to think about it, I realized that I knew nothing about crystals except that they were a form of inorganic life and that this was not what I wanted to make. In my Cubist sculpture I always wanted to retain the sense of *organic* life, of humanity.   *[1972]*

FRANCIS PICABIA

(1879–1953)

Picabia encountered Marcel Duchamp and his brothers during their intense exploration of Cubist propositions that resulted in the 1912 exhibition of the Section d'Or group. His painting had mechanical overtones even before his visit to New York in 1913, but afterward, it became notable for its strange and often ironic, machinelike impo-sitions on organic forms. From 1915, when Duchamp arrived in New York, Picabia was prominent in the Dada movement and produced some of the funniest visual critiques of modernism in his drawings for Alfred Stieglitz's magazine Camera Work, *an important international vanguard review that was founded in 1902 and continued publication until 1917.*

If you want to have clean ideas, change them as often as you change your shirts.

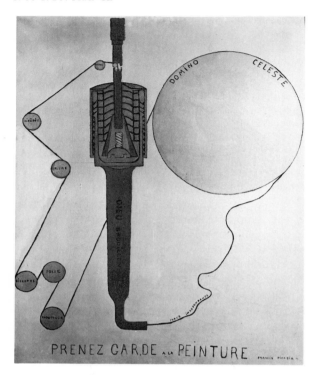

FRANCIS PICABIA   *Prenez Garde à la Peinture*
(Beware of Wet Paint). C. 1916. Oil, enamel, metallic
paint. 36½ x 28¾".

A conviction is a disease.

There is only one way to save your life: sacrifice your reputation.

One must go through life, be it red or blue, stark naked and accompanied
by the music of a subtle fisherman, prepared at all times for a celebration.

We are not responsible for what we do; we are ignorant of our acts until we
accomplish them.

When I have finished smoking, I am not interested in the butts.

Crime is less criminal than human justice.

What improves our personality represents what is good; what harms it
represents evil. That's why God has no personality.

There's nothing modern about making love; however, it's what I like to do
best.

Everything for today, nothing for yesterday, nothing for tomorrow. *[1920]*

ERNST BARLACH *Head* (detail, *War Monument*, Gustrow Cathedral). 1927. Bronze. 13½" high.

GERMANY

ERNST BARLACH

(1870–1938)

The outstanding sculptor of the German Expressionist period, Barlach began as a modeler, but around 1906 he began to explore medieval German wood sculpture and set himself the task of retrieving the tradition in modern terms. His sculptures were strongly composed in large, simple planes and usually depicted human figures symbolizing various emotions.

Just like a dramatist who feels the need for an absolute standard and then with the consciousness of this standard within him forms and elevates, simplifies, and clarifies, so too there lives in the sculptor's soul something which compels him to imbue his intention with a heroic boldness and with a joy in achieving monumental effects, in overcoming triviality and in transforming the unnatural into the natural. The rules which he obeys are no longer the petty ones of common sense but the great ones of a free intelligence. . . .

People have suppressed visions in favor of merely looking at things. Creating visions is a godlike act, art in a higher and therefore better sense than just realistic imitation which involves mere technical know-how. Shouldn't this "feast of vision" be a higher sacrament than the others? Are visions unreal? Actually, they are the basis for such ideas as "self-evident," "correct," as much as they are for physical objectivity.

The most conscientious studies can be experienced as false just like the most audacious vision can be experienced as true.

Merely to demonstrate how mystical everything is is futile since it only reminds the public that it must continue living in this gloomy world. But when the artist gives sensuous form to the mystical in such a way that it becomes intimately familiar he has elevated the observer above what is conventional and has placed him in the realm of the infinite. And he has revealed: see, the whole world is grand, everywhere, since the commonplace, everywhere, has mystical significance. . . .

Making something simple, making something monumental gives me a conception of eternal ideas. Part of nature's face is stripped of its wrinkles and little hairs and I try to show myself how it really looks. This process signifies an exaltation of my individuality to a status equal to nature, person to person. *[1906]*

ERNST LUDWIG KIRCHNER

(1880–1938)

When Kirchner founded Die Brücke (the Bridge) group in 1905 together with Erich Heckel, Karl Schmidt-Rottluff, and Fritz Bleyl, he was groping toward the personal expression that emerged only after his exposure to Van Gogh, Munch, and the French Fauves, particularly Matisse. He eventually developed a spirited painterly idiom that he referred to as "hieroglyphs" from nature, in which he infused his strong feeling for early German expressionist artists such as Dürer and Grunewald, as well as the results of his studies of Rembrandt's drawings. Kirchner was one of the early-twentieth-century artists who saw the spiritual as well as aesthetic character of non-European art, especially the art of Polynesia, and sought to recast it in European terms.

Years went by as I continued my studio study, mostly drawing on the streets, in city squares, and in cafés. I attempted to translate these drawings

ERNST LUDWIG KIRCHNER *Artillerymen.* 1915.
Oil on canvas. 55¼ x 59⅜".

into pictures. Technically, I first used thick oil colors, then in order to cover larger surfaces I applied the colors more thinly with a painting knife, and then I used benzine (my secret for the mat finish) with a wax additive. Every day I studied the nude, and movement in the streets and in the shops. Out of the naturalistic surface with all its variations I wanted to derive the pictorially determined surface. This is why I rejected academically correct drawing. Old masters like Cranach and Beham supported me in this effort. When the simple two-dimensional surface was purified I began shading the surface in order to enrich the composition, first with black and white, nowadays with other colors. At the same time I gained a deeper understanding of human psychology by getting to know my subjects better as human beings. I never had real models in the academic sense. Of course, you have quite a bit of private information about all this. Then, with insight into the limits of human interaction, I undertook the withdrawal of the self from itself and its dissolution within the other person's psyche for the sake of a more intense expression. The less I was physically involved, something which quickly occurred as a result of my mood, the more easily and completely I entered into and depicted my subject. My technique kept pace with this inner development until my induction into the army made me afraid of people and revealed new things to me in landscape.   *[1916]*

What *you* write about art, and creation in general, is easy for me to understand. I also understand what *you* mean about the artist and philosopher creating their own world. Actually, such a world is only a means of making contact with others in the great mystery which surrounds all of us. This great mystery which stands behind all events and things (sometimes like a phantom) can be seen or felt when we talk to a person or stand in a landscape or when flowers or objects suddenly speak to us. We can never represent it directly, we can only symbolize it in forms and words. Think of it, a person sits across from us and we talk, and suddenly there arises this intangible something which one could call mystery. It gives to his features his innate personality and yet at the same time it lifts those features beyond the personal. If I am able to join him in such a moment, I almost call it ecstasy, I can paint his portrait. And yet this portrait, as close as it is to his real self, is a paraphrase of the great mystery and, in the last analysis, it does not represent a single personality but a part of that spirituality or feeling which pervades the whole world.

I don't know whether I can express myself intelligibly. I can only give you an example of what I understand by passivity. It is the ability of so losing one's own individuality that one can make this contact with others. It takes immense effort to achieve this, yet it is achieved without willing it, to some extent unconsciously without one's having to do with it. To create at this stage with whatever means—words or colors or notes—is art. *[1917]*

E M I L   N O L D E

(1867–1956)

Although Nolde was briefly associated with the Bridge group around 1906–1908, his own Expressionism always set him apart from the various vanguard groups in pre–World War I Germany. Working through the influences of Van Gogh and Edvard Munch, Nolde arrived at a style that stressed strong emotional contrasts. He was interested in both myth and the Bible and frequently worked with religious motifs. An extended voyage in 1913–1914 took him to the Far East and Polynesia, where his interest in primitive art was stimulated. During the Nazi period Nolde was forbidden to paint but secretly produced a group of watercolors that have been widely praised for their moody and profound statements of nature.

Art is exalted above religions and races.

Not a single solitary soul these days believes in the religions of the

Assyrians, the Egyptians, and the Greeks. And their races are exhausted, crossbred, and spoiled. Only their art, whenever it was beautiful, stands proud and exalted, rising above all time.

Ancient artists often did not receive the respect which they deserved. Hardly any of their names are recorded even though they did more for the happiness of their people and of mankind in general than the pharaohs, generals, and world rulers whose pride and actions filled the world with sorrow and required the sacrifice of thousands upon thousands of human lives; and what remained for future generations?

Art elevates itself to the loftiest heights.   *[1911]*

GREAT BRITAIN

PERCY WYNDHAM LEWIS

(1882–1957)

Both as a writer and as an artist, Lewis made a terrific impact on his time. Contentious, brilliant, energetic, he shocked the London art world, first with his abstract drawings around 1912, and then with his foundation of the movement he called "Vorticism," which picked up threads from the Italian Futurists and French Cubists and wove them into explosive, deliberately provocative patterns. In 1915 he edited the first of two issues of the radical magazine BLAST.

LONG LIVE THE VORTEX!

Long live the great art vortex sprung up in the center of this town!

We stand for the Reality of the Present—not for the sentimental Future, or the sacripant Past.

We want to leave Nature and Men alone.

We do not want to make people wear Futurist Patches, or fuss men to take to pink and sky-blue trousers.

We are not their wives or tailors.

The only way Humanity can help artists is to remain independent and work unconsciously.

We need the unconsciousness of humanity—their stupidity, animalism, and dreams.

We believe in no perfectibility except our own.

Intrinsic beauty is in the Interpreter and Seer, not in the object or content.

We do not want to change the appearance of the world, because we are not Naturalists, Impressionists, or Futurists (the latest form of Impressionism), and do not depend on the appearance of the world for our art.

We only want the world to live, and to feel its crude energy flowing through us.

It may be said that great artists in England are always revolutionary, just as in France any really fine artist had a strong traditional vein.

BLAST sets out to be an avenue for all those vivid and violent ideas that could reach the Public in no other way.

BLAST will be popular, essentially. It will not appeal to any particular class, but to the fundamental and popular instincts in every class and description of people, *to the individual.* The moment a man feels or realizes himself as an artist, he ceases to belong to any milieu or time. *BLAST* is created for this timeless, fundamental Artist that exists in everybody.

The Man in the Street and the Gentleman are equally ignored. . . .

Education (art education and general education) tends to destroy the creative instinct. Therefore it is in times when education has been nonexistent that art chiefly flourished.

But it is nothing to do with "the People."

It is a mere accident that that is the most favorable time for the individual to appear. . . .

We want to make in England not a popular art, not a revival of lost folk art, or a romantic fostering of such unactual conditions, but to make individuals, wherever found.

We will convert the King if possible.

A Vorticist king! Why not?

Do you think Lloyd George has the Vortex in him?

May we hope for art from Lady Mond?

We are against the glorification of "the People," as we are against snobbery. It is not necessary to be an outcast bohemian, to be unkempt or poor, any more than it is necessary to be rich or handsome, to be an artist. Art is nothing to do with the coat you wear. A top hat can well hold the Sistine. A cheap cap could hide the image of Kephren.

Automobilism (Marinettism) bores us. We don't want to go about making a hullo-bulloo about motor cars, any more than about knives and forks, elephants or gas pipes.

Elephants are *very big.* Motor cars go quickly.

Wilde gushed twenty years ago about the beauty of machinery. Gissing, in his romantic delight with modern lodging houses, was futurist in this sense.

The futurist is a sensational and sentimental mixture of the aesthete of 1890 and the realist of 1870.

The "Poor" are detestable animals! They are only picturesque and amusing for the sentimentalist or the romantic! The "Rich" are bores without a single exception, *en tant que riches!*

We want those simple and great people found everywhere.

BLAST presents an art of Individuals.   *[1915]*

ITALY

GIACOMO BALLA

(1871–1958)

Teacher of prominent Futurists such as Boccioni and Severini, Balla was an intrepid experimenter. He signed the Futurist painting manifesto in 1910, but moved away toward his own vision when, in 1913–1914, he produced a series of paintings called "Iridescent Interpenetrations"—totally abstract symbolizations of the movement of light and color. Balla's audacity in the exploration of the dynamics of color was noted by scores of painters during the 1960s, when so-called Op Art flourished, and by others who turned to kinetic expressions.

With the perfecting of photography, static traditionalist painting has completely fallen from repute; photography kills static contemplation. Watching a cinematographic performance we find ourselves in front of a painting in movement that consecutively transforms itself to reproduce a given action.

Static traditionalist painting was vanquished because it was obliged to transfix one single point among the infinite variety of aspects of nature. Mechanics have overtaken the traditionalist painter and forced him into becoming a pitiable imitator of static and exterior forms. It is imperative therefore not to halt and contemplate the corpse of tradition, but to renew ourselves by creating an art that no machine can imitate, that only the artistic Creative Genius can conceive. Futurism, predestined force of progress and not of fashion, creates the style of flowing abstract forms that are synthetic and inspired by the dynamic forces of the universe.

GIACOMO BALLA OF TURIN
Temperament: daring, intuitive.
Art — 1st Period: Objective personal realist — rebel against the academic schools — Analysis of our life — solution in Divisionist researches (light, environment, psyche, objects, people) — Struggles toils enjoyments — achievement of glorious career with recognition from public, artists, critics.

2nd Period: FUTURISM. *Evolution:* Total repudiation of own work-career. Public, artists, critics dismayed — incomprehensibility — accusations — madness — bad faith — derision — pity — Received with smiling indifference — First plastic researches in movement (speeding automobiles, people in movement) — public curiosity — laughs, insults, derision, incredulity — violent arguments (Italians, poverty and grandeur, brimful of a great indigestion — Germanophilia!!!)

Continuation researches. Analysis reality abandoned definitively. Creation new Futurist style: synthetic abstract subjective dynamic forms.

GIACOMO BALLA *Automobile Dynamics.* 1913.

Still research more struggle.
ON WITH FUTURISM. . . .   *[1915]*

Any store in a modern town, with its elegant windows all displaying useful and pleasing objects, is much more aesthetically enjoyable than all those passéist exhibitions which have been so lauded everywhere. An electric iron, its white steel gleaming clean as a whistle, delights the eye more than a nude statuette, stuck on a pedestal hideously tinted for the occasion. A typewriter is *more architectural* than all those building projects which win prizes at academics and competitions. The windows of a perfumer's shop, with little boxes and packets, bottles and futurcolor triplicate phials, reflected in the extremely elegant mirrors. The clever and gay modeling of ladies' dancing shoes, the bizarre ingenuity of multicolored parasols. Furs, traveling bags, china—these things are all a much more rewarding sight than the grimy little pictures nailed on the gray wall of the passéist painter's studio.

[1918]

RUSSIA

NATALIA SERGEEVNA GONCHAROVA

(1881–1962)

Goncharova's upper-class family background enabled her to complete her education with extensive travels in Europe. She visited Paris in 1906, where she and her companion Mikhail Fedorovich Larionov eagerly examined the art of the Fauves and the proto-Cubist work of Picasso. When Goncharova returned to Russia, she began to paint in a style fusing the vanguard approaches she had observed in Paris. However, she soon turned her attention to the Russian folk legacy, influencing others, including Kasimir Malevich, to find motifs in peasant art. Her interest in Futurism led her to collaborate with Larionov in the development of an abstract style they called "Rayonism." In 1915 she and Larionov settled permanently in Paris, where Goncharova turned her attention to stage design.

I am convinced that modern Russian art is developing so rapidly and has reached such heights that within the near future it will be playing a leading role in international life. Contemporary Western ideas (mainly of France; it is not worth talking of the others) can no longer be of any use to us. And the time is not far off when the West will be learning openly from us.

If we examine art from the artistic monuments we have at our disposal without bearing time in mind, then I see it in this order:

The Stone Age and the caveman's art are the dawn of art. China, India, and Egypt with all their ups and downs in art have, generally speaking, always had a high art and strong artistic traditions. Arts proceeding from this root are nevertheless independent: that of the Aztecs, Negroes, Australian and Asiatic islands—the Sunda (Borneo), Japan, etc. These, generally speaking, represent the rise and flowering of art.

Greece, beginning with the Cretan period (a transitional state), with its archaic character and all its flowering, Italy right up to the age of the Gothic, represent decadence. Gothic is a transitional state. Our age is a flowering of art in a new form—a painterly form. And in this second flowering it is again the East that has played a leading role. At the present time Moscow is the most important center of painting.

I shake off the dust of the West, and I consider all those people ridiculous and backward who still imitate Western models in the hope of becoming pure painters and who fear literariness more than death. Similarly, I find those people ridiculous who advocate individuality and who assume there is some value in their "I" even when it is extremely limited. Untalented individuality is as useless as bad imitation, let alone the old-fashionedness of such an argument.

NATALIA SERGEEVNA GONCHA-
ROVA *La Femme au Chapeau.* 1912. Oil on canvas. 35½ x 26".

I express my deep gratitude to Western painters for all they have taught
me.

After carefully modifying everything that could be done along these lines
and after earning the honor of being placed alongside contemporary Western
artists—in the West itself—I now prefer to investigate a new path. *[1913]*

MIKHAIL FEDOROVICH LARIONOV

(1882–1964)

*Born in the Ukraine, Larionov came to Moscow to study painting at the Moscow
Institute of Painting, Sculpture, and Architecture, and quickly became a leader of
rebellious art students there. In 1908 he was drafted into the army, where he continued
to paint, infusing his canvases with a raw vernacular quality derived, he felt, from*

the authentic peasant tradition. By 1912 he had been sufficiently impressed by the Italian Futurists to shift into an abstract idiom that, in this 1913 manifesto, he called "Rayonism." After settling in Paris in 1915 with his companion Natalia Goncharova, he did a great deal of scenographic work for the Ballets Russes and rarely returned to easel painting.

Every form exists objectively in space by reason of the rays from the other forms that surround it; it is individualized by these rays, and they alone determine its existence.

Nevertheless, between those forms that our eye objectivizes, there exists a real and undeniable intersection of rays proceeding from various forms. These interactions constitute new intangible forms that the painter's eye *can* see. Where the rays from different objects meet, new immaterial objects are created in space. Rayonism is the painting of these intangible forms, of these *infinite* products with which the whole of space is filled.

Rayonism is the painting of the collisions and couplings of rays *between* objects, the dramatic representation of the struggle between the plastic emanations radiating from all things around us; Rayonism is the painting of space revealed not by the contours of objects, not even by their formal coloring, but by the ceaseless and intense drama of the rays that constitute the unity of all things.

Rayonism might appear to be a form of spiritualist painting, even mystical, but it is, on the contrary, essentially plastic. The painter sees new forms created between tangible forms by their own radiation, and these are the only ones that he places on the canvas. Hence he attains the pinnacle of painting for painting's sake inspired by these real forms, although he would neither know how to, nor wish to, represent or even evoke them by their linear existence.

Pictorial studies devoted to a formal representation by no matter what kind of geometrical line—straight, curved, circular—still regard painting, in my opinion, as a means of representing forms. Rayonism wishes to regard painting as an end in itself and no longer as a means of expression. . . .

In Rayonist painting the intrinsic life and continuum of the colored masses form a synthesis-image in the mind of the spectator, one that goes beyond time and space. One glimpses the famous fourth dimension since the length, breadth, and density of the superposition of the painted colors are the only signs of the visible world; and all the other sensations, created by images, are of another order—that superreal order that man must always seek, yet never find, so that he would approach paths of representation more subtle and more spiritualized.

We believe that Rayonism marks a new stage in this development.

[1914]

KASIMIR MALEVICH *Suprematist Composition.* Undated.
Oil on canvas. 31⅝ x 31⅝".

KASIMIR MALEVICH

(1878–1935)

Like others in the pre–World War I Russian vanguard, Malevich was inspired both by the Italian Futurists and by the French Cubists, but he quickly transformed the received ideas of Western Europe into a powerful pictorial idiom that has left a permanent imprint on modern art. He called his new philosophy "Suprematism" and gave various and sometimes contradictory explanations of his intentions. But, from around 1913 on, his thoughts had turned to an art freed from reference to external objects, and this nonobjective vocabulary was couched in intensely lyrical, transcendent terms that verged on mysticism. His diction in the following letters and statements attests to the emotional undercurrent and the will to spring free of the material world that run through twentieth-century abstract painting and reach a high point with another Russian-born artist, the American painter Mark Rothko.

My new painting does not belong solely to the earth. The earth has been abandoned like a worm-eaten house. And an aspiration toward space is in fact lodged in man and his consciousness, a longing "to break away from the globe of the earth." Futurism was almost exclusively concerned with space, but because its form was linked with objectivity, it did not even provide the imagination with a sense of present universal space. Its space was confined to the space separating objects on earth. On the other hand, a suspended surface of painted color on a sheet of white canvas imparts direct to our consciousness a strong sensation of space. It transports me to a boundless desert where one perceives around one the creative points of the universe.   *[1916]*

But we will discover something else, we will disclose on earth that which cannot be disclosed in heaven. Christ disclosed heaven on earth, having put an end to space, and established two limits, two poles, so that they should exist in themselves—or "over there." But we will pass by a thousand poles, just as we pass over billions of grains of sand on the shore of a sea or river. Space is greater than heaven, stronger and more powerful, and our new book is the teaching of the desert's space.   *[1916]*

It has become clear to me that new frameworks of pure color-painting should be created, constructed at color's demand; and, secondly, that color should leave the painterly mixture and become an independent factor, entering the construction as an individual of a collective system and individual independence.

The system is constructed in time and space, independently of all aesthetic beauties, experiences, and moods: it is more a philosophical color system for realizing the latest achievements of my ideas, as knowledge.

At the present time man's path lies through space, and Suprematism is a color semaphore in its infinite abyss.

The blue color of the sky has been defeated by the Suprematist system, has been broken through, and entered white, as the true real conception of infinity, and therefore liberated from the color background of the sky.

The system, hard, cold, and unsmiling, is brought into motion by philosophical thought, or else within the system its real strength is already moving.

All the colorings of utilitarian intention are insignificant and narrow, having the already completed purely applied significance of what was found by cognizance and the result of philosophic thought, on the horizon of our vision of little corners either serving a philistine taste or else creating a new one.

In one of its stages Suprematism has, through color, a purely philosophical movement, and in a second, as a form which may be applied, formed a new style of Suprematist decoration.

But it can appear on things as a transformation or incarnation of space in them, banishing from consciousness a thing's wholeness.

Through Suprematist, philosophical color thinking it has been made clear that the will can reveal a creative system when the artist annuls the thing as a painterly framework, as a means; as long as things remain a framework and means, his will is bound to revolve in the midst of a compositional circle and forms of objects.

All that we see has arisen from a color mass turned into plane and volume, and any machine, house, man, table—they are all painterly volume systems designated for definite purposes.

The artist ought also to transform painterly masses and produce a creative system, but not paint little pictures and fragrant roses, for this will all be dead representation reminding one of the living.

And even if it is constructed nonobjectively but based on color interrelations, its will will be confined inside the walls of aesthetic planes instead of philosophical penetration.

I am only free when my will, on a critical and philosophical basis, can bring from what already exists the basis for new phenomena.

I have torn through the blue lampshade of color limitations, and come out into the white; after me, comrade aviators sail into the chasm—I have set up semaphores of Suprematism.

I have conquered the lining of the heavenly, have torn it down, and, making a bag, put in colors and tied it with a knot. Sail forth! The white, free chasm, infinity is before us.   *[1919]*

OLGA VLADIMIROVNA ROZANOVA

(1886–1918)

Very active in all the avant-garde formations from 1911 until her death, Rozanova had a keen analytical mind. She wrote one of the earliest statements advocating nonrepresentational art and very probably influenced certain of Malevich's conclusions.

The art of painting is the decomposition of nature's ready-made images into the distinctive properties of the common material found within them and the creation of different images by means of the interrelation of these properties; this interrelation is established by the Creator's individual attitude. The artist determines these properties by his visual faculty. The world is a piece of raw material—for the unreceptive soul it is the back of a mirror, but for reflective souls it is a mirror of images appearing continually.

How does the world reveal itself to us? How does our soul reflect the world? In order to reflect, it is necessary to perceive. In order to perceive, it is necessary to touch, to see. Only the Intuitive Principle introduces us to the World.

And only the Abstract Principle—Calculation—as the consequence of the active aspiration to express the world, can build a picture.

This establishes the following order in the process of creation:

1. Intuitive Principle
2. Individual transformation of the visible
3. Abstract creation

The fascination of the visible, the charm of the spectacle, arrests the eye, and the artist's primary aspiration to create arises from this confrontation with nature. The desire to penetrate the World and, in reflecting it, to reflect oneself is an intuitive impulse that selects the Subject—this word being understood in its purely painterly meaning.   *[1913]*

SWITZERLAND

FERDINAND HODLER

(1853–1918)

A significant symbolist painter at the turn of the century, Hodler in his last years painted Alpine landscapes that in their vigor and sweep satisfied modern demands for simple, expressive forms. After a long eclipse, Hodler's reputation was retrieved during the 1970s with major exhibitions in both Europe and the United States.

Color exists simultaneously with form. Both elements are constantly associated but sometimes color strikes you more—a rose for instance—sometimes form—the human body.

WHAT IS DIFFERENT AND WHAT IS SIMILAR

Uniformity as well as diversity exist within human beings.

We are different from each other, but we are even more alike.

What unites us is greater and stronger than what divides us.

When you look up at the sky, you have a feeling of unity which delights you and makes you giddy. The very expanse is striking.

When I am on the sea, I can only see the sky and water, a long line of infinite horizon.

When I look at the night, that is another instance of a large expanse.

When I see a dead man, the eternity of his silence moves me, impresses me deeply.

When I see similar forms, a certain order, I am also pleasantly affected. Why should a flower delight me? Because it consists of similar forms grouped around a center. Nothing delights us more than orderly forms.

For twenty years I have noted similar phenomena and reproduced those resemblances, those similarities.

There is also diversity—the different faces and characters of various people. And on the other hand, what is similar, analogous, general characteristics, the same feelings of humanity. There is a small truth and a larger Truth.

Art unites us. Long live art!

What makes us one is greater than what divides us.

I have expressed my likings: a rose, the sound of an organ.

EXPLANATION OF MY PICTURES

Night: A large expanse of a natural phenomenon, a large expanse of black shades.

Tired of Living: The sound of an organ.

Eurythmy: Five men representing humanity, marching toward death.

[1917–1918]

UNITED STATES

ARTHUR GARFIELD DOVE

(1880–1946)

A trip to Europe in 1907 stimulated Dove to embark on a series of paintings that were perceived as abstractions. He exhibited them in 1910 and caused a furor in the public press. As a member of Stieglitz's circle before the First World War, Dove was interested in theories of synesthesia, and his paintings were about his sense of natural phenomena such as wind, water, sounds. Although his work appeared abstract, he thought of it as always rooted in his experience of nature.

At the age of nine I painted, studying with Newton Weatherly of Geneva, New York.

I was unable to devote all of my time to it until 1907–1908 in France, where I was free for eighteen months, working in the country.

Then back to America and discovered that at that time it was not possible to live by modern art alone. Made a living farming and illustrating to support the paintings.

To understand painting one must live with it. The speed of today leaves very few [sic] time to really live with anything, even ourselves. That too painting has to meet.

Then there was the search for a means of expression which did not depend upon representation. It should have order, size, intensity, spirit, nearer to the music of the eye.

If one could paint the part that goes to make the spirit of painting and leave out all that just makes tons and tons of art. . . .

There was a long period of searching for a something in color which I then called "a condition of light." It applied to all objects in nature, flowers, trees, people, apples, cows. These all have their certain condition of light, which establishes them to the eye, to each other, and to the understanding.

To understand that clearly go to nature, or to the Museum of Natural History and see the butterflies. Each has its own orange, blue, black; white, yellow, brown, green, and black, all carefully chosen to fit the character of the life going on in that individual entity.

After painting objects with those color motives for some time, I began to feel the same idea existing in form. This had evidently been known by the Greeks, as in going over conic sections again, with this in mind, I found that they were called "Maenechmian Triads." Maenechmus was an early Greek sculptor, and invented these triads.

This choice of form motives of course took the paintings away from representation in the ordinary sense.

Then one day I made a drawing of a hillside. The wind was blowing. I chose three forms from the planes on the sides of the trees, and three colors, and black and white. From these was made a rhythmic painting which expressed the spirit of the whole thing. The colors were chosen to express the substances of those objects and the sky. There was the earth color, the green of the trees, and the cyan blue of the sky. These colors were made into pastels carefully weighed out and graded with black and white into an instrument to be used in making that certain painting. . . .

Later the choice of form motive was reduced from the plane to the line. That happened one day in trying to draw a waterfall. The line was the only thing that had speed enough.

The Cow (1911) is an example of the line motive freed still further.

The line at first followed the edges of planes, or was drawn over the surface, and was used to express actual size, as that gave a sense of dimension; later it was used in and through objects and ideas as force lines, growth lines, with its accompanying color condition.

Feeling that the "first flash" of an idea gives its most vivid sensation, I am at present in some of the paintings trying to put down the spirit of the idea as it comes out. To sense the "pitch" of an idea as one would a bell.

It is the form that the idea takes in the imagination rather than the form as it exists outside.

This is no rule, nor method, but leaves the imagination free to work in all directions with all dimensions that are or may have been realized.

[before 1920]

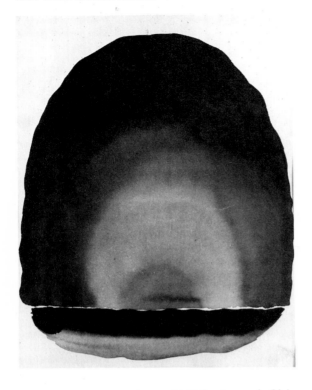

GEORGIA O'KEEFFE   *Light Coming on the Plains III.* 1917. Watercolor. 12 x 9".

GEORGIA O'KEEFFE

(1887–)

From her earliest exhibition at the 291 Gallery of Alfred Stieglitz in 1916, O'Keeffe demonstrated an uncanny ability to abstract essential characteristics of natural phenomena. Although at times her paintings and watercolors verged on total abstraction, they were always derived from her communion with the places and objects—both organic and inorganic—she directly experienced.

It is surprising to me to see how many people separate the objective from the abstract. Objective painting is not good painting unless it is good in the abstract sense. A hill or tree cannot make a good painting just because it is a hill or a tree. It is lines and colors put together so that they say something. For me that is the very basis of painting. The abstraction is often the most definite form for the intangible thing in myself that I can only clarify in paint.   *[1976]*

MAURICE BRAZIL PRENDERGAST

(1859–1924)

Prendergast studied in France long enough to master a Post-Impressionist, quasi-pointillist technique and returned to America to become one of the most original of the early-twentieth-century modernists. His watercolors in particular sparkle. They are informed by the techniques of the French, but Prendergast took creative liberties that gave his small works a monumental character that set them apart from all other American works of the period.

Very blue this afternoon. I suppose it comes from abstaining from the customary afternoon cup of coffee. You must make yourself a strong man. You are on the threshold as an artist. Be firm and determined.

Accustom yourself to master things which you seem to despair of.

The love you liberate in your work is the only love you keep.   *[1905]*

1920-
1940

BELGIUM

RENÉ MAGRITTE

(1898–1976)

Like many of his French colleagues in the Surrealist movement, Magritte was deeply inspired by the work of Giorgio de Chirico in the early 1920s. Magritte was one of the important figures in the Belgian Surrealist movement that flourished between the wars and also frequently participated in activities initiated by André Breton in Paris. His paintings, with their emphasis on the disparity between the thinking and seeing processes, were regarded as among the purest elucidations of Surrealist philosophy.

To equate my painting with symbolism, conscious or unconscious, is to ignore its true nature. . . . People are quite willing to use objects without looking for any symbolic intention in them, but when they look at paintings, they can't find any use for them. So they hunt around for a meaning to get themselves out of the quandary, and because they don't understand what they are supposed to think when they confront the painting. . . . They want something to lean on, so they can be comfortable. They want something secure to hang on to, so they can save themselves from the void. People who look for symbolic meanings fail to grasp the inherent poetry and mystery of the image. No doubt they sense this mystery, but they wish to get rid of it. They are afraid. By asking "what does this mean?" they express a wish that everything be understandable. But if one does not reject the mystery, one has quite a different response. One asks other things.

The images must be seen *such as they are*. Moreover, my painting implies no supremacy of the invisible over the visible. (The letter hidden in the envelope is not invisible; neither is the sun when it is hidden by a curtain of trees.) The mind loves the unknown. It loves images whose meaning is unknown, since the meaning of the mind itself is unknown. The mind doesn't understand its own *raison d'être*, and without understanding *that* (or why it knows what it knows), the problems it poses have no *raison d'être* either.

The word "dream" is often misused concerning my painting. We certainly wish the realm of dreams to be respectable—but our works are not oneiric. *On the contrary*. If "dreams" are concerned in this context, they are very different from those we have while sleeping. It is a question rather of *self-willed* "dreams," in which nothing is as vague as those feelings one has when escaping in dreams. . . . "Dreams" which are not intended to make you sleep but wake you up.

If one is a determinist, one must believe always that one cause produces the same effect. I am not a determinist, but I don't believe in chance either. It serves as still another "explanation" of the world. The problem lies precisely

RENÉ MAGRITTE   *The Palace of Curtains, III.* 1928–1929. Oil on canvas.
32 x 45⅞".

in not accepting any explanation of the world, either through chance or determinism. I do not believe that man decides anything, either the future or the present of humanity. I think that we are responsible for the universe, but this does not mean that we decide anything.

The other day someone asked me what the relationship was between my life and my art. I couldn't really think of any, except that life obliges me to do something, so I paint. But I am not concerned with "pure" poetry nor with "pure" painting. It is rather pointless to put one's hopes in a dogmatic point of view, since it is the power of enchantment which matters.

[1959]

GEORGES VANTONGERLOO

(1886–1965)

Vantongerloo participated in the de Stijl movement in his youth but later developed theories about the mathematical basis of abstract art that distanced him from Mon-

drian. His constructions and sculptures were often explorations of mathematical principles embodied in curves and spirals. In 1927 he settled in Paris, where he became an active member of the between-the-wars group Abstraction-Création: Art Non-Figuratif.

In art there are always two problems and therefore two solutions. The problem of the Subject, the manner of envisaging it and resolving it. And the problem of Art, which is the manner of combining functions and of incorporating into them a sensibility, which is individual. And finally, the solution to be given to the problem of Art. On the result of these two problems taken together depends the value of the work of Art. These problems must therefore be resolved with elegance.

In order to avoid a dominant in a work, it is also necessary that the solutions be in harmony and that one not infringe on the other. The sensibility of the author guides this harmony. No conventional rules which would lead to dogma. Each work has its own rules; it is a totality in itself. The same rules encountered in another work would be a tautology resulting, as often happens with artists, in the copying of one's own works.

I see a flower. It gives me a sensation of the beautiful. I wish to paint it. At this moment I see the whole subject—flower—changed. It is no longer the same beauty. Is it the environment, the light? In short, the vision is no longer the same. I attempt then to resolve the problem, the subject flower. In painting it, I strive after composition; the value of one color in relation to another, their harmony. Likewise with the lines. The process passes through my sensibility and the result is a work of artistic . . . or botanical value. I see a work by Nicolas Fouquet. By what am I moved? By the religious subject or by the Art? I am free to believe that it is the religious subject that moves me. But it is only through Art that the Great Emotion can reach me. Then Art is the harmony of relations accompanied by Fouquet's sensibility. It is not an illustration; it is a work of art.

Consider the work of Cézanne, it has nothing of nature, but everything of art. . . .

What is it that attracts us in art? Is it not the imponderable? Does the artist not wish to express his sense of the incommensurable? Does the spectator not wish, through the intermediary of a work of art, to feel the incommensurable? The means and the pretext for approaching it is a subject. Primitive peoples had recourse to fetishes. After this stage was superseded, the subject became mythological, then religious. Through the development of science, the subject assumes a character of observation, comparison, reflection. One paints directly from nature not in order to copy, but in an effort to penetrate the mystery of nature through observation and to express the feelings of grandeur received from the phenomenon observed. One does not paint a flower as if illustrating a botany text, as an analysis of the flower, but paints rather the atmosphere and the feeling that the scene releases. One uses colors which *seem* to be improvised, with a view to approaching the incommensurable. As man's knowledge develops, and according to his temperament, geometry comes to seem more qualified, not to produce an *industrial* art, but to reveal the incommensurable.   *[c. 1947]*

FRANCE

J E A N   A R P   (Hans Arp)

(1887–1966)

Before he became a member of the French vanguard in the 1920s Arp had participated enthusiastically in the Dada movement in both Germany and Switzerland, where he experimented with chance in torn-paper collages and in sound poems—poems in which sound alone, divested of meaning, expressed his intentions. He was associated with the Surrealists and later with groups of abstract artists formed in the early 1930s. His curvilinear sculptures in stone won him international acclaim. In the statement below he explains his long-standing attitude toward the evocation of nature, using the term concrete art *in an entirely personal way, distinct from that of Theo van Doesburg. Van Doesburg also wrote about concrete art in 1930, but asserted that it should receive nothing from "nature's formal properties or from sensuality or sentimentality."*

We don't want to copy nature. We don't want to reproduce, we want to produce. We want to produce like a plant that produces a fruit, and not reproduce. We want to produce directly and not by way of any intermediary.

Since this art doesn't have the slightest trace of abstraction, we name it: concrete art.

Works of concrete art should not be signed by the artists. These paintings, sculptures—these objects—should remain anonymous in the huge studio of nature, like clouds, mountains, seas, animals, men. Yes! Men should go back to nature! Artists should work in communities as they did in the Middle Ages. In 1915, O. van Rees, C. van Rees, [Otto] Freundlich, [Sophie] Taueber, and myself made an attempt of that sort.

That year I wrote: "These works are constructed with lines, surfaces, forms, and colors that try to go beyond the human and attain the infinite and the eternal. They reject our egotism. . . . The hands of our brothers, instead of being interchangeable with our own hands, have become enemy hands. Instead of anonymity, we have renown and masterpieces; wisdom is dead. . . . Reproduction is imitation, play acting, tightrope walking."

The Renaissance bumptiously exalted human reason. Modern times with their science and technology have turned man into a megalomaniac. The atrocious chaos of our era is the consequence of that overrating of reason.

The evolution of traditional painting toward concrete art, from Cézanne by way of the Cubists, has been frequently explained, and these historical explanations have merely confused the issue. All at once, "according to the laws of chance," around 1914, the human mind underwent a transformation: it was confronted with an ethical problem.

When I exhibited my first concrete reliefs, I put out a little manifesto declaring the art of the bourgeois to be sanctioned lunacy. Especially these naked men, women, and children in stone or bronze, exhibited in public squares, gardens, and forest clearings, who untiringly dance, chase butter-flies, shoot arrows, hold out apples, blow the flute, are the perfect expression of a mad world. These mad figures must no longer sully nature. Today, as in the day of the early Christians, the essential must become known. The artist must let his work create itself directly. Today we are no longer concerned with subtleties. My reliefs and sculptures fit naturally into nature. On closer examination however they reveal that they were formed by human hand, and so I have named certain of them: *Stone Formed by Human Hand*.

[c. 1942]

CONSTANTIN BRANCUSI

(1876–1957)

After studying at the École de Beaux Arts in his native Rumania, Brancusi settled in Paris for more studies in 1904. From around 1907 Rodin's influence, and that of African sculpture, seem to have turned Brancusi toward the abstraction and simplicity of form for which he is celebrated. His wood sculptures directly carved and his early stones bespeak his interest in primitive art. Later, Brancusi developed casting techniques as well, all in the interest of finding essential forms. His most celebrated monumental sculpture was completed in Rumania in 1937, where an ensemble of works in a park is crowned by the Endless Column.

After Michelangelo, sculptors wanted to make grandiose sculpture. They only succeeded in making grandiloquent sculpture. In the nineteenth century, the situation of sculpture was desperate. Rodin arrived and transformed everything. Thanks to him, man became again the measure, the module after which the sculpture was organized. Thanks to him sculpture became human again in its dimensions, in its signification, in its content. The influence of Rodin was and remains immense. While he was still alive and I showed at the Beaux Arts National of which he was president, certain friends and protectors, among them the queen [of Rumania], tried, without consulting me, to have me admitted to his studio. Rodin accepted me as a student. But I refused because nothing grows under large trees. My friends

CONSTANTIN BRANCUSI *View of the Artist's Studio.* 1918.
Gouache and pencil. 13 x 16¼".

were angry, ignorant as they were of Rodin's reaction. When he learned of
my decision, he simply said, "Basically he's right. He is as stubborn as I
am." Rodin had a modest attitude toward his art. When he finished his
Balzac, which remains the incontestable point of departure for modern
sculpture, he declared, "It is now that I would like to begin work."

The beautiful is absolute equity.

Things are not difficult to make; what is difficult is putting ourselves in the
state of mind to make them.

When we are no longer children, we are already dead.

What is the use of using a model? It only ends in sculpting cadavers.

Theories are samples without value. What counts is action.

Direct cutting is the real road to sculpture, but also the worst for those who
don't known how to walk. And, in the end, direct cutting or indirect—that
doesn't mean a thing. What counts is the thing made.

Simplicity is not an end in art, but one arrives at simplicity in spite of
oneself in drawing near to the reality in things.

Don't look for obscure formulas or mystery in my work. It is pure joy that I offer you. Look at my sculptures until you see them. Those closest to God have seen them.

To see far is one thing; going there is another.

There is a goal in all things. To arrive there you must remove yourself from yourself.

Create like a god, command like a king, work like a slave.

Glory doesn't give a damn about us when we run after her, but when we turn our back on her, it is she that runs after us.   *[1925–1957]*

VICTOR BRAUNER

(1903–1966)

Active in his native Rumania as a Dadaist, Brauner settled in Paris in 1930 and became associated with the Surrealist movement. The interest in magic prevalent in the later phases of Surrealism was strong in Brauner, whose series of "spectral" paintings won him a special place in the Surrealist pantheon.

My latest pictures are without external reference to the world of reality of these gentlemen, but so much the worse. They are documents on the "mist" of inspiration. To "their reality" I oppose "my mist."
    And the "mist" says to me:
    I *invade* slowly, quite softly, imperceptibly, on muffled steps.
    I *invade* the far horizons as I approach, leaving but a diminishing zone of visibility.
    I *invade* and the all disappears, all glimpses itself through me, for I am the new optics of transparence and opaqueness.
    . . . I am the birth of the object.
    . . . I am the end of the object.
    I am the spectre and the apparition.   *[1941]*

ANDRÉ DERAIN

(1880–1954)

During the 1920s, Derain, who had been a major figure in the Fauve group and was closely associated with Picasso during the Cubist years, turned back to the old masters for inspiration. His conviction that there would have to be a "return to order," as Jean Cocteau called it, led him to reject abstract art and even Cubism.

Everything comes from nature and everything returns there. . . . It is impossible to produce an art anterior to or exterior to the real . . . or then you're working with more poverty than reality itself . . . which is typical of decadent art. To use lines, planes, volumes, color that we borrow necessarily from nature without giving them a function constitutes a decadent practice that is equivalent to a truncated and failed parody of the exterior world. Do you know a painter who has invented a color different from those that compose the solar spectrum?

One must seize nature in her economy, her course, her imaginative process. In other words, one must adapt her style, putting oneself in the interior of this style instead of trying to recopy the effects, the externals.

Style is the constant coming and going of man toward the real, a perpetual interpolation of the subjective and objective. . . . It tends to identify what we have of *esprit* with the *esprit* of things. One must not say more nor less than the subject demands. That is what nature does. That is what Racine, Chardin, Corot, and Balzac did.   *[1939]*

MAX ERNST

(1891–1976)

Ernst had already distinguished himself in his native Germany as a leader in the Dada movement and one of the prime explorers of montage techniques, before he settled in France in 1922. He soon joined André Breton in vigorously propagating the Surrealist movement, pouring forth both texts and works of visual art in the spirit Breton described in his first Surrealist manifesto. Of all the Surrealists, Ernst was the most deliberate in the application of Surrealist principles, as his description here of frottage, one of his many techniques to induce "pure psychic automatism," indicates. The literary underpinnings of the movement are evident in his important citation of one of the Surrealist heroes: the child prodigy, nineteenth-century rebel-poet Arthur Rimbaud.

The procedure of *frottage*, resting thus upon nothing more than the intensification of the irritability of the mind's faculties by appropriate technical means, excluding all conscious mental guidance (of reason, taste, morals), reducing to the extreme the active part of that one whom we have called, up to now, the "author" of the work, this procedure is revealed by the following to be the real equivalent of that which is already known by the term *automatic writing*. It is as a spectator that the author assists, indifferent or passionate, at the birth of his work and watches the phases of its development. Even as the role of the poet, since the celebrated *lettre de voyant* of Rimbaud, consists in writing according to the dictates of that which articulates itself in him, so the role of the painter is to pick out and *project that which sees itself in him.*[1] In finding myself more and more engrossed in this activity (passivity) which later came to be called "critical paranoia,"[2] and in adapting to the technical means of painting (for example: the scraping of pigments upon a ground prepared in colors and placed on an uneven surface) the procedure of frottage which seemed applicable at first only to drawing, and in striving more and more to restrain my own active participation in the unfolding of the picture, and, finally, by widening in this way the active part of the mind's hallucinatory faculties I came to assist *as spectator* at the birth of all my works, from the tenth of August, 1925,[3] memorable day of the discovery of frottage. A man of "ordinary constitution" (I employ here the words of Rimbaud), I have done everything to render my soul monstrous.[4] Blind swimmer, I have made myself see. *I have seen.* And I was surprised and enamored of what I *saw*, wishing to identify myself with it.

[1] Vasari relates that Piero di Cosimo sometimes sat plunged in contemplation of a wall upon which certain sick persons had formed the habit of spitting. Out of these stains he formed equestrian battles, fantastic towns, and the most magnificent landscapes. He did the same with the clouds of the sky.

[2] This rather pretty term (and one which will probably have some success because of its paradoxical content) seems to me to be subject to precaution inasmuch as the notion of paranoia is employed there in a sense which doesn't correspond to its medical meaning. I prefer, on the other hand, the proposition of Rimbaud: "The poet becomes a *seer*, by a long, immense, and conscious disorder of all the senses."

[3] With the exception of *The Virgin Spanking the Infant Jesus* (1926), picture-manifesto, painted after an idea of André Breton.

[4] "Monstrous," in this sense, is meant to convey the idea of nobility, greatness, immensity. (Translator's note.)

[1948]

ALBERTO GIACOMETTI   *The Artist's Mother.* 1937.
Oil on canvas. 23½ x 19⅝".

ALBERTO GIACOMETTI

(1901–1966)

Giacometti, son of a well-known Swiss painter, settled in 1922 in Paris, where he began his study of sculpture with Antoine Bourdelle (1861–1929), a pupil of Rodin. By the end of the 1920s he was experimenting with forms derived from the free association advocated by the Surrealists, with whom he remained identified until the mid-1930s. He then embarked on his painful search for the means to re-present the human figure in its real situation in space—a space that he interpreted increasingly in both paintings and sculptures as an element actively affecting the bodies within it. His ideas on the subject, developed in the late 1930s, were moving in directions similar to those of the major phenomenological philosophers in France, particularly Maurice Merleau-Ponty and Jean-Paul Sartre, both of whom developed fresh theories of perception that influenced the post–World War II artists.

One day when I was drawing a young girl I suddenly noticed that the only thing that was alive was her gaze. The rest of her head . . . meant no more to me than the skull of a dead man. . . . One does want to sculpt a living person, but what makes him alive is without a doubt his gaze. The heads from the New Hebrides are true, *are more than true*, because they have a gaze. Not the imitation of eyes, but really and truly a gaze. Everything else is only the framework for the gaze. . . . If the gaze, that is, life, is the main thing, then the head becomes the main thing . . . the rest of the body is limited to functioning as antennae that make people's life possible—the life that is housed in the skull. . . . At a certain point in time I began to see the people in the street as if their living essence was very tiny. I saw living beings exclusively through their eyes.   *[1951]*

If one sets one's heart on grasping as much as possible of what one sees, be it in science or art, the procedure is the same. The scholar specialized in any field will find that the more he knows, the more he will have to learn, and never should he hope to reach full knowledge. Besides, full knowledge would be death itself. Art and science mean trying to understand. Failure or success plays a secondary role. This adventure is of recent date—it started approximately in the eighteenth century with Chardin, when one began to be interested more in the artist's vision than in serving the church or giving pleasure to kings. At last, man given to himself!

One could not express in words what one feels with one's eyes and one's hand.

Words pervert thoughts, writing distorts words—one no longer recognizes oneself. I do not believe in the problem of space; space is created solely by the objects; an object that moves without any relation to another object could not give the impression of space. The subject alone is decisive. Space, shapes, canvas, plaster, bronze . . . so many means. The only important thing is to create a new object which conveys an impression as close as possible to that received when contemplating the subject. . . . Sculpture rests in the void. One hollows out space so as to construct the object, and the object as such creates space, the space that exists between the subject and the sculptor.   *[1962]*

It might be supposed that realism consists in copying a glass as it is on the table. In fact, one never copies anything but the vision that remains of it at each moment, the image that becomes conscious. You never copy the glass on the table; you copy the residue of a vision. . . . Each time I look at the glass, it has an air of *remaking* itself, that's to say, its reality becomes uncertain, because its projection in my head is uncertain, or partial. One sees it as if it were disappearing, coming into view again, disappearing, coming into view again—that's to say, it really always is between being and not being. And it's this that one wants to copy.   *[c. 1963–1964]*

JULIO GONZÁLEZ

(1876–1942)

The Spanish-born González came to Paris at the turn of the century and was a familiar of Picasso and his circle. Toward the late 1920s he abandoned painting for sculpture and produced a remarkable group of works, first in forged and welded planes that often took on masklike lineaments reminiscent of earlier Picasso works, and later in open configurations of rods and slender planes in which open spaces functioned as virtual planes. These works had an enormous influence on the evolution of metal sculpture, suggesting variations to artists from Picasso himself to the American David Smith.

The age of iron began many centuries ago by producing very beautiful objects—unfortunately for a large part, arms. Today, it provides as well bridges and railroads. It is time this metal ceased to be a murderer and the simple instrument of a supermechanical science. Today the door is wide open for this material to be, at last, forged and hammered by the peaceful hands of an artist.

Only a cathedral spire can show us a point in the sky where our soul is suspended!

In the disquietude of the night the stars seem to show us points of hope in the sky; this immobile spire also indicates to us an endless number of them. It is these points in the infinite which are precursors of the new art: *To draw in space.*

The important problem to solve here is not only to wish to make a work which is harmonious and perfectly balanced—No! But to get this result by the marriage of *material* and *space.* By the union of real forms with imaginary forms, obtained and suggested by established points, or by perforation— and, according to the natural law of love, to mingle them and make them inseparable, one from another, as are the body and the spirit.   *[n. d.]*

To protect and design in space with the help of new methods, to utilize this space, and to construct with it, as though one were dealing with a newly acquired material—that is all I attempt.

The synthetic deformities of material forms, of color, of light; the perforations, the absence of compact planes, give the work a mysterious, fantastic, indeed diabolical aspect. The artist, in the very process of transposing the forms of nature, in breathing new life into them, collaborates at the same time with the space which ennobles them.   *[n. d.]*

JUAN GRIS

(1887–1927)

After the First World War, there were various calls to order, manifested in a renewed interest in the objective representation of the objects and figures encountered in daily life. Although Juan Gris was among the prewar Cubists, his style was more hieratic and always directed toward the clear if stylized symbolization of conventional motifs such as still life and figure. It was readily adaptable for the many who worked in a rather subdued Cubist idiom between the wars.

I work with the elements of the intellect, with the imagination. I try to make concrete that which is abstract. I proceed from the general to the particular, by which I mean that I start with an abstraction in order to arrive at a true fact. Mine is an art of synthesis, of deduction. . . .

I want to endow the elements I use with a new quality; starting from general types I want to construct particular individuals.

I consider that the architectural element in painting is mathematics, the abstract side; I want to humanize it. Cézanne turns a bottle into a cylinder, but I begin with a cylinder and create an individual of a special type: I make a bottle—a particular bottle—out of a cylinder. Cézanne tends toward architecture, I tend away from it. That is why I compose with abstractions (colors) and make my adjustments when these colors have assumed the form of objects. For example, I make a composition with a white and a black and make adjustments when the white has become a paper and the black a shadow: what I mean is that I adjust the white so that it becomes a paper and the black so that it becomes a shadow.

This painting is to the other what poetry is to prose.

Though in my *system* I may depart greatly from any form of idealistic or naturalistic art, in practice I cannot break away from the Louvre. Mine is the method of all times, the method used by the old masters: there are technical *means* and they remain constant. *[1921]*

HANS HARTUNG

(1904–)

Trained in Germany, where he encountered the theories of the Blue Rider (Der Blaue Reiter) group, led by Kandinsky, Hartung fled to France in 1935. He began experimenting with informal abstract compositions (for which he became well known only after the Second World War) during the 1930s, developing a calligraphic approach based on his philosophic conceptions of the cosmos.

I could very well one day return to doing my old spots or my earlier signs. One must never forbid oneself anything. One must also be able to go back, one must always be able to change. The outer world tries to put a label on people and, especially, on the artist: classicism, romanticism, humanism, anarchism, figuration, abstraction, geometrics. You're hunted out, and there is a single goal: to enclose you in a box. The first and most important thing is to remain free, free in each line you undertake, in your ideas and in your political action, in your moral conduct. The artist especially must remain free from all outer constraint. Everything we feel deeply must be expressed. What concerns me is more the law than the object. What fascinates me is to see on canvas or paper at least part of the immutable and complex laws which govern the world, laws that bring about the vibration of the electrons and other parts of the atom, that combine to form matter, traverse the cosmos, form worlds, create light, heat, and even consciousness and intelligence; those laws without which nothing exists. In my youth I wanted to become an astronomer and even now there remains, alongside the personal psychic life which tends to express itself, that desire to approach or at least sense this absoluteness of laws, those laws which interminably create the world of order which is behind everything.   *[1974]*

JEAN HÉLION

(1904–)

During the 1930s Hélion was a forceful member of groups fostering geometric abstraction, such as Abstraction-Création and Cercle et Carré. His basically Cubist approach, modified by an extensive use of the curving plane reminiscent of the Russians

*and Léger, set him apart. Later, as he relates in the pithy account below, he was no
less admired for his switch to figurative motifs, for which he is again greatly admired
today.*

I am not preoccupied in justifying [painting] in the world of objects. Painting
belongs to the world of concepts, and I expect to find a short cut through
everything, to constitute a plan of projection common for ideas, instincts,
and perceptions. I compose the products of my instincts as they reach my
eyes, each accepted as a fact or energy, with structures intellectually conscious, and with experiences of colors patiently and tenderly carried out
through numerous charts.

I understand abstract art as an attempt to feed imagination with a world
built through the basic sensations of the eyes.

In the enthusiasm of the discovery or rediscovery of the fundamental
perception of the eyes, color and form in their primary stages and all that
is known as plastic, the raw material is often confused with a work of art.
Materials, though, however exciting, have no meaning in themselves; too
much emphasis put upon them impedes the possibilities of conception, and
the image starts drifting into a limbo, blind and chrysalis-like.

A painter does not necessarily limit his thoughts and feelings to what the
colors and forms provoke directly. But he must train his thoughts and
feelings in circles and cycles having to pass through color and through form
at one stage of their journey, thus taking flesh in painting and in return
vitalizing it.

Art degenerates if not kept essentially the language of the mysterious
being hidden in each man, behind his eyes. I act as if this hidden man in
me got life only through manipulations of plastic quantities, as if they were
his only body, as if their growth was his only future. I identify him with
his language. Instead of a description, an expression, or a comment, art
becomes a realization with which the urge to live collaborates as a mason.

This language is personal, and cannot pretend to become immediately
and equally intelligible to all; though it may be made very clear, as a new
object may be clear though unexplained. The spectator can enjoy painting
first as a voyage, and through its motion get an emotion going deep into
himself, where perhaps we meet.   *[1937]*

My pictorial course is in clear stages:
• From 1925 to 1929: painting of force, reaction, instinctive work before
nature and objects;
• From 1929 to 1933: elaboration of a system of signs;
• From 1934 to 1939: an effort to express the world in an abstract manner;
• From 1939 and from 1943 to 1946: effort to sing of the immediate world
with my abstract structures;
• From 1947 to 1951: search for archetypes both visual and human;

• From 1951 to 1954: effort to express everything through the narrow contact with the object. Effort to include the appearance in the essence;
• From 1955 to 1958: light;
• After 1958: free zone: *everything at once.*   *[1973]*

A U G U S T E   H E R B I N

(1882–1960)

One of the founders of Abstraction-Création in 1931, an international organization embracing nonobjective artists of many tendencies, Herbin was an important prose-lytizer for a purely formal art based on principles developed earlier by Mondrian's circle. Herbin's strict rationalization of color and geometric form would be elaborated upon after the Second World War by such artists as Victor Vasarely, who advocated an alphabet of pure geometric colored forms that he hoped would be universal.

Having renounced the representation of the object, we have renounced at the same time all *quantitative* characteristics: weight, matter, three-dimensional proportions, linear perspective. . . . Our imagination can in no case draw from these characteristics definition and enrichment of the composition of the work. It is the opposite in considering only *qualitative* characteristics (color and its spatial function . . . its close connection with shapes).

[The painter] begins by studying the object, [then] he will decompose light into color sacrificing the importance of the object and its shape.

The deterioration of the idea of an object is going to result in confusion by separating . . . the idea *volume* and the idea *color.* Color demanding the two-dimensional surface, by liberating itself of the problem *light* indispensable to the volume expressed in three dimensions, this will result in . . . a weakening of the idea *object;* . . . the technique must speak between two contradictory (imperatives), making unity impossible, stressing . . . impurity.

The idea *object* will be abandoned but the idea *volume,* the idea *light,* and the idea *color* will be maintained: same determination and same impurity; the appearance *object* has disappeared but . . . the work remains objective in its means, in its technique: *it is improper that this work be called abstract.*

                                                                                     [1948]

GERMANY

OTTO DIX

(1891–1969) '

During the 1920s, Dix brought a devastatingly critical eye to bear on the disorders of German society. His brutally honest paintings of the war were perhaps the most searing produced in Germany. His portraits were equally frank, and among the outstanding products of the Neue Sachlichkeit ("New Objectivity") movement.

You know, if one paints someone's portrait, one should not know him if possible. No knowledge! I do not want to know him at all, want only to see what is there, the outside. The inner follows by itself. It is mirrored in the visible. As soon as one knows him too long, one gets irritated. The visual immediacy is lost. The first impression is the right one. Once I have finished his picture, I can perhaps revise my impression and say, he really isn't such a beast as it seemed. Or he is not as decadent or as greedy as Flechtheim was at that time, or not so naïve as the Trillhaases. . . . It's all the same to me. I must keep the first impression fresh. If it is lost, I must find it again.   *[c. 1965]*

GEORGE GROSZ

(1893–1959)

During the First World War, Grosz had produced strong satirical drawings of the military, and, with John Heartfield, had developed a technique of photomontage in order to indict the ruling caste. He participated in Dada activities for a couple of years after the war. At the same time, he was beginning to work on his extraordinary drawings of the various groups within German society that were either victims or victimizers during the chaotic aftermath of the war. His trenchant characterizations based on observed reality were considered the motivating force for a movement that came to be called Neue Sachlichkeit.

The artistic revolutions of painters and poets are certainly interesting and aesthetically valuable—but still, in the last analysis, they are studio problems and many artists who earnestly torment themselves about such matters end up by succumbing to skepticism and bourgeois nihilism. This happens because persisting in their individualistic artistic eccentricities they never

GEORGE GROSZ *A German at Home*
(illustration from Daudet).

learn to understand revolutionary issues with any clarity; in fact, they rarely
bother with such things. Why, there are even art-revolutionary painters who
haven't freed themselves from painting Christ and the apostles; now, at the
very time when it is their revolutionary duty to double their efforts at
propaganda in order to purify the world of supernatural forces, God and
His angels, and thereby sharpen mankind's awareness of its true relationship
to the world. Those symbols, long since exhausted, and the mystical raptures
of that stupid saint hocus-pocus, today's painting is full of that stuff and
what can it possibly means to us? All this painted nonsense certainly can't
stand up to reality. Life is much too strong for it.

What should you do to give content to your paintings?

Go to a proletarian meeting; look and listen how people there, people just
like you, discuss some small improvement of their lot.

And understand—these masses are the ones who are reorganizing the
world. Not you! But you can work with them. You could help them if you
wanted to! And that way you could learn to give your art a content which
was supported by the revolutionary ideals of the workers.

As for my works in this portfolio, I want to say the following: I am again trying to give an absolutely realistic picture of the world. I want every man to understand me—without that profundity fashionable these days, without those depths which demand a veritable diving outfit stuffed with cabalistic and metaphysical hocus-pocus. In my efforts to develop a clear and simple style I can't help drawing closer to [Carlo D.] Carrà. Nevertheless, everything which is metaphysical and bourgeois about Carrà's work repels me. My work should be interpreted as training, as a hard workout, without any vision into eternity! I am trying in my so-called works of art to construct something with a completely realistic foundation. Man is no longer an individual to be examined in subtle psychological terms, but a collective, almost mechanical concept. Individual destiny no longer matters. Just as the ancient Greeks, I would like to create absolutely simple sport symbols which would be so easily understood that no commentary would be necessary.

I am suppressing color. Lines are used in an impersonal, photographic way to construct volumes. Once more stability, construction, and practical purpose—e.g., sport, engineer, and machine but devoid of Futurist romantic dynamism.

Once more to establish control over line and form—it's no longer a question of conjuring up on canvas brightly colored Expressionistic soul-tapestries—the objectivity and clarity of an engineer's drawing is preferable to the uncontrolled twaddle of the cabala, metaphysics, and ecstatic saints.

It isn't possible to be absolutely precise when you write about your own work, especially if you're always in training—then each day brings new discoveries and a new orientation. But I would like to say one thing more: I see the future development of painting taking place in workshops, in pure craftsmanship, not in any holy temple of the arts. Painting is manual labor, no different from any other; it can be done well or poorly. Today we have a star system, so do the other arts—but that will disappear.   *[1920]*

CARL HOFER

(1878–1956)

After sojourns in Rome and Paris between 1903 and 1913, Hofer settled in Berlin. There, he established his name as a painter somewhat apart from the German Expressionist movement, but sharing many of its ideals and brooding on similarly pessimistic themes.

We stand today at one of the great turning points of culture, one unfelt by the majority. Our points of view are fluctuating. A new, deeper, and subjective approach to nature has created new forms of art, and the events of our innermost spiritual experience clamor for tangible expression. During the past five years my principal task has been to achieve, by artistic means, the purely pictorial aspect of these perceptions of form and color.

My character was solidly anchored in traditional forms, within whose bounds I endeavored to express my personality. Rejected by the opinions of a new order, these forms are no longer adequate, but where I can use them I try to fill them with new life. . . . For me no difference exists in principle between nonobjective and objective representation. If a picture has been experienced and created according to the rules of graphic counterpoint, it is immaterial whether its theme is form visually or intuitively apprehended. The entire gamut of possible expression and representation lies between the objective and nonobjective methods, and I claim license for the artist who feels attracted to them, so that he may make use of these manifold opportunities.

For me each picture has its own laws; I try to develop its form from the inmost nature of the thing painted. It will differ characteristically from the next picture, for only paintings done from the same sequence of images can be similar. . . . I want my work to be known, not only by its exterior peculiarities: color, "palette," or uniqueness, but by its spiritual affinity and intricate consistency. . . . I profess no theories, for then I should have to carry them to their conclusion, which is to say, *ad absurdum.* Degree of novelty is for me no criterion of value. *[1931]*

KÄTHE KOLLWITZ

(1867–1945)

Kollwitz first achieved fame in Germany in 1897–1898 with her series of prints and drawings based on Gerhart Hauptmann's play The Weavers. *Her profound concern with social injustice was deepened during her marriage to Dr. Karl Kollwitz, who practiced medicine in the poorest quarter of Berlin. After their son was killed during the First World War, Käthe Kollwitz turned her attention to the expression of strong pacifist convictions. During the early 1920s, her prints and drawings showed tremendous compassion for the sufferings of women and children during the war's aftermath. During the Nazi period, her work was banned and she lost her teaching post. The crowning achievements of her life were her self-portraits of this period, and her series of lithographs on the theme of death—great and moving masterpieces.*

On All Souls' Day Karl and I went together to the Reichstag memorial meeting for the dead of the World War. At such moments, when I know I am working with an international society opposed to war I am filled with a warm sense of contentment. I know, of course, that I do not achieve pure art in the sense of Schmidt-Rottluff's, for example. But still it is art. Everyone works the best way he can. I am content that my art should have purposes outside itself. I would like to exert influence in these times when human beings are so perplexed and in need of help. Many people feel the obligation to help and exert influence, but my course is clear and unequivocal. Others must follow vague courses. Pl., for example. In the spring he wants to clear out, go around wandering and preaching. He wants to preach *action*, but inward action, a turning away from the outmoded forms of life that have proved wrong. Preparing the soil for a new life of spiritual liberation. And then there are all the groups preaching a new eroticism ("religious bohemia"). It is reminiscent of the Anabaptists, of the times when—as now—the great turning point in history is proclaimed and it is announced that the millennial kingdom is upon us.

Compared with all these visionaries my activities seem crystal clear. I wish I might go on working for many long years as I am working now.

[1922]

LÁSZLÓ MOHOLY-NAGY
(1895–1946)

Born in Hungary, Moholy-Nagy settled in Berlin in 1921 and taught at the Bauhaus from 1923 to 1928. There he experimented with light and mechanical devices to produce a variety of works ranging from photographic images to kinetic sculptures. His interest in machines and in technology in general led him to theorize about art in the future in several important publications. His pioneering spirit brought him to America in 1937, where he founded the New Bauhaus and where his principles found new adherents in various fields, ranging from industrial design and architecture to the fine arts.

All technical achievements in the sphere of optics must be utilized for the development of *this* standard language. Among them the *mechanical and technical* requisites of art are of primary importance.

Until recently they were condemned on the grounds that manual skill, the "personal touch," should be regarded as the essential thing in art. Today they already hold their own in the conflict of opinions; tomorrow they will triumph; the day after tomorrow they will yield results accepted without question. Brushwork, the subjective manipulation of a tool is lost, but the clarity of formal relationships is increased to an extent almost transcending the limitations of matter; an extent in which the objective context becomes transparently clear. Maximum precision, the law of the norm, replaces the misinterpreted significance of manual skill.

It is difficult today to predict the formal achievements of the future. For the formal cystallization of a work of art is conditioned not merely by the incalculable factor of talent, but also by the intensity of the struggle for the mastery of its medium (tools, today machines). But is safe to predict even today that the optical creation of the future will not be a mere translation of our present forms of optical expression, for the new implements and the hitherto neglected medium of light must necessarily yield results in conformity with their own inherent properties.   *[1923–1926]*

THE FUNCTION OF THE ARTIST

Art is the senses' grindstone, sharpening the eyes, the mind, and the feelings. Art has an educational and formative ideological function, since not only the conscious but also the subconscious mind absorbs the social atmosphere which can be translated into art. The artist interprets ideas and concepts through his own media. Despite the indirectness of his statement, his work expresses allegiance to the few or many, to arrogance or humility, to the fixed or visionary. In this sense, he must take sides, must proclaim his stand and no true artist can escape this task. Otherwise his work would be no more than an exercise in skill. What art contains is not basically different from the content of our other utterances but art attains its effect mainly by subconscious organization of its own means. If that were not so, all problems could be solved successfully through intellectual or verbal discourse alone.

The so-called "unpolitical" approach to art is a fallacy. Politics is taken here, not in its party connotation, but as a way of realizing ideas for the benefit of the community. Such a Weltanschauung is transformed, in the arts, into an organized, felt form by the concrete means of the different modes of expression. This content can be generally grasped directly through the senses, on a subliminal level, without a conscious thinking process. Art may press for a socio-biological solution of problems just as energetically as social revolutionaries may press for political action. The difficulty is that few people are sensitive and, at the same time, educated enough to receive the real message of art, whether contemporary or old. As a young painter I often had the feeling, when pasting my collages and painting my "abstract" pictures, that I was throwing a message, sealed in a bottle, into the sea. It might take decades for someone to find and read it. I believed that abstract art not only registers contemporary problems, but projects a desirable future order, unhampered by any secondary meaning, which the customary departure from nature usually involves because of its inevitable connotations. Abstract art, I thought, creates new types of spatial relationships, new inventions of forms, new visual laws—basic and simple—as the visual counterpart to a more purposeful, cooperative human society.   *[1928]*

OSKAR SCHLEMMER   *Study for Triadic Ballet*. 1922. Gouache, ink, and collage of photographs. 22⅝ x 14⅝" (irregular).

OSKAR SCHLEMMER

(1888–1943)

Schlemmer taught at the Bauhaus from 1920 to 1929. He shared with his colleagues Kandinsky and Klee a deep respect for "inner vision" and tried, in his paintings and stage designs, to endow the human figure with a hieratic dignity. In the 1920s, the movement toward a representational vanguard art, or a "new objectivity," drew considerable strength from Schlemmer's vigorous approach, particularly in costume and set design for avant-garde dance and theater.

I view future developments as follows (the general outlines are already more or less visible): the ways will part. The architectural, Constructivist trend in recent art will be channeled into direct application, the answer to many of the problems we are experiencing now. Application: shaping the objects of everyday use, or better yet, designing houses and their entire contents. At the same time, the rumor of art's demise will be laid to rest; it was originally spread by the advocates of applied art (the *real* Constructivists, who do not paint); as I see it, the picture, painting, the metaphysical, will be rescued by precisely those Constructivist methods which can either be applied to the real, practical world or used to express the realm of the ideal.

"Absolute" art, the art of "pure" form and color, belongs to architecture and all that implies. Painting needs a medium borrowed from the visible world. The most appropriate subject matter: man. Does that suggest a restoration of the old aesthetics? I believe it does. Certain old principles seem unshakable, eternally fresh. If their restoration in a new guise were not a reality, someone would have to invent it.

Proud, new, noble tasks ahead.

"Abstract" figures, completely divested of corporeality, and mere hieroglyphs: mysterious marks, cliff paintings, stone engravings are, seen in this light, one extreme. The other would be embedding the figure in space, coloration, *valeur*. Objective: a felicitous synthesis of nature and abstraction which—still—seems to be the criterion of true art.

This style of depiction: imbedding in space, coloration, *valeur*, will appear conventional, and in a sense it will be just that, for it incorporates the old, proven truths of painting. Nevertheless, or perhaps for that very reason, this method will be capable of revealing the most profound original insights, and Otto Meyer's* great wisdom consists in his use of a comprehensible language to express new, unheard-of visions. It looks like compromise. Perhaps the ultimate wisdom is: compromise.

Developments in Germany and in art are cut off before their prime. They are falling victim to the tempo of the times. I feel absolute freedom and metaphysical fulfillment have not yet been attained; the degree of formal perfection, or of classic form, necessary to the development of grand style has not been reached. *[1924]*

* A Swiss painter.

K U R T   S C H W I T T E R S

(1887–1948)

After the First World War, Schwitters settled in Hanover, where he flourished as an independent Dadaist, writing sound and nonsense poems and making innumerable small collages with found objects such as bus tickets and wine bottle labels. His exceptional grace softened the absurdist thrust of Dada and certain of his collages can be seen in a purely aesthetic, Constructivist light. These collages followed a principle of additive assembling that led him to build a sculpture room, a "Merzbau," which might be considered the first environmental sculpture, prefiguring the work of post–World War II artists such as Allan Kaprow and Lucio Fontana.

I call small compositions that I have pasted and occasionally overpainted "Merz-drawings." In reality the expression *drawings* is not sufficient because these small works are, essentially, painted, that is, colored and flatly formed. But by some chance this mistaken expression happened to creep in quite early and now this word cannot be changed very easily. But please regard the small "Merz-drawings" as paintings.

I called my new way of creation with any material "merz." This is the second syllable of "Kommerz" (commerce). The name originated from the "Merzbild," a picture in which the word *Merz* could be read in between abstract forms. It was cut out and glued on from an advertisement for the Kommerz und Privatbank. This word *Merz* had become a part of the picture through being attuned to the other part of the picture, and so it had to stay there. You will understand that I called a picture with the word *Merz* the "Merz-picture" in the same way that I called a picture with *und* the "Und-picture" and a picture with the word *Arbeiter* the "Arbeiter-picture." When I first exhibited these pasted and nailed pictures with the Sturm in Berlin, I searched for a collective noun for this new kind of picture, because I could not define them with the older conceptions like Expressionism, Futurism, or whatever. So I gave all my pictures the name *Merz-pictures* after the most characteristic of them and thus made them like a species. Later on I expanded this name *Merz* to include my poetry (I had written poetry since 1917), and finally all my relevant activities. Now I call myself Merz.   *[c. 1927]*

GREAT BRITAIN

SIR WILLIAM COLDSTREAM

(1908–   )

Coldstream's generation, as he describes below, explored the various sources of the modern idiom and—under the severe stress of the world Depression and the disturbing political events of the 1930s—greatly questioned their value. Coldstream was one of the most forceful dissenters and, in 1937, was a founder of what came to be known as the Euston Road School—painters who committed themselves to a representational approach of a rather sober, restrained character.

I lived in a room with a north light, near the Tottenham Court Road, and belonged to a set of about a dozen friends, all painters who had just left the Slade. We read Clive Bell and Roger Fry and spent a great deal of time discussing aesthetics. All the more intelligent books on art which we read taught us to regard subject-matter merely as an excuse for good painting. Our discussions were usually on the question of which contemporary style was best and most progressive. None of us ever sold any pictures; we had the idea that only second-rate artists could sell their work before they were dead. Once a year we sent our work to the London Group. We hoped to have important one-man shows some day. The set was divided roughly into two groups. I belonged to that which admired Sickert, Matisse, and Duncan Grant, as opposed to that which followed Picasso and Braque.

The slump had made me aware of social problems, and I became convinced that art ought to be directed to a wider public; whereas all ideas which I had learned to regard as *artistically* revolutionary ran in the opposite direction. It seemed to me important that the broken communications between the artist and the public should be built up again and that this most probably implied a movement toward realism.

At present I paint directly from nature without much conscious selection except in the initial selection of the subject. I do not choose subjects in the first place because they strike me as exciting patterns or interesting shapes or color. I choose them for their general interest—literary interest if you like. Possibly because I am a painter I am drawn to subjects suitable to painting, but if so I am not aware of the fact. On the whole I prefer living subjects, as I am more interested in people than things. When I am painting I make no conscious attempt to bring out the literary interest or character, and I do not consciously alter the shapes, colors, or positions of objects, though I should not hesitate to do so if I wanted to. I am just as likely to want to paint a man because he is a doctor—and I am interested in doctors— as because of the shape of his head. In any case I should be interested in the shape of his head once I had started. As far as I can remember once I have started painting I am occupied mainly with putting things in the right place. That is to say, in trying to make each part occupy its right position in space. Certainly one designs, modifies, modulates, simplifies, selects, and exaggerates, since painting is not a scientific record of fact but a record of fact enlarged and modified by one's reaction to it, and the most realistic painting can be nothing like reality. *[1938]*

HENRY MOORE

(1898–)

Moore's interest in non-Western sculpture led him to experiment with forms drawn from sources as varied as Sumerian and pre-Columbian artifacts, in addition to natural formations such as pebbles, rocks, and bones. His audacious address to new sculptural problems such as the inclusion of negative, or empty, spaces, as part of the whole, won him a singular position in the British avant-garde, and, during the 1940s, international acclaim. Most contemporary British sculptors of younger generations owe something to Moore's point of view, which he also put forward during many years of teaching.

The human figure is what interests me most deeply, but I have found principles of form and rhythm from the study of natural objects such as pebbles, rocks, bones, trees, shells, etc.

Pebbles and rocks show nature's way of working stone. Smooth, sea-worn pebbles show the wearing away, rubbed treatment of stone and principles of asymmetry.

Rocks show the hacked, hewn treatment of stone, and have a jagged nervous block rhythm.

Bones have marvelous structural strength and hard tenseness of form, subtle transition of one shape into the next and great variety in section.

Trees (tree trunks) show principles of growth and strength of joints, with easy passing of one section into the next. They give the ideal for wood sculpture, upward twisting movement.

Shells show nature's hard but hollow form (metal sculpture) and have a wonderful completeness of single shape.

My aim in work is to combine, as intensely as possible, the abstract principles of sculpture along with the realization of my idea. . . .

Abstract qualities of design are essential to the value of a work, but to me of equal importance is the psychological, human element. If both abstract and human elements are welded together in a work, it must have a fuller, deeper meaning.   *[1934]*

A piece of stone can have a hole through it and not be weakened—if the hole is of a studied size, shape, and direction. On the principle of the arch, it can remain just as strong.

The first hole though a piece of stone is a revelation.

The hole connects one side to the other, making it immediately more three-dimensional.

A hole can itself have as much shape-meaning as a solid mass. . . .

The mystery of the hole—the mysterious fascination of caves in hillsides and cliffs.   *[1937]*

The most striking quality common to all primitive art is its intense vitality. It is something made by people with a direct and immediate response to life. Sculpture and painting for them was not an activity of calculation or academism, but a channel for expressing powerful beliefs, hopes, and fears. It is art before it got smothered in trimmings and surface decorations, before inspiration had flagged into technical tricks and intellectual conceits. But apart from its own enduring value, a knowledge of it conditions a fuller and truer appreciation of the later developments of the so-called great periods, and shows art to be a universal continuous activity with no separation between past and present.

All art has its roots in the "primitive," or else it becomes decadent, which explains why the "great" periods, Pericles' Greece and the Renaissance for example, flower and follow quickly on primitive periods, and then slowly fade out. Underlying the individual characteristics and featural peculiarities of the different primitive schools, a common world language of form is apparent . . . ; through the working of instinctive sculptural sensibility, the same shapes and form relationships are used to express similar ideas at widely different places and periods in history, so that the same form-vision may be seen in a Negro and a Viking carving, a Cycladic stone figure and a Nukuoro wooden statuette. . . . It eventually became clear to me that the realistic ideal of physical beauty in art which sprang from fifth-century Greece was only a digression from the main world tradition of sculpture, whilst, for instance, our own equally European Romanesque and Early Gothic are in the main line. *[1941]*

BEN NICHOLSON

(1894–1982)

Nicholson was a major figure in the British avant-garde during the 1930s, when many other British artists turned away from modern abstraction. He associated himself with the international groups, based largely in Paris, that advocated nonobjective art, but his own reliefs often suggest the presence of still life or landscape motifs.

1. It must be understood that a good idea is exactly as good as it can be universally applied, that no idea can have a universal application which is not solved in its own terms and if any extraneous elements are introduced the application ceases to be universal. "Realism" has been abandoned in the search for reality: the "principal objective" of abstract art is precisely this reality.

2. A different painting, a different sculpture are different experiences just as walking in a field or over a mountain are different experiences and it is only at the point at which a painting becomes an actual experience in the artist's life, more or less profound and more or less capable of universal application according to the artist's capacity to live, that it is capable of becoming a part, also, of the lives of other people and that it can take its place in the structure of the world, in everyday life.

3. "Painting" and "religious experience" are the same thing. It is a question of the perpetual motion of a right idea.

4. You cannot ask an explorer to explain what a country is like which he is about to explore for the first time: it is more interesting to investigate the vitality of the present movement than to predict its precise future development; a living present necessarily contains its own future and two things are indisputable—that the present constructive movement is a living force and that life gives birth to life. *[1937]*

About space-construction: I can explain this by an early painting I made of a shop window in Dieppe, though, at the time, this was not made with any conscious idea of space but merely using the shop window as a theme on which to base an imaginative idea. The name of the shop was Au Chat Botté, and this set going a train of thought connected with fairy tales of my childhood and, being in French, and my French being a little mysterious, the words themselves had also an abstract quality—but what was important was that this name was printed in very lovely red lettering on the glass window—*giving one plane*—and in this window were reflections of what was behind me as I looked in—*giving a second plane*—while through the window objects on a table were performing a kind of ballet and forming the "eye" or life-point of the painting—*giving a third plane*. These three planes and all their subsidiary planes were interchangeable so that you could not tell which was real and which unreal, what was reflected and what was unreflected, and this created, as I see now, some kind of space or an imaginative world in which one could live.

The same process takes place in making an abstract painting or an abstract relief, where, for instance, as the simplest example—you can take a rectangular surface and cut a section of it in one plane lower and then in the higher plane cut a circle deeper than, but without touching, the lower plane. *One is immediately conscious that this circle has pierced the lower plane without having touched it*—even a dog or a cat will realize instantly—and this creates space. The awareness of this is felt subconsciously and it is useless to approach it intellectually, as this, so far from helping, only acts as a barrier. This language is comprehensible to anyone who doesn't set up barriers— the dog and cat set up no barriers and their eyes, whiskers, and tails are alive, without restriction, but the whiskers of an intellectual do not give off the necessary spark, and contact cannot be made.

I think that so far from being a limited expression, understood by a few, abstract art is a powerful, unlimited, and universal language.   *[1941]*

GREECE

NIKOLAS GHIKA

(1906–   )

Trained in Paris, Ghika first worked in a post-Cubist idiom, but during the 1930s he became concerned with restoring Greek characteristics in modern art, and fused references to Greek landscape and folk art with a semi-abstract formal style.

Are you aware of a particular tradition of painting which has special relevance for a Greek artist, and if so to what extent does it condition your work? Can you describe this tradition?

I should say at once that I am historically minded—I can't help it. And at times it carries me to extremes. You may hear me say quite seriously about two colors in somebody's picture: "These are not historically right colors." This sounds rather pompous and you might well question such circumspection. It is awfully difficult to explain. But I tend to see color in more or less definite modes. In music, they used to speak of the Lydian mode, the Frygian, and so on; or, as you say, the Ionic order or the Doric.

If you have an Ionic column which is of a certain proportion and a certain shape, you must, of necessity, match all the parts of the architecture with it, and this makes it impossible to use any other proportion—which belongs, say, to the Doric order.

I would call, for instance, a basic combination of cerulean blue, crocus yellow, and Chinese vermilion, Ionic. Light red, ochre yellow, and ultramarine, Doric. There are of course endless scales. This is only to show you the peculiar way in which my mind works.

Of course, as somebody said, you are born a colorist or you are not, but then there are certain rules which I do not like to see transgressed. For instance if one uses, as they did on Greek vases, a flat color to represent the mantle of a young virgin one can on top of it draw lines, many or a few, black or white, or colored or both, to show the movement, the folds or the creases.

But if one uses the same uniform tint on the mantle of the Virgin, as was later sometimes done, and models it in light and dark in the same hue, this is wrong, because to model means to represent surfaces which have a different orientation, catch the light in a different way, and therefore change hue all the time. Who rediscovered this? The Impressionists.

You might say that this could apply perhaps to European art which stems from the Greek, but does not necessarily apply to other continents, or to the modern abstraction or spontaneity.

My answer to that would be that there have been only a relatively small number of totally isolated centers of really important creative art. More often than not there has been interrelation between them. I do not seem really to believe in a completely pure parthenogenesis. One can generally find a germ brought by migrating tribes on camels or ships or in a merchant's luggage which gives the initial kickoff. If the soil where it is dropped is fertile, a great artistic center develops in which the native gifts are grafted on to the foreign sample and proliferate into a perfectly original creation. And this new style may fire back at its origins.   *[1968]*

OSVALDO LICINI   *Ritmo.* 1956. Card. 6¹¹⁄₁₆ x 4⁵⁄₁₆".

ITALY

OSVALDO LICINI

(1894–1958)

Together with Alberto Magnelli and Atanasio Soldati—for whom he also speaks in the passage below—Licini made a forceful entry into Italian artistic life as an advocate of abstraction. His strong Constructivist style of painting of the 1930s was later modified with the introduction of organic, free forms.

Art for us is of a mysterious nature and cannot be defined. . . . Enemies of all formulas, we refuse to give an exact definition to abstractionism. . . . We are abstractionists and we believe that nothing human is lacking in our work. But we are accused of being cerebral. . . . We are abstractionists by the psychological law of compensation, that is, in reaction to the excessive materialism and naturalism of the century.

We are abstractionists because we maintain that classicism, romanticism, realism, etc., are closed cycles and it is vain to try to return to them. Art transforms and renews itself rigorously following the irresistible spirit that doesn't turn back. We take the occasion to recall that painting is the art of color and signs. The signs express the force, the will, the idea. Color expresses magic. We have said signs [*segni*] and not dreams [*sogni*]. [*c. 1935*]

ALBERTO MAGNELLI

(1888–1971)

Magnelli's early works were affected by his contact with Futurist and Metaphysical painters in Italy. However, when he went to Paris in 1933, he began to veer toward the geometric practices of the Abstraction-Création group and eventually developed a highly personal mode of expressive abstraction for which he was celebrated there after the war.

If you consider that nature is a reality, that the human being is himself part of this reality, his spirit is an element and prolongation of that reality. The human spirit acts necessarily in the heart of the real. . . . Each gesture of man is human and the movements of the creative imagination are also. . . . I am always astonished when they refuse painters the right to "invented figuration" or "the imagination of forms," since they recognize so easily the rights of imagination in engineers. . . .

Too often the spectator sees only the superficial aspect of the work, but it has to do with much more. In its forms, through its forms, the naturally invented subject expresses a myth—I mean invented by the artist who opens his way through nature. Thus, the abstract painting carries the traces of signs that come from afar. The work is a concentration, a making explicit of our sensory vision. All powerful works, by the fact of being powerful, provoke necessarily social resonances. It is false to think that to provoke such resonances the painter must represent anecdotes reflecting social life. . . .

In order for the human community to benefit from the contributions of the artist, it must learn the language that he uses in his work. In order to understand what is said in a language, you first have to learn that language. . . .

I believe that these days, to elevate humanity by means of art, there is no need to look for realism, naturalism, or formal materialism, but on the contrary, to touch the essential in the poetic forces that are in man. *[1947]*

MARINO MARINI

(1901–1980)

During the Fascist years many Italian artists lost heart, but Marini, holding himself apart, developed a vigorous sculptural style that won him international recognition. His themes were often related to traditional equestrian monuments that he managed to give a modern symbolic intonation. He was, in addition, one of the century's most distinguished portrait sculptors.

I do not think that space is a problem. I do not believe that it is necessary for the artist to preoccupy himself with more or less ephemeral, constantly changing theories.

The artist attempts to create a work of art; and if he succeeds, it is because his inspiration and the docility of his hand in following his inspiration necessarily bring about a solution of the problem. Besides, if there were a problem, it would be different for each new work.

I do not make any distinction between abstract and figurative sculpture, provided it is really sculpture in either case. What matters above all is the quality of a work of art. As for myself, since I am a Mediterranean, I can express myself freely only through the human. But I accept and admire every other form of expression, provided the artist succeeds in transmitting his message through it. A match may be more moving than a Doric column, but it would be absurd to concede a priori that a box of matches might constitute a message on the same level as the Parthenon.   *[1953]*

GIORGIO MORANDI

(1890–1964)

Morandi studied at the Academy of Fine Arts in his native Bologna. He was associated with the Metaphysical School for a short time around 1918, and later with the Valori Plastici movement, which advocated a kind of neoclassical realism. From the mid-1920s to his death, however, Morandi remained an isolated artist whose muted still lifes of such objects as bottles and pitchers generated a poetic response. His drawings, etchings, still life paintings, and occasional landscapes are often compared with those of Chardin and Cézanne in their architectonic harmony, but a lyrical, softened, tonal atmospheric aura distinguishes them.

I have always avoided suggesting any metaphysical implications. I suppose I remain, in that respect, a believer in Art for Art's sake rather than in Art for the sake of religion, of social justice or of national glory. Nothing is more alien to me than an art which sets out to serve other purposes than those implied in the work of art in itself. . . .

I believe that nothing can be more abstract, more unreal, than what we actually see. We know that all that we can see of the objective world, as human beings, never really exists as we see and understand it. Matter exists, of course, but has no intrinsic meaning of its own, such as the meanings that we attach to it. Only we can know that a cup is a cup, that a tree is a tree.   *[c. 1959]*

MEXICO

DAVID ALFARO SIQUEIROS

(1896–1974)

Along with Diego Rivera and José Clemente Orozco, Siqueiros was a leader in the Mexican mural movement of the 1920s. Like many other Mexican artists after the 1910–1911 revolution there, he believed that art should be a force for social and political change. His forceful personality and his writings contributed to the renown of Mexican painters elsewhere and influenced many artists in the United States. The statement below, composed by several artists, including Siqueiros, was read by him to the American Artists' Congress in New York in 1936, and is a summary of his view of the evolution of socially committed Mexican art.

Modern Mexican painting of revolutionary tendency arose at the same time as the Mexican Revolution and followed its contingencies. Thus the first unrest in art corresponded to the beginnings of social and political unrest. Toward the end of the Díaz regime, the thoughts of the artists were exclusively fixed on Europe. Their artistic tendencies reflected the mentality of the dominant feudal aristocracy. It was naturally at this period that unrest first appeared. The artistic unrest was manifested in the form of a movement for a folk art. Saturnino Herrán, for the first time, took as his subjects scenes of popular life. In greater or lesser degree all other painters took the same path. Armed insurrection had already broken out in the North and South. In 1911 students of the School of Fine Arts—The National Academy of Carlos—organized a strike which included economic and political as well as educational demands. It called for the abolition of academic methods and the establishment of open-air schools. They supposed that they were expressing in this way their revolutionary position. They childishly abolished

DAVID ALFARO SIQUEIROS
Proletarian Victim. 1933. Duco on burlap.
6'9" x 47½".

the black pigment from their palette as a revolutionary protest. Our strike insinuated itself into the struggle for land for the peasants, reforms for the workers, and against imperialism, but only in a more or less general manner. We received considerable support among the students of the National University. This was converted into a general protest against the existing methods of intellectual oppression in the universities themselves, and thus our strike assumed a definitely political character. Its leaders were arrested and the demand for their liberation became a matter of national interest. Six months later came the triumph of Madero and with it the fulfillment of our most elementary demands. In this way there appeared the first open-air schools and the traditional academic methods were replaced by Impressionism.

Our Europeanism, the reflection of dying Porfirism, began to be replaced by a nationalistic aesthetic. We began to discover that Mexico had a great archaeological tradition and also a rich folklore. Works by artists who had been ignored previously now assumed a very important place in our artistic thought. The popular drawings by [José Guadalupe] Posada became highly esteemed; so did the paintings in the *pulquerias* (drinking rooms). We did not yet think about the political content of art. By 1913 there began to appear the first manifestations of social consciousness in our art with reference to workers, as, for example, in the works of Romano, Guillemin, Ortega, Furter, and many others. This social art resulted in conflicts with the Ministry of Education. The growth of the revolution converted our first open-air school into a political center. Unanimously we joined the struggle of the masses against the dictatorship of Huerta. This make it impossible for us to continue work, and most of us entered the army of the revolution as soldiers. This fact put us for the first time in direct contact not only with the people, but also with the geography of the country. This converted the bohemian painters into a new type of artist. In a hiatus during the armed conflict of 1915 José Clemente Orozco and [Francisco] Goitia produced works of art which were important for the subsequent development of our Art. Orozco's anticlerical drawings and Goitia's revolutionary scenes illuminated contemporary life, for the Mexican youth. A little later, in 1919, the work in the School of Fine Arts was resumed, absorbing a larger part of the youth restlessness. At the same time Siqueiros was sent to Europe by a similar group of artists that had emerged, in Guadalajara. This caused the contact between the restlessness of the Mexican youth with a certain degree of mature technique in Europe which was represented by Rivera. It made it possible to publish our manifesto *Vida Americana*—American Life— which appeared in Barcelona in 1921. Here for the first time Rivera and Siqueiros tried to express the theory of a muralist movement which developed a little later. This movement, however, had certain practical antecedents in the group formed by Dr. Atl called the Society of Painters and Sculptors which wanted to paint in a collective for the walls of the amphitheater of the Prepatorium.

With the appointment in 1922 of José Vasconcelos as minister of education the impulse toward mural painting became a reality. Orozco, Rivera, and Siqueiros obtained big contracts to paint murals, and various others obtained contracts to paint smaller panels. This circumstance produced groupings among the artists. Our manifesto talked about mural art for the masses. But the moment we began our actual work, having come to mural painting as easel painters we were primarily absorbed in new technical problems. We neglected the real problems of content and created murals of neutral or socially irrelevant character. As soon as we had acquired our technique we became more conscious of the social possibilities of our work and organized our revolutionary syndicate of painters, sculptors and engravers. It was then possible to give more consistency to our political attitude. At first our political confusion was a natural consequence of the uncertainty and confusion of the Mexican revolution as a whole and also our lack of revolutionary political education. None of us had had experience with trade unions, with strikes or social struggles. We gave little thought to questions of revolutionary strategy in the placing of our works. We were at this time Utopians in our conceptions of revolutionary art with little direct contact with the masses. The appearance of the organ of our syndicate, *El Machete*, was the beginning of our direct contact with the organized masses, and at the same time the beginning of our conflict with the government. Our murals were in places more or less inaccessible to the masses. But the moment we began to reach the masses through our drawings and prints the government became antagonistic to us. Our first audiences were students and teachers, only intellectuals; our second audience the large masses of people. This new broadening of contact in turn reacted on us to develop our political and social views and to direct our work along new lines. At the same time around 1924 and 1925 that we were perfecting the content of our work, some of us were little by little transformed from merely passive spectators of the revolution into active participants. *[1936]*

THE NETHERLANDS

THEO VAN DOESBURG

(1883–1931)

A prime mover in the de Stijl movement, Doesburg was a prolific lecturer, writer, and proselytizer as well as a graphic artist, painter, and architect. He played an important role in the founding of the periodical de Stijl, *in which he broadened the discussion of Neoplasticism to include current tendencies such as the Dada movement. As a result, he had access to art institutions all over Europe and for a time was influential at the Bauhaus. In 1930 he settled in Paris, where he had already been extremely active in propagating the principles of nonobjective art.*

1. I speak here for the de Stijl group in Holland which has arisen out of the necessity of accepting the consequence of modern art; this means finding practical solutions to universal problems.

2. Building, which means organizing one's means into a unity (*Gestaltung*) is all-important to us.

3. This unity can be achieved only suppressing arbitrary subjective elements in the expressional means.

4. We reject all subjective choice of forms and are preparing to use objective, universal, formative means.

5. Those who do not fear the consequences of the new theories of art we call progressive artists.

6. The progressive artists of Holland have from the first adopted an international standpoint. Even during the war . . .

7. The international standpoint resulted from the development of our work itself. That is, it grew out of practice. Similar necessities have arisen out of the development of . . . progressive artists in other countries.

THEO VAN DOESBURG   *Composition (The Cow).* 1916–1917.
Oil on canvas. 14¾ x 25".

The artist speaks from within his interior and the exterior worlds in words and images which come easily to him because they are elements of the world in which he alone belongs. The public's worlds, however, are totally different and the words with which it expresses its ideas are entirely characteristic of its own world.

The perceptions of different people, each of whom inhabit different interior and exterior worlds, clearly cannot coincide. . . .

The modern artist uses the phrase *space formation* in order to enable the observer to look at his work. The artist whose occupation consists in space formation and is closely involved with it, regards this expression as as much a matter of course as does the surgeon the word *fracture.* The layman, however, has totally different conceptions of space and formation. At best he takes *space* to mean a hollow or a measurable surface. The word *formation* will awaken in the observer an uncertain memory of a physical shape. The combination of the two words *space* and *formation* will therefore convey to him a physical form having spatial depth and shown in perspective in the manner of the artists of the past.

To the modern creative artist space is not a measurable, delimited surface, but rather the idea of extent which arises from the relationship between one means of formation (e.g., line, color) and another (e.g., the picture plane). This idea of extent or space touches the fundamental laws of all the visual arts because the artist must understand its principles. Furthermore, *space* means to him a special tension created in the work by the tightening of forms, planes, or lines. The word *formation* means to him the visible embodiment of the relationship between a form (or color) and space and the other forms or colors. . . .

Just as Spanish flies are no longer prescribed in medicine, so in painting it has become impossible to cling to a Vitruvian hypothesis. Vitruvius says in the Sixth Book of his work on architecture: "A painting is the representation of a thing which exists or which can exist, e.g., a man, a ship or other things for which rigidly outlined physical forms have served as models."

Experience proves that this idea still persists, both among laymen and among many artists too. With so primitive a conception of art many good articles and books about the new visual art must inevitably fail to bring proper results. All these studies (most of them by art historians) evince too personal an interpretation. These writings are the products of a system of thought and feeling which has an individualistic bias and as such are not suited to elucidate a creative principle rooted in universality. Personal interpretation of the various expressional forms of the new visual art must be replaced by a synthesis of its nature, which alone can answer the purpose.

One of the most significant points of difference between it and earlier concepts of art consists of the fact that in the new art the artist's temperament is no longer so prominent. The new plasticism is the product of a universal stylistic intent. . . .

The modern artist desires no intermediary. He wishes to address himself to the public directly, through his work. If the public does not understand him it is up to him to provide his own explanations.

The main reason why the public is on the wrong tack where the new art is concerned lies in the irrelevance of lay criticism, which obscures with unclear clarifications the unprejudiced vision and experience of works of art.

There is only one way to restore the unprejudiced way of looking, destroyed by the ignorance and complacency of traditional art criticism: *elementary and universally intelligible principles of visual art must be established—which is what is attempted here.*

[1925]

POLAND

HENRYK BERLEWI

(1884–1967)

Born in Warsaw, Berlewi traveled in Europe before the First World War, and in 1922 met both El Lissitzky and Theo van Doesburg, who spurred his interest in nonobjective painting. His theory of Mechanofaktur, *in which the principles of engineering were brought to bear on painting, was launched in 1924. In 1926 he left Poland for Paris and returned to figurative painting. He died an opponent of abstract art.*

The technical means of painting must be readjusted—applied to the tasks of the scheme. The old technique of painting, still lingering, with all its features of skillful virtuosity, accidentality, dependence on transient moods and whims of a painter, has been quite well fitted to the ends of the impressionistic and naturalistic, individualistic and subjectivist art of yesterday. However, the old technique is no longer appropriate for the principles of art of today which can be summarized as follows: a breaking with all imitation of objects (even if it is the most free), autonomy of forms, discipline in the broadest sense of the word, clarity permitting everyone to grasp the artist's intention, schematism, geometry, precision that facilitates everyone [in] the ordering of his impressions obtained from the given work. The technique of craftsmen is even more helpless when it comes to a creation of a new schematic textural system. And in that case, it is only the mechanistic technology, modeled after the industrial methods as independent from individual whims and based upon a strict and precise functioning of a machine, that can give us a hand. Thus, the painting of today, the art of today, should be based upon the principles of machine production. *[1924]*

HENRYK STAŻEWSKI

(1894–)

When Kasimir Malevich visited Warsaw in 1924 he made a great impression on several young artists, who immediately banded together to form a group to explore Suprematist ideas. Stażewski and his colleague Władysław Strzeminski were among the founders of Blok, *an important periodical for the Polish avant-garde. After moving to France in 1930, Stażewski was active in Parisian groups defending the nonobjective point of view.*

To struggle against society is an unavoidable fate of artists. What form did this take in the past and what form does it take in the present? A typical example was provided by Impressionism. The world of thought in the paintings of the Impressionists was completely incomprehensible to the general public, and it formed a world separated from the rut of ordinary everyday life and bourgeois Philistinism. Artists, cut off from Society by a wall of antagonism, formed their own communities (the Bohemia) differing from the world of the bourgeoisie by their way of life as well as by their attire—long hair, capes, broad-brimmed hats.

It was only when the public began to understand the Impressionists' work that their way of life and dress became fashionable. Impressionism then transformed itself into bourgeois art. Soon it had to make way for new trends such as Cubism, Dadaism, Surrealism.

It is only by creating art for the general public, bringing one's influence to bear on it, that one can produce a mental world for the people. The artist forms a pictorial language which it is only possible to recognize when it is an expression of our common conceptions as well as our mutual relationships.

Nature, in its kaleidoscopic variety and in its disorder, can contain experience of a world of images, conscious of an order representing unity of experienced impressions. This search for order which brings closer subjects and objects to a unity, a sameness of people and things, has to use a more precise way of conveying ideas than that of typical works of art, with all their inaccuracies and fallacies, by using pronouncements and an occasional lack of credibility as far as their essence is concerned.

In our daily concept of reality there occur moments lasting only seconds when everything seems to get blurred, as would happen if the world was surrounded by layers of ether. A phenomenon is then born of an illusion of distance and of all measures as regulated by mathematical physics. After a little while light rainbow colors appear; then, in no time, everything vanishes, to go back to a normal condition.

Similar conditions appear in our intellectual life when, just for a moment our reality, conceived through our eyes, transforms itself into something oscillating between an aboveground and a subterranean universe. What we see seems to us to exist in that moment on some remote planet at a distance of billions of light years.   *[1982]*

WŁADYSŁAW STRZEMINSKI

(1893–1952)

Born in Minsk, Strzeminski came to Warsaw in the early 1920s. There, in 1924, he helped to found the Blok group, which consisted of Cubists, Suprematists, and Constructivists, all highly influenced by the Russian vanguard painters, most particularly Malevich. Along with his friend Stażewski, he formulated a theory called "unism," based on the principles outlined below.

I define art as creating
the unity of organic form by its
organicity parallel with nature

reproducing the existing
forms of the world is—reproduction
rather than creation

and thus it is not art.

Every being attains its organicity according with a law, proper only for itself:

> THUS FOR DEFINING
> THE LAW OF ORGANICITY OF ARTISTIC
> ENTITIES WE CANNOT TAKE THE LAW OF
> STRUCTURE OF ANY OTHER THING.

(as it makes no sense to create a man on the image of a bridge or a house or in the shape of a wasp)
To make a picture into an object is violence against painting.

The principles of the law of forming pictorial entities:
• flatness, involved by the flatness of a canvas on its stretcher
• geometrism of some parts of a picture, involved by the geometrical shape of a stretcher
• localization of the painterly action within a picture
• an exponential growth of forms by a juxtaposition of discrepancies
• economy of approach. Simultaneity of the phenomena.
It cannot be doubted that the art of yesterday (Cubism, Suprematism) has an intense store of means, on which the most perfect style of contemporary applied art could be built, as the invention of electricity allowed to build up the electrotechnics of the present day.

Forward without a pause

But I believe, that this is not the task of the art of strict form, that it must investigate what has been achieved and steadily pursue a more perfect form, in order to warrant the possibility of a continuous development of art. While the application of what has already been won by it is the task of applied art. I sincerely wish it the greatest possible success in creating the style of the contemporary epoch.   *[1923]*

THE SOVIET UNION

N A U M   G A B O

(1890–1977)

Gabo and his brother Antoine Pevsner were active in the plethora of projects and organizations spawned immediately after the Russian Revolution. In 1920 they issued their famous Realistic Manifesto, *in which they propounded the Constructivist principles for sculpture, opting for pure forms for their own sake, thereby opposing the more utilitarian tendency propagated by Vladimir Tatlin called Productivist art. Gabo's experiments with kinetic principles and with transparent materials such as celluloid were influential in Western Europe, where he arrived in 1922.*

I would say that the real sources of the conception of space in sculpture are to be looked for in the whole state of our intellectual development and of the collective mind of time. Space did not play a great role in the previous arts, not because the previous artists did not know anything about space, but because space represented to them only something which is there together with or attached to a mass volume. The volume and the material world around them was the main peg on which they hung their ideas and vision of the world. I would say that the philosophic events and the events in science at the beginning of this century have definitely made a crucial impact on the mentality of my generation. Whether many of us knew exactly what was going on in science, or not, does not really matter. The fact was that it was in the air, and an artist, with his sensitiveness, acts like a sponge. He may not know about it but he sucks in ideas and they work on him. On the other hand, we sculptors, rejecting the old sculpture, found its means insufficient for us to express our new images. We had to find new means and introduce new principles and that is why the principles of space and structure became basic. By doing my constructions I discovered the importance of space in them. We realized that every engineering object is, apart from its functional character, acting on us as an image. I emphasized this fact in the manifesto and before, by saying that every object we see, be it an object of nature or created by man, a telephone, a table, a chair, a house, or a tree, has an image of its own, and what I meant was that it acts on us in the same way as a sculpture although it is not made for that purpose. We realized that the main core of a constructed object is its structure and structure demands greater participation of space than a monolithic volume does.

Constructive sculpture is not only three-dimensional, it is four-dimensional insofar as we are striving to bring the element of time into it. By time I mean movement, rhythm: the actual movement as well as the illusory one which is perceived through the indication of the flow of lines and shapes in the sculpture or in painting. In my opinion, rhythm in a work of art is as important as space and structure and image. I hope the future will develop these ideas much further.   *[c. 1956]*

EL LISSITZKY

(1890–1947)

Inspired by Kasimir Malevich, whom he met in 1919, Lissitzky combined distinctive spatial traits of Suprematist theory with his own tectonic tendencies, producing the works he called "Proun." He was active in the Soviet Union immediately after the Revolution and then spent considerable time wandering about Europe, where he made

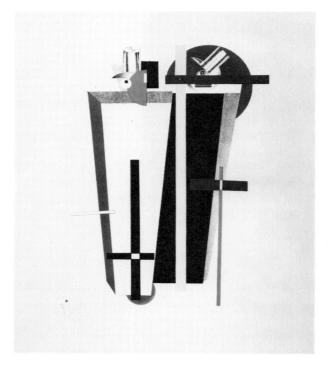

E L L I S S I T Z K Y   *The Gravedigger,* from *Figurines, Plastic
Representation of the Electromechanical Production
"Victory Over the Sun."* 1923. Lithograph. 21" x 17¹³⁄₁₆".

*contact with other vanguard artists, including those in the de Stijl movement and
the artists at the Bauhaus. During the 1920s, Lissitzky carried Russian experimental
ideas into Europe. In Germany, especially, his typography and structural designs were
greatly admired.*

I cannot define absolutely what Proun is, for this work is not yet finished;
but I can try to define a few things which are already clear. At my early
exhibitions in Russia, I noticed that the visitors always asked: What does it
represent?—for they were used to looking at pictures which had been produced on the basis that they were to represent something. My aim—and
this is not only my aim, this is the meaning of the new art—is not to
represent, but to form something independent of any conditioning factor.
To this thing I gave the independent name *Proun.* When its life is fulfilled
and it lies down gently in the grave of the history of art, only then will this
idea be defined. It is surely an old truth, dear friend, that had I defined
absolutely this idea which I have created, my entire artistic work would
have been unnecessary.

But in a few facts:

The painter of pictures uses his optical, psychological, historical, etc. abilities, and writes all that into the novel, the short story, the grotesque, etc. of his picture. The Proun creator concentrates in himself all the elements of modern knowledge and all the systems and methods and with these he forms *plastic elements*, which exist just like the elements of nature, such as H (hydrogen) and O (oxygen), and S (sulphur). He amalgamates these elements and obtains acids which bite into everything they touch, that is to say, they have an effect on all spheres of life. Perhaps all this is a piece of laboratory work: but it produces no scientific preparations which are only interesting and intelligible to a circle of specialists. It produces living bodies, objects of a specific kind, whose effects cannot be measured with an ammeter or a manometer.   *[1925]*

ALEXANDER RODCHENKO

(1891–1956)

Rodchenko joined Tatlin in enthusiastically endorsing the development of artistic forms suitable for mass consumption, working in the 1920s in many media, including typography and photomontage. During the late 1920s and 1930s, Rodchenko became increasingly interested in photography as an art form. Even the 1921 slogans below, however, find their natural extension in the mechanically produced art of the camera.

SLOGANS

• Construction is the arrangement of elements.
• Construction is the outlook of our age.
• Like every science, art is a branch of mathematics.
• Construction is the modern prerequisite of organization and the utilitarian employment of material.
• Art that is useless for life should be kept in museums of antiquities.
• The time has come for art to be an organic part of life.
• Constructively organized life is more than the enchanting and stifling art of magicians.
• The future is not going to build monasteries for priests, or for the prophets and clowns of art.
• Down with art as a glittering extravagance in the senseless lives of the wealthy!
• Down with art as a showy gem in the dark, grimy lives of the poor!
• Down with art as a means of escape from a senseless life!
• The art of our age is conscious, organized life, capable of seeing and creating.

• The artist of our age is the man able to organize his life, his work, and himself.
• One has to work for life, not for palaces, churches, cemeteries, and museums.
• Active work has to be done among the people, for the people, and with the people; down with monasteries, institutions, studios, studies, and islands!
• Consciousness, experiment . . . function, construction, technology, mathematics—these are the brothers of the art of our age.   *[1921]*

It is almost impossible to overlook how hard we endeavor to discover all the potentialities of photography.

As in a marvelous fairy tale or dream, we discover the miracles of photography in their amazing reality.

Applied photography imitating etchings, paintings, or carpets is following new paths of its own; it flourishes and emanates a characteristic scent. Possibilities never before seen lie open before it.

The numerous planes of images with finely traced outlines surpass the effects of photomontage. There are transitions from the complete whole to the finest tiny veins.

The contrasts of perspective. Light contrasts. Contrasts of forms. Viewpoints inaccessible to drawing or painting. Foreshortening with strong distortion of the photographed object and the rough texture of the material.

Perfectly new, unprecedented representation of movement by man, animal, machine, etc. Moments we didn't know of or, if we did, couldn't see, like the flight of a bullet, for example.

Compositions whose boldness surpasses the imagination of the painter; a formal wealth that leaves Rubens's works far behind.

Compositions with an extremely complex play of lines, which the Dutch and the Japanese cannot approach.

Then there is also the creation of nonexistent moments by the use of montage on a photo.

The negative picture conveys totally new stimulations to the senses.

Not to mention the double exposure (in film: dissolving), optical distortions, the photography of reflections, and similar possibilities.

The photographers have shown themselves to be masters with individual taste, style, and manner. They continue working on their subjects and style with perseverance.

Photographic art is developing rapidly, conquering more and more ground. . . . Its development matches the advances witnessed in painting.

Technically, photography is simple and quick; it has become such an indispensable requisite of science, life, and technology, and a thing within such easy reach, that it is still not considered able to act as its own prophet . . . nor is its right to its own creative artists recognized.

The love of photography must be fostered until people begin to collect photographs. (Photo collections and immense photo exhibitions must be assembled.)

Instead of so-called salons, international photo exhibitions should be organized.

Periodicals and books on photography must be published.

Photography has every right and every merit to claim our attention as the art of our age.   *[1934]*

VLADIMIR TATLIN

(1885–1953)

Tatlin's insistence on the "culture of materials" made him a natural rival of Kasimir Malevich, whose exalted views of the function of aesthetics Tatlin vehemently opposed. After the Revolution Tatlin applied himself to developing and teaching principles of design for the new Soviet society, making both utilitarian objects and his famous model for a monument to the Third International. Toward the late 1920s Tatlin began work on a poetically conceived glider that he called "Letatlin," in which he tried to fuse his interest in an art for a new technologically oriented society with a secret dream, as his writing on Letatlin below indicates.

1. The lack of variation in the forms (which is not in reality necessitated by technical requirements) leads to a limitation in the use of materials, to a monotonous use of materials, and creates to some extent a ready-made attitude to the cultural and material shaping of objects; this in its turn leads to monotonous solutions to the constructive tasks set.

2. An artist with experience of a variety of different materials (who, without being an engineer, has investigated the question which interests him) will inevitably see it as his duty to solve the technical problem with the help of new relationships in the material, which can offer new opportunities of concentration; he will try to discover a new, complicated form, which in its further development will naturally have to be technically refined in more detail. The artist shall in his work, as a counterpart to technology, present a succession of new relationships between the forms of the material. A series of forms determined by complicated curvatures will demand other plastic, material, and constructive relationships—the artist can and must master these elements, in that his creative method is qualitatively different from that of the engineer.

The further consequences are these:

1. I have selected the flying machine as an object for artistic composition, since it is the most complicated dynamic form that can become an everyday object for the Soviet masses, as an ordinary item of use.

2. I have proceeded from material constructions of simple forms to more complicated: clothes, articles of utility in the environment—as far as an architectural work to the honor of the Comintern. The flying machine is the most complicated form in my present phase of work. It corresponds to the need of the moment for human mastery of space.

3. As a consequence of this work, I have drawn the conclusion that the artist's approach to technology can and will lend new life to their stagnating methods, which are often in contradiction with the functions of the epoch of reconstruction.

4. My apparatus is built on the principle of utilizing living, organic forms. The observation of these forms led me to the conclusion that the most aesthetic forms are the most'economic. Art is: work with the shaping of the material, in this respect.   *[1932]*

MAX WALTER SVANBERG

(1912–)

Born in Malmö, Svanberg began his career as a sign painter. During the late 1930s he began to paint highly erotic fantasies that immediately caused a scandal in Sweden. The French Surrealists, particularly André Breton, held Svanberg in high esteem and, after the Second World War, invited him to exhibit in their various manifestations.

One can only reach complete beauty—the multiform and anguishing beauty—by means of an irrational game that finds itself in a universal poetic, capable of liberating the imagination, where form and color are not ends in themselves, but means of liberating the strongest functions of the image residing in the imagination. In order to reach supreme clarity, one must be so aware of the terrible presence of the perishing character of life that one actually suffers. . . . Suspicious of all taboos, I carve my art, diamond of my destiny. . . . My art is a hymn to woman, composed by one who adores her, on his knees before this strange hybrid of visions of reality, of convulsive beauty and chaste sensuality. She is solitary in a room the color of a rainbow. Her skin is composed of strange clothing and clouds of butterflies, of events and odors, of the rose fingers of dawn, transparent suns of full daylight, blue loves of dusk and night fish with huge eyes.   *[n.d.]*

UNITED STATES

CHARLES JOSEPH BIEDERMAN

(1906–)

Known for both his theoretical writings and his Constructivist reliefs, Biederman has enjoyed an underground reputation for many years. After a sojourn in New York and a trip to Paris in the 1930s, Biederman retreated to Red Wing, Minnesota, where he has lived ever since, making his relief constructions and sending out tracts on his theory of structurism (as reflected in the statement below). His ideas were influential in Great Britain and the Netherlands after the Second World War.

The new art I pursue brings to a conclusion the "research" which Cézanne felt he would not live to "realize" and answers his hope for a "continuator" of his efforts. I realized this goal, not by "going back" to Cézanne, but rather by experiencing an American evolution in my art which opened the way for the continuance of Cézanne's extraordinary achievements in the spatial world of light. This became possible because, like Monet and Cézanne, I sought solutions in the visual study of nature, and like them was able to extend my perception of the structural process of nature. This permitted a truly genuine nonmimetic creation of the artist's art (bereft of confusion and compromise with the now obsolete vision of mimesis), according to the creative potentialities inherently given in the creative structural process of nature—the only structural possibilities available to the artist. The alternative is the artist's false assumption of superiority to nature, his denial of nature, and his arrogant claim of being "his own nature." This alternative confuses and confounds the structural world of nature, and so art, by a naïve appeal to an unlimited freedom purportedly residing in the subconscious.

It is precisely out of this attitude that the post-Cézannian chaos has arisen in which art is *reduced* to the "puny" (Cézanne) concern of revealing the questionable value of the artist's personal "inner world." The new art I advocate, in the line of Monet-Cézanne, acts in the very opposite way. That is, not "reducing" but extending the past evolution of human art by ceasing any form of imitating what nature has already created, ceasing the limitation of imitating light as in painting, and ceasing the limited notion of form as in sculpture. The new art liberates the artist to create his own art in the full dimensions of the actualities of spatial reality. The artist is freed from conditioning to the biological creations of nature to adopt what is uniquely suited to human creation—geometric structuring. This mode of structuring, however, is submitted to the potentialities as given by the creative process of nature. It then becomes evident why neither the brush nor the chisel but rather the machine is now the ideal medium which enables the artist to engage the exactitude of geometric structuring in the spatial world of light and thus secure the full reality experience inherent in the new art of creation.

[c. 1951]

ALEXANDER CALDER

(1898–1976)

Son and grandson of sculptors, Calder first studied mechanical engineering and later painting, before he came back to the family tradition with linear wire sculptures and small figures for his private circus in 1927. Calder's first moving constructions, made in Paris in 1932, were dubbed "mobiles" by Marcel Duchamp. By 1934, Calder had perfected his floating mobiles, depending entirely on natural forces in their movements. His lyrical approach distinguished his work from other kinetic works in the Constructivist tradition. Calder also differed from most other modern artists in that he brought humor into his conceptions, feeling free to compose visual jokes in much the same way that Mozart liked to compose musical ones. His pioneering in motion sculpture has had important results in subsequent kinetic art.

The underlying sense of form in my work has been the system of the universe, or part thereof. For that is a rather large model to work from.

What I mean is that the idea of detached bodies floating in space, of different sizes and densities, perhaps of different colors and temperatures, and surrounded and interlarded with wisps of gaseous condition, and some at rest, while others move in peculiar manners, seems to me the ideal source of form. . . .

When I have used spheres and discs, I have intended that they should represent more than what they just are. . . . A ball of wood or a disc of metal is rather a dull object without this sense of something emanating from it.

When I use two circles of wire intersecting at right angles, this to me is a sphere . . . what I produce is not precisely what I have in mind—but a sort of sketch, a man-made approximation. *[1951]*

Which has influenced you more, nature or modern machinery?

Nature. I haven't really touched machinery except for a few elementary mechanisms like levers and balances. You see nature and then you try to emulate it. But, of course, when I met Mondrian I went home and tried to paint. The basis of everything for me is the universe. The simplest forms in the universe are the sphere and the circle. I represent them by disks and

ALEXANDER CALDER   *The Only Only Bird.* 1952. Tin and wire. 15″ high.

then I vary them. My whole theory about art is the disparity that exists between form, masses, and movement. Even my triangles are spheres, but they are spheres of a different shape.   *[c. 1958]*

JOSEPH CORNELL

(1903–1973)

Among the few Americans immediately fired by European Surrealism in the early 1930s, Cornell began by making collages similar to those of Max Ernst. He soon took to constructing shadow boxes containing found objects and old texts, in which he wove nostalgic fantasies often based on French romantic poetry and his collection of memorabilia of the ballet and theater of the nineteenth century. Cornell was discovered and celebrated by the French Surrealists during the 1930s, but it was not until after the Second World War that he became well known in the United States as an inspired eccentric.

Shadow boxes become poetic theaters or settings wherein are metamorphosed the elements of a childhood pastime. The fragile, shimmering globules become the shimmering but more enduring planets—a connotation of moon and tides—the association of water less subtle, as when driftwood pieces make up a proscenium to set of the dazzling white of sea foam and billowy cloud crystallized in a pipe of fancy.   *[1946]*

. . . impressions intriguingly diverse . . . that, in order to hold fast, one might assemble, assort, and arrange into a cabinet . . . the contraption kind of the amusement resorts with endless ingenuity of effect, worked by coin and plunger, or brightly colored pinballs . . . traveling inclined runways . . . starting in motion compartment after compartment with a symphony of mechanical magic of sight and sound borrowed from the motion picture art . . . into childhood . . . into fantasy . . . through the streets of New York . . . through tropical skies . . . into the receiving trays the balls come to rest releasing prizes. . . .   *[1948]*

STUART DAVIS

(1894–1964)

During the 1920s, Davis had assimilated the vocabulary of European Cubism to a lively realistic impulse that resulted in paintings inspired—as he said again and again—by the American environment. When the Depression brought forward local voices insisting on a strictly American realism, Davis rose to defend modern art. He was committed to an international view, both artistically and politically, and was one of the prime movers of the important American Artists' Congress in 1936, in which most prominent American artists met to discuss the implications of political crises, in both Europe and the United States, for contemporary art. Unlike many other politically radical artists of the period, Davis never accepted social realism as a legitimate artistic direction. He remained faithful to the innovations of the great modern masters, while incorporating what he felt to be a distinctive American note in his own work.

Modern art rediscovered humanity in painting, an essential social service unrestricted by racial or national boundaries. I refer to the discovery that an artist had the power to see the world with a fresh eye. Whether he painted people, still life, landscape, or invented subjects, every picture was an objective proof of that power to see beyond the traditional. Man's senses were restored to him. It is natural, of course, that people who had forgotten they owned any found no reflection of themselves in these pictures. They attacked them as the vicious jokes of dissolute bohemians.

STUART DAVIS

STUART DAVIS *Ready to Wear.* 1955.
Oil on canvas. 56¼ x 42".

It has been often said, even by proponents of those pictures known in aesthetic slang as Cubist and abstract, that they have no subject matter. Such a statement is equivalent to saying that life has no subject matter. On the contrary, modern pictures deal with contemporary subject matter in terms of art. The artist does not exercise his freedom in a nonmaterial world. Science has created a new environment, in which new forms, lights, speeds, and spaces are a reality. The perspectives and chiaroscuro of the Renaissance are no longer physically with us, even though their ghosts linger in many of the best modern work.

In my own case, I have enjoyed the dynamic American scene for many years past, and all of my pictures (including the ones I painted in Paris) are referential to it. They all have their originating impulse in the impact of the contemporary American environment. And it is certainly a fact that the relevant art, literature, and music of other times and places are among the most cherished realities of that environment. I mention this last point only because there is a continuing trend by strong groups in American art who, in this way or that, have sought to deny it.

Some of the things which have made me want to paint, outside of other paintings, are: American wood and iron work of the past; Civil War and skyscraper architecture; the brilliant colors on gasoline stations; chain-store fronts, and taxicabs; the music of Bach; synthetic chemistry; the poetry of Rimbaud; fast travel by train, auto, and airplane which brought new and multiple perspectives; electric signs; the landscape and boats of Gloucester, Mass.; 5 & 10 cent store kitchen utensils; movies and radio; Earl Hines's hot piano and Negro jazz music in general, etc. In one way or another the quality of these things plays a role in determining the character of my paintings. Not in the sense of describing them in graphic images, but by predetermining an analogous dynamics in the design, which becomes a new part of the American environment. Paris School, Abstraction, Escapism? Nope, just Color-Space Compositions celebrating the resolution in art of stresses set up by some aspects of the American scene.   *[1943]*

CHARLES DEMUTH

(1883–1935)

Demuth's delicate watercolors of the 1920s often depicted the architectural visage of America in a modified Cubist style known as Precisionism. But his interest in the formal characteristics of landscape and still life extended to the human figure as well, and his sophisticated modernist attitudes, shared with several major contemporary American poets, among them William Carlos Williams, found expression in a varied oeuvre that ranged from abstraction to objective realism.

Across a Greco, across a Blake, across a Rubens, across a Watteau, across a Beardsley is written in larger letters than any printed page will ever dare to hold, or Broadway façade or roof support, what its creator had to say about it. To translate these painted sentences, whatever they may be, into words— well, try it. With the best of luck the "sea change" will be great. Or, granting a translation of this kind were successful what would you have but what was there already, and as readable—and perhaps, on repetition, a trifle boring.

Paintings are; and, I call complete drawings paintings too, to be looked at. If the "inner eye" does not glitter before certain contemporary "Calla Lilies," certain American watercolors, certain of Florine's, or Peggy's portraits,* added physical words will not cause it to glitter—even though spoken or written by Pater or Joyce. Your choice—ladies!

For the painter, paintings are, wet or dry, just paintings. They are not

* The references are probably to Florine Stettheimer and Peggy Bacon.

CHARLES DEMUTH *Incense of a New Church.* 1912.
Oil on canvas. 26 x 20⅛".

arguments. They are not signs on the way to that supposed Nirvana: Culture. They are not—however, this must be printed in our new world, so perhaps that: "They are not," cannot be said.

Paintings must be looked at and looked at and looked at—they, I think, the good ones, like it. They must be understood, and that's not the word either, through the eyes. No writing, no talking, no singing, no dancing will explain them. They are the final, the nth whoopee of sight. A watermelon, a kiss may be fair, but after all have other uses. "Look at that!" is all that can be said before a great painting, at least, by those who really see it.

"And cannot words, written or spoken, help those who have partial or little sight for painting?"

My answer to this question is: No. Only prayer, and looking, and looking, and looking at painting and—prayer can help.   *[1929]*

BURGOYNE DILLER

(1906–1965)

Diller was the preeminent American disciple of the de Stijl movement, working in its austere vocabulary from the early 1930s. His steadfast attitude encouraged other artists during a period when abstract art was under fire. As an administrator on the Federal Arts Project (the WPA), which employed out-of-work artists on "socially useful" projects during the Depression, Diller protected such artists as Gorky, de Kooning, and Guston, and fought off the detractors who sought to reduce American art to social realist aims. Diller never wrote about his art, but his principles are succinctly stated in the diagram below.

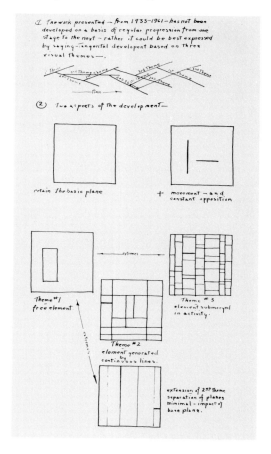

[1961]

PHILIP EVERGOOD

(1901–)

The impact of the Depression turned Evergood toward social themes, and, during the years he participated in the Federal Arts Project, Evergood painted many striking works commenting on social injustices in America. He was never sympathetic to the American scene painters who tended toward illustration, and he strived to give his works an imaginative cast that occasionally paralleled European Expressionism.

Diverse emotions stir in different humans when exposed to the same experiences and when confronted with the same objects. Compare the differences of reaction (both inner and outer) in separate individuals to the sight of a picket line, for example. The sleek member of the *haute monde* sunning her poodle looks upon the picketers with hatred, fear, and nausea, for they appear to jeopardize security and menace the pampered life which means the complete world to that individual. The unemployed worker with no coat and holes in his shoes is warmed by the sight of these marchers who are sacrificing the loss of wages to win a fight for better living conditions.

I feel the search of an artist should be for the richest and fullest of human experiences and that he should look for both the visual manifestations and those transmitted intuitively. The more the artist contacts the inner qualities of people the more he will understand Life and where he fits into it. The more mature he gets in his relationships to other human beings the more vital will be what he says in print or stone.

Thoughts like these are very much a part of aesthetics.   *[1946]*

BEN SHAHN

(1898–1969)

Born in Kovno, Lithuania, Shahn came to the United States in 1906. During the Depression his work expressed a social commitment, and he became well known through his series of gouaches based on the Sacco-Vanzetti case. He painted murals, worked as a government photographer, and produced posters until the Second World War. Afterward, his work was less overtly political, but never lost the graphic character that lent itself so readily to socially committed art.

Generalities and abstractions and vital statistics had always bored me. Whether in people or in art it was the individual peculiarities that were interesting. One has sympathy with a hurt person, not because he is a generality, but precisely because he is not. Only the individual can imagine, invent, or create. The whole audience of art is an audience of individuals. Each of them comes to the painting or sculpture because there he can be told that he, the individual, transcends all classes and flouts all predictions. In the work of art he finds his uniqueness affirmed.

Yes, one rankles at broad injustices, and one ardently hopes for and works toward mass improvements; but that is only because whatever mass there may be is made up of individuals, and each of them is able to feel and have hopes and dreams.

   Nor would such a view invalidate a belief which I had held about the unifying power of art. I have always believed that the character of a society is largely shaped and unified by its great creative works, that a society is molded upon its epics, and that it imagines in terms of its created things— its cathedrals, its works of art, its musical treasures, its literary and philo- sophic works. One might say that a public may be so unified because the highly personal experience is held in common by the many individual members of the public. The great moment at which Oedipus in his remorse tears out his eyes is a private moment—one of deepest inward emotion. And yet that emotion, produced by art, and many other such private and pro- found emotions, experiences, and images bound together the Greek people into a great civilization, and bound others all over the earth to them for all time to come.   *[1957]*

JOSEPH STELLA

(1877–1946)

A sojourn in Italy and France from 1909 to 1912 introduced Stella to the work of the Cubists, and more importantly, the Futurists, whose style he transmuted into a cooler, more structured version upon his return to America. His famous views of the Brooklyn Bridge were followed by works in the later 1920s that were often grouped with those of the Precisionist artists, among them Charles Sheeler, Morton Schamberg, and Charles Demuth.

Seen for the first time, as a weird metallic Apparition under a metallic sky, out of proportion with the winged lightness of its arch, traced for the conjunction of Worlds, supported by the massive dark towers dominating the surrounding tumult of the surging skyscrapers with their gothic majesty sealed in the purity of their arches, the cables, like divine messages from above, transmitted to the vibrating coils, cutting and dividing into innumerable musical spaces the nude immensity of the sky, it impressed me as the shrine containing all the efforts of the new civilization of America . . . the eloquent meeting point of all the forces arising in a superb assertion of powers, in Apotheosis.

To render limitless the space on which to enact my emotions I chose the mysterious depth of night . . . and to strengthen the effective acidity of the various prisms composing my Drama I employed the silvery alarm rung by the electric light.

Many nights I stood on the bridge—and in the middle alone—lost—a defenseless prey to the surrounding swarming darkness—crushed by the mountainous black impenetrability of the skyscrapers—here and there lights resembling suspended falls of astral bodies or fantastic splendors of remote rites—shaken by the underground tumult of the trains in perpetual motion, like the blood in the arteries—at times, ringing as alarm in a tempest, the shrill sulphurous voice of the trolley wires—now and then strange moanings of appeal from tugboats, guessed more than seen, through the infernal recesses below—I felt deeply moved, as if on the threshold of a new religion or in the presence of a new Divinity.   *[1929]*

URUGUAY

JOAQUÍN   TORRES-GARCÍA

(1874–1949)

Torres-García received his art training in Barcelona, where he worked for several years before going first to the United States and then to Paris. He remained there from 1924 through 1932 and was active in groups of nonobjective artists, among them Theo van Doesburg and Piet Mondrian. In 1933 he returned to Uruguay, where he exercised enormous influence, propagating his theory of Universal Constructivism. By developing a symbolic language that incorporated ideographic references to Latin America, particularly its pre-Columbian past, Torres-García helped artists throughout South American to understand and develop the abstract plastic language formulated in Europe.

One day [Amédée] Ozenfant said to me: *L'art moderne n'est pas amusant.* He was right. It poses problems too serious for most people, it is too pure. For that same reason, the sculptor Lipchitz told me many times that my art was too austere, that it made no concession to sensuality, that it was excessively abstract. And he would add: Look at nature, the way it functions; how, in

JOAQUÍN TORRES-GARCÍA *Constructive Composition.* 1932. Oil on board. 41½ x 30½".

order to preserve the species, it has invented love, which is, after all, a trap. Well, by appealing to the sensuality, art carries the viewer to more profound truths; it is the necessary vehicle.

I did not allow myself to be seduced by such reasonings, since opposed to them was this other: that beauty is a resultant, but the goal of art is beyond the creation of beauty. Shall we do something fine only because it may be beautiful? Art responds to the same concept of deep seriousness as that of ethics and of life; like these, it should have absolute sincerity as its standard. *[1944]*

1940
TO THE
PRESENT

ARGENTINA

MARCELO BONEVARDI

(1929–   )

After studying architecture at the University of Córdoba, Bonevardi turned to painting and soon evolved a technique of construction in which he inserted handmade, enigmatic objects in niches and depressed planes, suggesting his mythic sources in the art of ancient civilizations. His fantasy has often been compared with that of his countryman, the great writer Jorge Luis Borges.

If my dreams had the obsessive persistence of time, if in meditation I could contemplate the mystery of my own skeleton and ascend the Rainbow until I reached the Great Silence, and then dared to venture in my boat through the labyrinths of a mystic geography, perhaps one day I could construct that object—of which I once caught a glimpse in a small wooden box with a dead scarab—   *[1965]*

AUSTRIA

FRITZ WOTRUBA

(1907–1975)

Wotruba worked first as a direct carver in stone in a naturalistic, almost classical vein. After the Second World War, however, he began to reduce his forms to simple essentials, making large stone sculptures that were at once reminiscent of the human figure and abstract enough to stand as vigorous formal statements.

The point of working directly in stone is this: by the deliberate choice of limitations and constraints, to force the image to emerge clearly and simply. I also believe there are laws which the stone imposes on us. Whoever violates them endangers more than a mere aesthetic conception. He who perforates the stone destroys the plastic impression that dwells in it. A hole in the block of a piece of sculpture is in most cases nothing but the expression of weakness and of impotence.

The power and force of stone reside in its mass, its weight, and its density.

A good piece of sculpture must combine barbarism and culture: two unique elements in a work of art.

No material, nor any formal intention, however sure and precise, can replace spirit and genius. The material is destined, in the end, to remain a mere auxiliary, just good enough to enable stammering to become speech.

F R I T Z W O T R U B A *Standing Figure*. 1958. Bronze. 33⅛" high.

The question arises as to the justification and the meaning of folklore forms. Does the power of a work of art lie in the limitations imposed by origin and race, or can its absolute greatness be achieved only by divesting it of such essentially insignificant rudiments of human history? Theoretical reflections of this kind cannot deter me from my belief in the absolute necessity of art for man. Art is probably the very soul of man.

At the present time the artist stands alone, and this is well, for no ideology can be of help to him. He must understand that there are things which are irrevocably dead for art, and that nothing will ever revive them. These things none the less cling to him and suck his substance like vampires; only when he has freed himself of them can the New and the Living emerge.

Technique today takes the place of the dynamic: man is caught in his own snare. From the outset, the mechanical in technique goes against everything living. In technique lurks death. The apparent facility and freedom which technique lends to things is a diabolical deception. Even the meaning of material is falsified. Which is why the choice of material is decisive for the artist. He must know just how far he can yield to the mechanical, physical, and chemical charms which surround him. The atrophy of the soul that threatens us nowadays cannot be resisted, so universal is the fascination which technique exerts. In the long run neither political ideals nor religious creeds will be able to resist it.

I dream of a sculpture in which landscape, architecture and city become one.

It may be a city like Marseilles, a city roaring in the heat, which is suddenly transformed, and becomes a grandiose sculpture, a gigantic figure, built of white blocks and divided by vast level terraces, laid out in a bare and motionless landscape.

This image has majesty, but I am incapable of reproducing it, even though I know that this is one of the rare great themes which fill an artist's life.

What is not contained in a city!

A city is expressed by its people, for its houses are nothing more than places where they keep their vices, hopes, desires, and dreams—but the blood and the souls of animals likewise belong to the city and to the land-scape.   *[c. 1950–1960]*

BELGIUM

PIERRE ALECHINSKY

(1927–   )

Alechinsky's experience with the international COBRA group opened the way to extensive experimentation with free association, calligraphy, and collaborative works. His commitment to an expression of deep psychological sources places him in the larger modern tradition of Expressionism, mitigated by Surrealist principles.

COBRA was my school. I was twenty-two when I met the writer Christian Dotremont, and the painters Jorn, Appel, and Corneille. Working with the group, helping to publish a review, fighting calculated abstractionism on the right and social realism on the left kept me pretty busy until 1951. I was so engrossed in all this activity that, thinking back, I realize that I did very little painting during that time. Which at least saved me from painting all the bad pictures which I would certainly have turned out otherwise.

When I paint, I liberate monsters, my own monsters—and for these I am responsible. They are the manifestation of all the doubts, searches, and groping for meaning and expression which all artists experience, and at the same time they represent my doubts, my searches, and my most profound and diffuse difficulties. One does not choose the content, one submits to it.

A man may be so affected by some exterior, political event which wounds him so deeply that he is forced to purge himself of it. But that is a far cry from availing oneself of an opportunity, from dispelling the horrors of

PIERRE ALECHINSKY *L'Esprit des Chutes*. 1978. Ink. 76 x 47".

everyday existence by describing them in one's diary, from appointing oneself a social arbiter. . . . Neither the world's shame and guilt nor one's own guilt and shame can be cured by some kind of abracadabra. Suffering cannot be paid for in the currency of a few pictorial "good deeds."

Ensor wrote repeatedly: *"Les suffisances matamoresques appellent la finale crevaison grenouillère."* And he is right: the deliberate expansion of means and methods does not automatically bring a new dimension of value. There is ink, a sheet of paper, a canvas, a few colors, the usual paintbrush, the hand: less than nothing, yet more than enough. One single stroke is capable of creating the essential mood. A picture exists in its own right, it refers to nothing, no exterior scheme or idea. I start a painting. Will anything become of it? Will I be distracted, will I block the essential moment of inspiration? I don't know. Let's just go on. How far? Until the point when laziness takes over again. Is that why I suddenly stop? But no, I do not stop, I go on, I start again. . . . Ideas and their consequences, facts and the consequences they draw from Ideas, arrive, flow, die, flounder in depths, reappear.   *[1961]*

POL BURY

(1922–)

Bury had been deeply impressed by the Belgian Surrealist poets and painters in his youth, and something of their high-spirited challenge to rationality remained when he turned to sculpture in the 1950s. His initial experiments with moving planes that could be rotated by the spectator gave way to motorized sculptures of clustered forms that moved in random patterns in very slow tempi, producing strangely paradoxical organic effects.

When he wishes to bring to life things that are inert, the sculptor immediately feels Gravity sinking down with all its weight into the scale pan. This image may possibly raise a smile. And yet . . .

Is it really necessary to encumber oneself with this anxiety to bring to life things that have no apparent reason for stirring? A psychoanalyst would diagnose some lingering remnant of a trauma of birth. Here, the causes justify the effects but do not explain them. We are what we are. And if Newton's apple reveals the complications that attended his birth, that same apple explains even more effectively the laws of gravitation of the universe. Certain persons do not hesitate to deduce laws from such phenomena, and yet are not distressed to have to admit that there are forces which attract apples towards the center of the earth, forces which permit things not to stay put.

A circular cutting tool and a mallet together make it possible to restructure images, from the simplest to the most complex ones. If we take the image of a straight line, snip it into short lengths, and paste the fragments back together end to end but with a very slight displacement, we have a straight line which has adventured for a moment outside its destiny, and the traces of that adventure remain in this collage. This first state of the straight line, in which it has become gently undulating, can be subjected to a similar process of cutting into short lengths and reglueing slightly askew to produce a second state. The operation can be repeated until the complete destruction of the line, its atomization into an infinity of dots. The line is a simple example. Geometric figures, on the other hand, offer a very wide field of action.

From the "cinetization" of straight lines to the "cinetization" of skyscrapers involves nothing more than a change of image. This forest of steel and concrete verticals which constitutes New York offers an excellent field of action for cutting out and pasting together again. More effectively than with horizontal architecture, the "cinetized" skyscraper restores the process of

Gravity, but slowed down, so that the building is eternally trembling on the brink of collapse.

It seems that such interventions in the image could be construed as representing a vicious desire to destroy, but on the contrary one should see nothing more in them than the aspiration to give an air of freedom to things that have pretensions to be immutable. The idea of illustrating the end of the world, of destroying a world, represents a morose delectation which has its partisans but remains, ultimately, an anecdotal preoccupation.

It can be satisfying to intervene in the respectable dispositions of geometry, scenery, faces, and to fancy that in this way one is able to tickle Gravity.   *[1966]*

CANADA

PAUL-ÉMILE BORDUAS

(1905–1960)

Indisputable master of the postwar Canadian vanguard, Borduas had been the first among them to accept Surrealist innovations, particularly automatism, during the early 1940s. He inspired younger artists both with his abstract paintings in the automatist mode and with his emotional writings, one of which was the influential 1948 manifesto "Refus Globale" ("Global Refusal"), signed by a number of his younger admirers, including Jean-Paul Riopelle.

Magic booty, magically wrested from the unknown, lies at our feet. It has been gathered by the true poets. Its power to transform is measured by the violence shown against it and by its resistance in the end to exploitation. After more than two centuries, de Sade is still not found in bookstores, and Isidore Ducasse, dead for more than a century of revolutions and carnage, remains too virile for flabby contemporary consciences, in spite of the cesspool customs of today.

The items of this treasure reveal themselves, inviolable, to our society. They remain the incorruptible, sensitive legacy for tomorrow. They were ordained spontaneously outside of and in opposition to civilization, and await freedom from its restraints to become active in the social scheme.

Therefore, our duty is simple:

To break definitively with all conventions of society and its utilitarian spirit! We refuse to live knowingly at less than our spiritual and physical potential; refuse to close our eyes to the vices and confidence tricks perpetuated in the guise of learning, favor, or gratitude; refuse to be ghettoed in an ivory tower, well-fortified but too easy to ignore; refuse to remain silent—

do with us what you will, but you shall hear us; refuse to make a deal with *la gloire* and its attendant honors: stigmata of malice, unawareness, or servility; refuse to serve and to be used for such ends; refuse all *intention*, evil weapon of *reason*—down with them, to second place!

Make way for magic! Make way for objective mysteries!
Make way for love!
Make way for necessities!

To this global refusal we contrast full responsibility.

The self-seeking act is fettered to its author; it is stillborn.

The passionate act breaks free, through its very dynamism.

It is naïve and misleading to consider the men and things of history through the magnifying glass of fame, which lends them qualities beyond the reach of clever academic monkey tricks, although such qualities come automatically when man obeys the deep necessities of being—when he elects to become a new man in a new age (the definition of any man, of any time).

[1948]

J E A N - P A U L   R I O P E L L E   *Lointain.* 1962. Oil on canvas. 15 x 21⅝".

J E A N - P A U L   R I O P E L L E

(1923–)

Riopelle was a member of Borduas's circle and exhibited with them from 1946. In later years he settled in France but continued to participate actively in the artistic life of Canada. He has one of the strongest international reputations of any contemporary Canadian artist.

Since I'm Canadian, they always talk about the great Canadian forests apropos of my paintings. . . . I am not a painter of virgin forests or infinite prairies . . . a leaf of a tree, that's enough. It is the whole forest. You have only to see it. My conception is not that of abstracting: is it going *toward* it with a free gesture (I'm not talking about automatism) to try to understand what nature is, departing not from the destruction of nature but rather, toward the world.   *[1972]*

CHILE

ROBERTO MATTA ECHAURREN

(1911–   )

Matta left Chile for Paris in 1933, where he became a draftsman in Le Corbusier's studio. His association with the major Surrealists during the late 1930s brought him to experiment with "psychological morphologies"—figurative and cosmic themes that greatly influenced American artists when he lived in New York from 1939 to 1948.

When I started painting, it was through necessity, of trying to find an expression which I call a morphology, of the functioning of one's thinking, or one's feeling.

I tried to use, not my personal psychic morphology, but a social morphology. Using the totemic images involved in a situation which was more historical: the torture chambers and so on. I tried to pass from the intimate imagery, forms of vertebrae, and unknown animals, very little known flowers to cultural expressions, totemic things, civilizations.   *[1975]*

CUBA

WIFREDO LAM

(1902–1982)

Of mixed Chinese, black, and Spanish parentage, Lam early experienced the problems in Cuba that led to the eventual revolution, which he supported. He left Havana for Spain in 1923 and went on to Paris in 1938, where he soon met the Surrealists and Picasso, who befriended him. Lam's fusion of modern painterly idiom with motifs drawn from Afro-Cuban life won him acclaim first in Europe and then in the United States.

I was born in Cuba at the very time the republic was founded and the island detached from Spain, although still continuing to live as a Spanish colony. I lived in the black quarter. It was the uprooted Africans brought to settle and work in Cuba who influenced the birth of democracy and gave it its character. They brought their primitive culture, their magical religion with its mystical side in close correspondence with nature. My first contact with life, in this burning context was very violent. . . .

My pictures are a reflection, an intimate confession of my existence. They

W I F R E D O   L A M   *The Jungle*. 1943. Gouache on paper
mounted on canvas. 7'10¼" x 7'6½".

have a deep relation with the "interior" and with the movement of my
childhood. André Breton in his first manifesto wanted to penetrate the
essence of creation and stressed that the psychological behavior of man,
acquired after birth, appeared clearly in his creative evolution. . . .

In Cuba and in Spain I painted in the manner imposed by my milieu. I
belonged to the Surrealist movement later. . . . Breton transmitted to me
the poetic impulse: that of being more than ever independent in spirit. The
tragic spectacle of the Spanish Civil War—that bloody conflict among brothers—touched me profoundly. After this confrontation, intensely felt, I cast
all the energy of my mind in pursuit of a truth and I left in my painting a
trace of that pain. . . . There is a dualism between the thrusts of consciousness and those of the unconscious. It is above all the idea delivered by the
painting that interests me. I efface myself before it. . . .   *[c. 1973]*

I decided that my painting would never be the equivalent of that pseudo-
Cuban music for nightclubs. I refused to paint cha-cha-cha. I wanted with
all my heart to paint the drama of my country, but by thoroughly expressing
the Negro spirit, the beauty of the plastic art of the blacks.   *[c. 1975]*

JIŘÍ KOLÁŘ   *Reverence to Columbus.* 1969. Paper collage on plaster, metal, wood.
35½ x 81½ x 48¼".

CZECHOSLOVAKIA

JIŘÍ KOLÁŘ

(1914–   )

Operating in the interstice between painting and poetry, Kolář was a leading voice in postwar Czechoslovakia. Younger artists were inspired by his use of words in visual compositions and constructions.

Art has nothing whatever to do with what is private or public, political or poetic, beautiful or ugly, everyday or absurd, nude or symbolic, but with a domain in which the private and public, the political and the poetic, the beautiful and the ugly, the everyday and the absurd, the nude and the symbolic, are indissociable—of a domain in which beauty and death, history and nature, fantasy and reality, dream and memory are inseparable. *[1968]*

I believe that every creator must eventually attempt what may be termed a revolt, whether he wants to or not; he must, as I have, attempt an overhaul and reconstitution of poetry as a whole, regardless of its greater or lesser validity to date. . . . When later on I saw for the first time the great surveys of Kupka's and Kandinsky's work, I was overwhelmed by the realization that these creative acts were already accomplished in the year of my birth. What then was left for me to do. I asked, despite the fact that even then I had a good deal of work under my belt.   *[1975]*

If we take the term *primitive art* and we consider it in a European context then we accept the fact that this art is created by nonartistic means and for nonartistic purposes. The process of the creation would be nonartistic as well. But all of these creations were done by individuals endowed with innate feelings for plastic images, a sense for color, and an unbound fantasy— by those who were unconsciously sculptors, painters, and poets. Now I am touching upon my point. Naturally none of these primitive people knew how to read or write as we understand it. There is nothing special about that. There are millions of people today who do not know how to read or write. Aren't they the silent artists? The silent poets? What goes on in their minds when someone shows them a handwritten or printed poem? *[1978]*

DENMARK

A S G E R J O R N
(1914–1973)

Born in Denmark, Jorn studied during the 1930s with Léger and Le Corbusier, but after the Second World War abandoned formal painting for a febrile Expressionist manner. He not only painted, but also acted as the chief theorist of the COBRA movement founded in 1948 in Brussels and wrote serious essays about the origins of the art impulse.

People often ask me what I hope to achieve by my writings. They tell me that my intentions are not always very clear. But I am not aware of having any very definite intentions in this matter. When my intentions are too clear, it makes me feel rather sad. One reason why I write is to oppose any clear-cut schemes or directives about art, whether the motives are moral, scientific, or apparently liberal: like the attempt to *free* art by cutting it off from the rest of human activity.

The painter's relation to literature is that of a hostile accomplice, "hostile" because of the risk of becoming literary, "accomplice" because painting cannot exist without the inspiration of literature; but painting goes adrift if it fails to obey the inherent laws of painting.

ASGER JORN *Painting.*

Anything really *new* is repulsive, because it is abnormal and unreasonable. Real ugliness is just as rare as real beauty. Tension in a work of art is negative-positive: repulsive-attractive, ugly-beautiful. If one of these poles is removed, only boredom is left.

A creative train of thought is set off by: the unexpected, the unknown, the accidental, the disorderly, the absurd, the impossible.

In every real experiment there is a moment of zero predictability.

Even the most faithful copy of a work of art involves a loss of tension. The reason is simple. During every really creative act, the artist finds himself homeless (*dépaysé*). To overcome this state he has to call up his last reserves of strength. This mobilization of all his creative and formal resources, this passionate struggle with the medium, cannot be imitated. It is every man for himself. This explains the magic power of art.   *[1964]*

FRANCE

DANIEL BUREN

(1938–)

A polemical artist whose appearance on the art scene during the 1960s immediately stimulated contention, Buren has consistently maintained a stance of revolutionary critic. His installations most often incorporate a nonsignifying band of color repeated endlessly. These stripes have come to be identified with his revolt. The avowed "materialism" of Buren and certain other French artists of the 1960s was associated with political positions drawing upon the Marxist tradition.

I believe we are the only ones to be able to claim the right of being "looked at," in the sense that we are the only ones to present a thing which has no didactic intention, which does not provide "dreams," which is not a "stimulant." Each individual can dream himself and without doubt much better than by the trickery of an artist, however great he may be. The artist appeals to laziness, his function is emollient. He is "beautiful" for others, "talented" for others, "ingenious" for others, which is a scornful or superior way of considering "others." The artist brings beauty, dreams, suffering to their domiciles, while "the others," whom I myself consider a priori as talented as artists, must find their own beauty, their own dream. In a word, become adults. Perhaps the only thing that one can do after having seen a canvas like ours is total revolution. *[before 1973]*

JEAN DUBUFFET

(1901–1985)

When Dubuffet exhibited his "Mirobolus Macadam et Cie," the arch title he gave his paintings in the 1946 show in Paris, his work instantly roused controversy and won him a leading position in the informal school sometimes known as Tachism. His use of unorthodox painting materials such as sand, soot, pebbles, and even chicken droppings was seen as a blow to elegant French traditions, as he intended.

Many people, having made up their minds to run me down, have imagined that I take pleasure in showing sordid things. What a misconception! I had wanted to show them that these things, which they had considered ugly, are great marvels. Do, above all, refrain from talking of humor, of satire, as some people stupidly do, or of bitterness, which has also been spoken of; I do my best to rehabilitate objects regarded as unpleasing (do not, I beg of you, deny these despised objects all hope), and my work always stems from an attitude of celebration (of incantation). But a clear-sighted celebration, once all the smoke and camouflage is away. One must be honest. No veils! No shams! Naked, all things first reduced to their worst.   *[n.d.]*

It is true that, in the paintings exhibited, the manner of drawing is completely innocent of any of the conventional skills, such as we are used to finding in the works of professional painters, and is such that no special studies or natural gifts would be needed to carry out similar ones. I would reply that I hold to be useless those kinds of acquired skill, and those gifts, whose sole effect seems to me to be that of extinguishing all spontaneity, switching off the power and condemning the work to inefficacy.   *[n.d.]*

And now what happens with art? Art has been considered, since the Greeks, to have as its goal the creation of beautiful lines and beautiful color harmonies. If one abolishes this notion, what becomes of art?

I am going to tell you. Art then returns to its real function, much more significant then creating shapes and colors agreeable for a so-called pleasure of the eyes.

I don't find this function, assembling colors in pleasing arrangements, very noble. If painting was only that, I should not lose one hour of my time in this activity.

Art addresses itself to the mind, and not to the eyes. It has always been considered in this way by primitive peoples, and they are right. Art is a language, instrument of knowledge, instrument of communication.

I think this enthusiasm about the written language, which I mentioned before, has been the reason our culture started to regard painting as a rough, rudimentary, and even contemptible language, good only for illiterate people. From that, culture invented, as a rationalization for art, this myth of plastic beauty, which is, in my opinion, an imposture.

I just said, and I repeat now, painting is, in my opinion, a richer language than that of words. So it is quite useless to look for rationalizations in art. Painting is a language much more immediate, and, at the time, much more charged with meaning. Painting operates through signs which are not abstract and incorporeal like words. The signs of painting are much closer to the objects themselves. Further, painting manipulates materials which are themselves living substances. That is why painting allows one to go much further than words do, in approaching things and conjuring them.

Painting can also, and it is very remarkable, conjure things more or less, as wanted. I mean, with more or less presence: at different stages between being and not being. At last, painting can conjure things not isolated, but linked to all that surrounds them: a great many things simultaneously.

On the other hand, painting is a much more immediate language, and much more direct, than the language of words: much closer to the cry, or to the dance. That is why painting is a way of expression of our inner voices much more effective than that of words.

I just said, painting allows especially, much better than words, one to express the various stages of thought, including the deeper levels, the underground stages of mental processes. Painting has a double advantage over the language of words. First, painting conjures objects with greater strength, and comes much closer to them. Second, painting opens wider the doors to the inner dance of the painter's mind. These two qualities of painting make it an extraordinary instrument of thought, or, if you will, an extraordinary instrument of clairvoyance, and also an extraordinary instrument to exteriorize this clairvoyance, and to permit us to get it ourselves also with the painter.

Painting now, using these two powerful means, can illuminate the world with wonderful discoveries, can endow man with new myths and new mystiques, and can reveal, in infinite number, unsuspected aspects of things, and new values not yet perceived.

Here is, I think, for artists, a much more worthy job than creating assemblages of shapes and colors pleasing for the eyes.   *[1951]*

JEAN FAUTRIER

(1898–1964)

In 1943 Fautrier caused a furor by exhibiting a group of paintings he called "Hostages." His heavily impastoed images, with their faint allusions to figures, and his courageous confrontation of a forbidden subject, occupied France, captured the imaginations of younger artists. After the war, Fautrier was regarded as a seminal figure in the movement toward Expressionist abstraction called, in France, "Art Informel."

The unreality of an absolute informal aesthetic gives us nothing—a gratuitous game. There is no form of art that can give emotion if it doesn't mix in a part of the real. No matter how minute, how impalpable this allusion may be, this irreducible portion is like the key to the work. It renders it readable; clarifies meaning; opens its essential, profound reality to the aesthetic sensibility, which is true intelligence.

One only invents that which is, restores in nuances of emotion the reality that is incorporated in matter, form, color—products of the moment changed into that which changes no longer.   *[1957]*

ANDRÉ MASSON *Automatic Drawing.*
1925. Ink. 17 x 12⅛".

ANDRÉ MASSON

(1896–)

During the 1920s Masson was closely identified with the Surrealists, particularly Miró, but in later years he attempted to pass beyond the dicta of the official Surrealist movement. His free-style drawings and sand paintings became more abstract during the 1940s, most of which (1940–1946) he spent in the United States. He was greatly respected by the Abstract Expressionists in New York, some of whom were directly influenced by his work.

It was obvious that for Miró as for myself, poetry (in the broadest sense of the term) was of capital importance. Our ambition was to be painter-poets and in that we differed from our immediate predecessors who, while going around with the poets of their generation, were terrified of being labeled "literary painters." As painters purporting to work from poetic necessity, we were taking a great risk. Furthermore, but for a few rare exceptions, the verdict of the French critics observing our beginnings was: "Definition of a

Surrealist Painter: not a painter but a failed poet." This was in the best of cases. Often we were charitably advised to "go and have your heads examined."   *[1943]*

Fundamentally I am more a sympathizer with Surrealism, than a Surrealist or a non-Surrealist. In the beginning I tried to satisfy myself with the automatist approach. It was I who became the severest critic of automatism. I still cannot agree with the unconscious approach. I do not believe you can arrive by this means at the intensity essential for a picture. I recognize that there are intense expressions to be obtained through the subconscious, but not without selection. And in that I am not orthodox.

Only so much as can be reabsorbed aesthetically from that which the automatic approach provides should be utilized. For art has an authentic value of its own which is not replaced by psychiatric interest.

It is perhaps more difficult for a Frenchman to be an orthodox Surrealist than for artists of other races. I like Chardin too much ever to be a Surrealist. In Chardin we find no association with things outside the representation itself, or at any rate, a minimum of them. Plastic rigor cannot be replaced by even the richest literary imagination. A painting or sculpture does not have a survival value if it lacks this plastic rigor. The literary imagination in such work is never anything but a pretext of excuse for it and must be absorbed into the plastic form. If it is not, the literary imaginative element soon becomes dated.

As a consequence I am solitary: I am too Surrealist for those who do not like Surrealism, and not Surrealist enough for those who do. I accept the ambiguous situation much as Delacroix did—I do not compare myself with Delacroix, but I believe I understand Delacroix. If he had not the strength of plastic rigor Delacroix would have been a Redon.   *[1946]*

GEORGES MATHIEU

(1921–   )

One of the animators of the Art Informel, or Tachist, movement in postwar Paris, Mathieu was celebrated for his performance as a spontaneous painter who lunged and danced as he attacked his huge canvases. His activities as a writer and publicist, both for his French colleagues and the American Abstract Expressionists, were important in establishing an international context for new tendencies that emerged after the Second World War.

From the ideal to the real, from the real to the abstract, from the abstract one moves on to the possible. Becoming has passed from the realm of man to that of cybernetic machines. Logic is based on contradiction, physics on relations of uncertainty or indeterminacy. . . .

Evolution in art is produced by the saturation of the means of expression (significations) replaced by new means, of which the efficacy is unknown at the moment of use. The significance of these new means supposes a necessity, a structuring of the pictorial material, such as that realized to a lesser degree in psychic or biological facts. This intrinsic autonomy is, in fact, the only quiddity possible for the work of art in its relation with its own existence. . . . Art is in going beyond the signs. The sole chance, eventually, of an *informel* can only rest in the transcending of non-signs. The question is posed: it does more than put the basis of Western civilization at stake. . . .

In this *informel* which precedes the coming into existence, in this freedom to restructure, the signs, which are the structuring elements, have to be made, but how? The phenomenology of "the very act of painting" alone can tell us. . . . The phase which might be called "From the Abstract to the Possible" is more than a phase. It is a new era of art and of thought which is beginning.   *[1958]*

MARTIAL RAYSSE

(1936–   )

A member of the Nouveau Réaliste movement during the 1960s, Raysse used a technique of assemblage similar to that of the British and American Pop artists, stressing the derivation of his images from popular printed sources. Later, he branched out into installation works, using common objects and mirrors. More recently, he has moved toward an almost lyrical ironic mode of figurative painting.

The unconditioned eye does not exist. The general public sees the world today with eyes that were developed by the Impressionist painters . . . this education of perception being spread by means of newspapers, publicity, and so forth. A painter exerts an action upon perception, engineers vision, but what was I going to say? Oh yes . . . vision, a psychological phenomenon, subjective . . . and emotional . . . In a room where a definite color determines the prevailing tone, the beloved will change color in relation to her surroundings. If you look at a face and fix your attention on the nose, the nose will not only change its size but also its color in relation to the rest of the face. These were the observations that I wanted to translate in the works I termed "a geometric variable" (variable geometry). For example, in the big painting entitled *Paysage à Géométrie Variable et à Martial Raysse Kilométres-Heure* exhibited at Venice, each element was treated as a world in itself, with its own particular color scheme and scale, independently of the others, in order to express the attention that was directed to this specific part of the landscape at a given moment. All of those elements, taken together, constituted a picture which was a seismographic record of the psychological variations of the painting act considered as a life act. The special shape chosen permitted me to define a basic space that would convey my ideas the most conveniently. This choice is based on the following considerations and coming from the field of *l'art d'assemblage* where the objects I utilized were common property. I had for a long time felt the need for creating prefabricated objects of my own, my prototypes . . . to replace the stereotypes of society with my own personal ones. . . . It was in this sense that I defined a certain shape of mouth and eye, or certain elements like palm trees, chickens, boats, etc., which I could use in a given context to express certain personal psychological definitions.   *[1967]*

GERMAINE RICHIER

(1904–1959)

Richier's experiments with open surfaces, revealing structural members beneath their bronze exteriors, and her tendency toward metamorphosis of form, found favor during the last decade of her life. The Abstract Expressionists and the artists of France's Art Informel movement had by that time embraced a fusion of disparate idioms such as Surrealism and abstraction, figurative elements and formal ones.

The human image has never been forgotten in the arts. The sculptor is not protected from the crises which have jolted modern art, but in sculpture, an art of slower evolution according to some, the disruptions are of a different nature. In some way it is sculpture that knew how to preserve the human face from these upheavals (in fact, today's sculptors do not renounce the making of busts). The face: that is to say, an entity, a whole of expressions and gestures brought into accord with the form.

    What characterizes sculpture, in my opinion, is the way in which it renounces the full, solid form. Holes and perforations conduct like flashes of lightning into the material which becomes organic and open, encircled from all sides, lit up in and through the hollows. A form lives to the extent to which it does not withdraw from expression. And we decidedly cannot conceal human expression in the drama of our time.   *[1955]*

PIERRE SOULAGES

(1919–)

Soulages gained prominence during the 1950s with his large black-and-white paint-ings, whose stark imagery suggested Oriental ideograms. His sweeping black strokes have led critics to compare his paintings to those of the American Abstract Expres-sionists, particularly Franz Kline's.

Let's be done with the trees. What interested me was the drawing of the branches, their movement in space. One may find there a point of departure for my abstract painting. But if it offers a handwriting which is related to them it is just a chance. Window bars or the back of a chair would have furnished me the same point of departure.

. . . Black trees. There already was the black which is a color I like. But apropos of black, people so often speak of "an economy of means." I myself have only spoken of "a limited palette." There is no question of "economy" in art. When one likes something passionately, the rest is excluded from consideration, naturally. . . . The more the means are limited, the stronger the expression: that, perhaps, explains the choice of a limited palette.

Black has always been the base of my palette. It is the most intense, the most violent absence of color, that gives an intense appearance to colors with it, even to white, as a tree makes the sky blue.

A painting is a physical experience. It is an object which in the course of fabrication becomes suddenly alive because one throws into it at certain moments all that one experiences more or less confusedly: all that one is. I try, across the succession of my canvases, to find a path to follow. The denial of descriptive painting seems to me one possibility. For the adoption of this attitude on my part is not merely the outcome of a wish for purity or reserve in my work. It is the result of a profound need for pictorial intensity—I would say poetic intensity.

Painting is a play of opacities and transparencies.   *[c. 1967]*

NICHOLAS DE STAEL *Landscape in Vaucluse No. 2.* 1953. Oil on canvas.
25 x 32".

NICHOLAS DE STAEL

(1914–1955)

Russian-born, de Stael settled in France in 1938. He was one of the abstract painters whose impasto technique won him a place in the Art Informel movement of postwar France known as Tachism. But, in spite of his thick pastes, bright colors, and unorthodox compositions, de Stael was never really an "informal" painter, but rather based his work on the objectively perceived forms of nature.

An eye that rams . . .

You never paint what you see or think you see. You paint with a thousand vibrations the blow that struck you; how can you be struck and cry out, without anger. . . .

A gesture . . . a weight.

And all at slow combustion.

Never assess space too quickly, there are small fir cones all shriveled up, whose smell gives us such a feeling of immensity that one strolls through Fontainebleau just as if it were a dwarf's attic. The atmosphere does not volatilize.

There is a capacity for violence here.

With Rembrandt an Indian turban becomes a brioche. Delacroix sees it as an iced meringue, Corot as a dry biscuit, and it is neither turban nor brioche, nothing but a quick-life deception, as painting will always be, in order *to be*.

[1949]

PIERRE TAL-COAT

(1905–1985)

Son of a family of fishermen, Tal-Coat, whose real name was Pierre Jacob, had no formal training. His paintings during the 1930s were notably Expressionist, particularly his well-known series of Massacres *based on events during the Spanish Civil War. During the Second World War Tal-Coat turned to lyrical abstraction. Around 1947, Tal-Coat began to phrase his work in highly condensed, delicate tones, earning a prominent place in the postwar Parisian Art Informel movement.*

Prior to the naming of things invisible wave sweeping us out of our cell of insistent visitation. Seized by such an awareness, beyond the dull means of pastures old, I had to proceed toward that which, from the curves, from even our stammerings, can attempt to express what otherwise escapes fair reason. I mean that which cannot be partitioned off by fluctuating edges and escapes from the gilded frame, from the established patterns. And that it was the extreme precariousness of the enterprise at which every extremity gleamed a possibility of freedom which is beyond tensions.

Here, accosted by the world, overrun on all ideas, unable to claim I observe it, which always implies perception lagging behind for excess of reference. This said to explain my attempt to raise myself to the level of the experienced without the convention of the known. And the necessity to proceed forbids recapitulation, for all that belongs to the moment is its one guarantee in the ineffable of its presence.

And to yield to one's wonderment requires a necessary precariousness. But no less precarious the continuing awakening to preserve expressive harmony.

To thus proceed suits me, demanding neither courage nor special gift: that which is given to each in its emerging necessity.   *[c. 1980]*

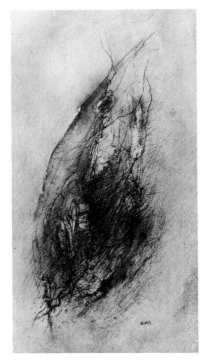

W O L S   *Vegetation.* 1947.
9¼ x 4¹⁵⁄₁₆″.

W O L S   (Alfred Otto Wolfgang Schulze-Battmann)

(1913–1951)

Born in Germany but a naturalized French citizen, Wols was trained as a musician and studied ethnology in Germany before settling in Paris in 1932. He earned his living as a photographer until the Second World War. While he was interned by France before it fell to the Germans in 1940, and then while living in extremely difficult circumstances in the South of France, Wols produced a great many drawings, watercolors, and poems marked with a searching fantasy and tragic vision. His free style and often labyrinthine linear configurations were noted by the postwar generation of French "informal" painters.

To believe in nature, including everything
seeming to be material, is enough.

The Image can be in rapport with nature
like the Bach fugue with Christ;
such a case is not a re-copy
but an analogous creation.

The Christian's mistake is
to appeal without prayers
to a kind of important person;
one must appeal to nobody
or to the void.

Whether God is represented
by circles or a straight line
is all the same to me.
But He cannot be represented
by people.

People with waking dreams get to
know of a thousand things
which escape those who only
dream in sleep.

Seeing is shutting one's eyes.

Seeing to the bottom of things
is merely seeing a solitary single thing.
Seeing deeply
is seeing a thing that is unique.

If you could see to the bottom of a thing,
you would realize it is one and the same as that
in your own me.
But is it possible to see right down there?
To feel it, to love it.   *[n.d.]*

(WEST) GERMANY

JOSEPH BEUYS

(1921–   )

*Beuys developed a way of working during the 1960s that included small drawings,
assembled refuse, and occasional handwritten commentaries that drew attention to his
anti-formal aesthetic. After ten years as a professor of sculpture at the Düsseldorf
Academy, he was dismissed in 1971 for having incited students to reject the orthodox
curriculum. Beuys then began to include a political dimension in his installations and*

Happenings, often inviting spectator participation. His use of felt, fat, and fur as working materials—a reference to his days as a prisoner of war in the Soviet Union—have led commentators to assess his work in terms of its mystical, political message.

My objects are to be seen as stimulants for the transformation of the idea of sculpture, or of art in general. They should provoke thoughts about what sculpture can be and how the concept of sculpting can be extended to the invisible materials used by everyone:

Thinking Forms	how we mold our thoughts or
Spoken Forms	how we shape our thoughts into words or
SOCIAL SCULPTURE	how we mold and shape the world in which we live: Sculpture as an evolutionary process; everyone an artist.

That is why the nature of my sculpture is not fixed and finished. Processes continue in most of them: chemical reactions, fermentations, color changes, decay, drying up. Everything is in a state of change.   *[c. 1975]*

J U L I U S   B I S S I E R

(1893–1965)

Before the Second World War, Bissier explored Chinese modes of painting in small black-and-white ink drawings. In the years after the war, he began to work on small, exceptionally delicate watercolors and temperas, often in irregular formats. These, in their extreme simplicity and luminosity, gained him a large public throughout the world.

Some forms in nature or in its states of transition are torn, others spongy, still others powdery. Some affect you agreeably, some disagreeably, as you observe them. Take such varied contrasts and project them onto a flat surface, whether in a "composition" or as handwritten notes accidentally jotted down. Think of such jottings as charged—well, with the way I am, and you have the essence of my works.

Now, if you imagine that even ideas can be combined with such notes— perhaps by arranging the surface characters in a particular set of conceptions such as vegetable, mineral, fire, earth, water, and their juxtaposition and opposition and mixture—you open up a second possibility. And if you go on to think that certain states of mind will make one prefer one "surface

JULIUS BISSIER   *6 July 1959.* 1959. Oil and tempera on canvas. 8¼ x 11¼".

character" or the other, and that in such a state one will directly use the characters as compositions corresponding to one's "mood," you have what in my work I call a "metaphor."   *[c. 1942–1949]*

HEINZ MACK

(1931–)

Concerned exclusively with the role of light in the art object, Mack worked with polished surfaces that he set in motion with an electric motor, producing light patterns in random order.

The dynamic structure of color and light delights my eye, disturbs my lazy thoughts, lends wings to the rhythm of my heart and to the quick breath of my wishes.

In my reliefs light itself becomes the medium instead of color, the movement—as well as causing the light vibrations—produces a new, immaterial color and tonality, and the intangible and entirely nonfigurative nature of these suggests a possible reality whose aura and secret beauty we already love.   *[1950]*

GÜNTHER UECKER

(1930–)

A member of Düsseldorf's Zero group, along with Otto Piene and Heinz Mack, Uecker worked with compositions of clustered forms raised from the picture surface to create illusions of light and movement.

I deliberately call my white structures "objects," as they are different from illustrative projections on a screen. I built them with prefabricated elements like nails. At first I used strictly arranged rhythms, mathematical sequences, but these dissolved into a free rhythm. Then I tried to achieve an integration of light which, by changing light, would set these white structures in motion, and which could be understood as a free, articulate area of light. I decided on a white zone, as it is the extreme of colorfulness, the climax of light, triumph over darkness. I believe that a white world is a humane world in which man can experience his colorful existence, in which he can be truly alive. These white structures can be a spiritual language in which we begin to mediate. The state of White can be understood as a prayer, its articulation can be a spiritual experience.   *[1950]*

WOLF VOSTELL

(1932–)

During the late 1950s Vostell began to exhibit his "décollages"—compositions of public posters torn from walls— and to produce Happenings in both Germany and America. He was active in Fluxus, an international group of neo-Dadaists, and was associated with a short-lived configuration called "destruction art," in which artists damaged or destroyed their own creations.

What fascinated me were the symptoms and the emanations of a constant metamorphosis in the environment and in which destruction in general, and in artistic expression, together with dissolution and juxtaposition, are the strongest elements. de-coll/age as production principle which makes use of destruction and autodestruction, in contradistinction to collage in which mostly undestroyed although heterogeneous objects are assembled.

Not only through the chaos of visual events, intermingling or superimposed in layers, but also through the psychological consequences in the field of perception which leads through the erosion of the image to an a-perception, I became aware that the constructive elements in life do not exist at all—but that everything is intermediate stages on the road to dissolution.

The artistic treatment of destruction is an answer! Documentation as permanent artistic protest and rebellion of the conscious and subconsious mind against the contradictions and inexplicabilities of life.   *[1968]*

GREAT BRITAIN

FRANK AUERBACH

(1931–)

Deeply impressed by the independence of the older Expressionist David Bomberg, Auerbach developed a vehement Expressionist idiom in which the human figure, with its existence in a palpably threatening atmosphere, predominates.

What I'm not hoping to do is to paint another picture because there are enough pictures in the world. I'm hoping to make a new thing for the world that remains in the mind like a new species of living thing. It sounds very grandiloquent. The only way I know how to do it, or to try and do it, is to start with something that I know specifically, so that I have something to cling to beyond aesthetic feelings and my knowledge of other paintings. Ideally one should have more material than one can possibly cope with.

The problem of painting is to see a unity within a multiplicity of pieces of evidence and the very slightest change of light, the very slightest, tiniest hairbreadth inflection of the form creates a totally different visual synthesis. I actually more or less start again every time the model rests and gets up again, but my mind has traveled along certain paths and tried out certain possibilities and created certain hopes, so that I somehow digest some of the possibilities. When the conclusion occurs and I feel I've been lucky enough to find some sort of whole for this overwhelming and unmanageable heap of sensations and impressions, I think that the previous attempts have contributed.

I mean, to put down an ideogram of a table so that people will recognize it as a table is not the work of a painter, but to sense it for a moment as a magic carpet with a leg hanging down at each corner is the beginning of a

FRANK AUERBACH   *Head of E.O.W.* 1961.
Oil on board. 24 x 20".

painter's imagination, and there would be a million ways of sensing this table on the floor, this invisible box. This is where the painter's imagination begins and this is what a painter's imagination is. It's not a question of fancy dress, or symbolic objects. It's this reinvention of the physical world, and everything else comes from that.   *[1978]*

FRANCIS BACON

(1910–   )

A self-taught painter, Bacon had worked only intermittently during the 1930s (like the French painter Dubuffet), but in 1944 he exhibited studies for figures at the base of the Crucifixion that brought him extraordinary attention. Bacon's horrifying imagery, his constant references to violently distorted figures, instantly caused a scandal in England, as Dubuffet's had in France, and established Bacon as one of the fiercest postwar figurative artists.

FRANCIS BACON *Man with Dog.* 1953.
Oil on canvas. 60 x 46".

I would like to make images which reflect all kinds of things that I feel instinctively about my own species, and I would like, in my arbitrary way, to bring one nearer to the actual human being. Now this is a very difficult thing. You would think my way of deforming images, which for myself brings me nearer to the human being than if I were to sit down and illustrate one, would probably put most others off, but somehow, on the instinctive level, there are exceptions. Whether it in fact really works I don't know—it does for me—it brings me nearer to the actual fact of being a human being. I get nearer by going farther away.

Any work that I like does the same to me—it makes me see other things. It makes me aware of reality, although it may not be very realistic in itself. I can only put it that way—that it unlocks the valves of sensation.

Death is the only absolute that we know in this life. Death is the one absolute certainty. Artists know they can't defeat it, but I think that most artists are very aware of their annihilation—it follows them around like their shadow, and I think that's one of the reasons most artists are so conscious of the vulnerability and the nothingness of life.

There are two sides to me. I like very perfect things, for instance. I like perfection on a very grand scale. In a way I would like to live in a very grand place. But as in painting you make such a mess, I prefer to live in the mess with the memories and the damage left with one. I think we all have this double side to us. One likes disorder and one likes order. We have to battle for order.

Painting is in a peculiar stage now because it's so difficult to be figurative, and abstract art seemed to be the logical continuation, but the trouble is, practically all the abstract school becomes like decoration because it's free fancy and you can just put anything down that looks pretty, whereas in figuration that is so difficult, it's almost impossible to avoid painting the human body like an illustrator. A photograph would be better.   *[1974]*

DAVID BOMBERG

(1890–1957)

First associated with Wyndham Lewis's Vorticism, Bomberg withdrew from the British vanguard in order to develop an Expressionist, figurative idiom during a long sojourn in Palestine in the 1920s. After the Second World War, he attracted a small but fervent group of admirers among young artists, including Lucian Freud and Frank Auerbach, whose work has increasingly come into prominence.

We gladly make known our acknowledgment to the source at the mountain peak, George Berkeley, Bishop of Cloyne, and to Paul Cézanne, father of the revolution of painting. We truly claim to be friends and appraisers for we knew the secrets of George Berkeley's philosophy of the metaphysic of mind and matter lay in its divinity and we could not follow in its footsteps unless we ourselves were of that. But we gathered sufficient from his theory of vision, in how we perceive distance to find our way, by the contemplation of the meaning of drawing and how it is related to the interpretation of form, to the study of its structure; gradually we were brought to comprehend how the part was not the organic whole and how the organic whole was part of the mystery of mass and this prepared the base for the understanding of the significance of Cézanne's contribution to painting whose secret passed on his death—for he spoke to many of all things but not of this, which was deep in the recesses of his mind—therefore to Berkeley who taught us how to think is the grandeur—he derives from Plato and Newton; the Cézanne who taught us how to invent is the glory—he derives from the Italians and his colleagues the French Impressionists.

The fundamental creativeness of all true artists, great or small, has been not only in making good works themselves but in inspiring others to follow them. Thus Cézanne often wished to communicate what was being revealed to him and desired a school—that might have prevented followers imitating him, for to understand is to avoid the weakness that permeates the blood stream. Thus the vigor and vibrant vitalities go unnurtured, which today is the outcome of the evil that was done yesterday.

Why British painting today shares with all other countries a decline is because it is so facile with its own virtuosity trying to imitate the virtues of others, and if artists do not feel sick it is because it has become the fashion of painting to mirror one another's complexions with the same ingredients of the "beauty" preparations—structure has become less important.

We are resolutely committed to the structure of the organic character of mass. We have no concern at all with the decorative properties of attractive superficialities. We do not admit a willful distortion which is another superficial appearance on the horrific side of the attractive. We conceive of art as the incomprehensible density of cosmic forces compressed into a small space, therefore any of the manifestations to the contrary will not find a habitation with us. For we are less concerned with man's condition and more with what he thinks and feels. The strength that gave the cave dwellers the means to express the spirit of their life is in us to express ours. We have no need to dwell on the material magnificence of man's achievement, but with the approach of the scientific mechanization and the submerging of individuals we have urgent need of the affirmation of his spiritual significance and his individuality. Our environment is there to distract us but a sufficiency of contemporaries are concerning themselves with this aspect. . . .

Whether the paintings or sculptures of the future are carried out in ferro-concrete, plastic, steel, wire, hydrogen, cosmic rays of helium and oil paint, stone, bronze, superseded as anachronisms, it is reality that man is yet subject to gravitational forces and still dependent on sustenance from nature and a spiritual consciousness, an individual with individual characteristics to remain so for eons of time.   *[1953]*

ANTHONY CARO

(1924—)

Caro developed as a gifted modeler and worked for a time as an assistant to Henry Moore. However, after a 1959 visit to the United States, where he admired the welded steel work of David Smith, Caro turned to welded techniques. Like Smith, he used prefabricated and found parts, but in placing his works without distinctions (such as pedestals) from their environs, Caro struck out on his own and opened the way for a vigorous new generation of sculptors that included his students Phillip King and William Tucker.

I think part of the trouble—part of the disadvantage—of sculpture, and also part of the advantage of it is the fact that it's heavy and real; I don't want to make sculpture which has an unreality. I want to make sculpture which is very corporeal, but denies its corporeality. I don't want to make sculpture which is like a . . . conjurer's trick. . . .

I would really rather make my sculpture out of "stuff"—out of something really anonymous, just sheets maybe which you cut a bit off. Angle iron and rolled-steel joists and all that, I think, are irrelevant: they are a thing I'd like to get away from in the end. . . . They'll bit by bit creep away out of the sculpture. The only thing is that certain things, like those heavy joists from which I think I've taken most of the bridge connotations, do have a weight about them, they do have the effect of being able to punctuate, they are a bit like a blob of color in a Monet painting or something like this. Much of the sculpture that I'm doing is about extent, and even might get to be about fluidity or something of this sort, and I think one has to hold it from becoming just amorphous. . . .

I have been trying, I think, all the time to eliminate references, to make truly abstract sculpture. It is using these things like notes in music. But the note must not remind you too much of the world of things, or of parts of noses or breasts or ears or anything—perhaps it's impossible to make a sculpture out of clay at this moment, at the moment it's too difficult for me anyway—there are too many reminders in it. And I think therefore one tries really to get a material with not too much art history in it. Although I think steel's got plenty of art history now, unfortunately. But I would be very happy to use another material. *[1965]*

ANDREW FORGE

(1923–)

Although known largely for his brilliant art criticism, Forge was one of the postwar British painters who broke with figurative precedents and developed a suggestive abstract painting style that draws upon Post-Impressionist techniques put in the service of a contemporary vision.

To recapture the studio monologue is like trying to tell a dream. Even as you reach for words you realize that you are not telling but translating, and that what you are trying to tell is shrinking away from you. And at best that monologue is no more than a kind of incantation.

My ambition is to construct a painting so that the whole of its surface is alive, however I look at it. Each mark and the interval between each mark must give something back on its own terms. It must be vivid. Dot placed by dot gives back location, interval, primitive pattern, agitation, dazzle. Extended in space (the picture surface) and time (the cycles of excitement and boredom that give shape to studio hours), the dots accrue, giving back pathways, constellations, geometries, and at last as the white ground of the canvas is overcome, unforseen color sensations.

I think of each canvas as a place, which is one reason why I paint in small dots and dashes. A less complex surface would surrender itself too quickly. The heart of the matter is in what the canvas gives back—invitations to be pondered, refused, turned around, or accepted and augmented. Each mark however small should be the upshot of a fully charged decision—but a decision made in the clearest possible awareness of its local terms, its here and now, and not with an eye to the "ending." Here is another way of looking at the dot: a way of excluding gestures and big statements and the temptation to will a painting into the world by persuasion or brute force.

I have felt that there is something unsatisfactory about the discussion of meaning as applied to abstract painting. It is either too sentimental in its tone or too dogmatic; too reliant on physiognomic projection, or too tied to a serial context, the series of art history, the series of a painter's oeuvre. I hate either extreme, not out of love for a middle way but because this either/ or seems to symbolize a poverty of spirit and a contempt for a difficult wholeness.

My slow painting, I tell myself, is like life: you don't know how it is going to end. But that doesn't release you from choosing from moment to moment, from point to point. How else can life be acknowledged except through such choices? *[1984]*

RICHARD HAMILTON

(1922–   )

Although trained as a painter, Hamilton worked in the advertising profession for many years, and drew from it the materials for his montage critique of modern society and culture. He was considered a seminal force in the Pop Art movement in England. His wide-ranging interests extended to mounting such important London exhibitions as "Man, Machine and Motion" at the ICA (1955); the "This Is Tomorrow" show at the Whitechapel Gallery (1956); and the Duchamp retrospective at the Tate Gallery (1966), for which Hamilton reconstructed Duchamp's shattered masterpiece Large Glass.

It seems to me that the artist, the intellectual, is not the alien that he was and his consumption of popular culture is due, in some measure, to his new role as a creator of popular culture. Popular art, as distinct from fine art, art created by the people, anonymously, crudely and with a healthy vigor, does not exist today. Its present-day equivalent, Pop Art, is now a consumer product absorbed by the total population but created for it by the mass entertainment machine, which uses the intellectual as an essential part of its technique. The results are highly personalized and sophisticated, but also have a healthy vigor.

In much the way that the invention of photography cut away for itself a chunk of art's prerogative—the pictorial recording of visual facts—trimming the scope of messages which fine art felt to lie within its true competence, so has popular culture abstracted from fine art its role of mythmaker. The restriction of his area of relevance has been confirmed by the artist with smug enthusiasm so that decoration, one of art's few remaining functions, has assumed a ridiculously inflated importance.

It isn't surprising, therefore, to find that some painters are now agog at the ability of the mass entertainment machine to project, perhaps more pervasively than has ever before been possible, the classic themes of artistic vision and to express them in a poetic language which marks them with a precise cultural date-stamp.

It is the *Playboy* Playmate of the Month pull-out pinup which provides us with the closest contemporary equivalent of the odalisque in painting. Automobile body stylists have absorbed the symbolism of the space age more successfully than any artist. Social comment is left to TV and comic strip. Epic has become synonymous with a certain kind of film and the heroic archetype is now buried deep in movie lore. If the artist is not to lose much of his ancient purpose he may have to plunder the popular arts to recover the imagery which is his rightful inheritance.

Futurism has ebbed and has no successor, yet to me the philosophy of affirmation seems susceptible to fruition. The long tradition of bohemianism which the Futurists made their bid to defeat is anachronic in the atmosphere of conspicuous consumption generated by the art rackets.

Affirmation propounded as an avant-garde aesthetic is rare. The history of art is that of a long series of attacks upon social and aesthetic values held to be dead and moribund, although the avant-garde position is frequently nostalgic and absolute. The Pop-Fine-Art standpoint, on the other hand— the expression of popular culture in fine art terms—is, like Futurism, fundamentally a statement of belief in the changing values of society. Pop-Fine-Art is a profession of approbation of mass culture, therefore also antiartistic. It is positive Dada, creative where Dada was destructive. Perhaps it is Mama—a cross-fertilization of Futurism and Dada which upholds a respect for the culture of the masses and a conviction that the artist in twentieth-century urban life is inevitably a consumer of mass culture and potentially a contributor to it.   *[after 1953]*

DAME BARBARA HEPWORTH
Solitary Eye. 1972. White marble. 16¾″ high.

DAME BARBARA HEPWORTH

(1903–1975)

Along with Ben Nicholson and Henry Moore, Hepworth sustained the abstract tradition of modern sculpture in England during the 1930s. After the war, she worked in direct carving on a large scale, perforating her stones with holes that she likened to caves and watery depths. Her relationship to nature was intense and won her admirers throughout the world.

Being a carver, I do have a complete conception in my mind of the form I'm making before I start carving or, indeed, making any work. It is, I suppose, simply a faculty one happens to be born with—being able to see mentally all around the form before one begins. And I do find that if, for instance, architects ask for a maquette for a given position, that is one of the most difficult things, because my whole idea is to make a small maquette which will live as a small sculpture but leave myself completely free and, indeed, I always have to stipulate this, that when I work on a bigger scale that it will change because scale is all important. Man is only up to six foot high, and our whole vision changes according to height and perhaps in depth, and it is a physical reaction which tells on all our spiritual perceptions. Therefore, I would prefer to make a maquette which looks terribly nice as a small sculpture and is exciting to me, and then act quite freely when I do much bigger work—to change and expand and alter wherever I feel the physical and spiritual necessity.

I think it would be true to say that it is perfectly possible to be on a lonely hill in Cornwall, considering man's philosophic development and relation to life, and create a work which could transport the whole of this environment of the world in its absolute beauty, unspoiled beauty, and place it, say, in the middle of Piccadilly and create the exact evocation of idea so that everything becomes quite stilled and controls the impetus, which I think we suffer from, of rushing and confusion, and create an exact response. I do believe, in abstract work, that it is possible for sculptors to create forms which, for instance, make man consider space, or traveling in space, or moving around the world as we now do, and produce this in the middle of the biggest hurly-burly but still make it completely valid. That is, I don't wish to make a work fit for Piccadilly, but I would like to make what I most truly feel and put it in Piccadilly and say, "Here is something of myself, of Cornwall, of sky, sea, space," and let it tell in that environment. *[c. 1962]*

ROGER HILTON

(1911–1975)

After the Second World War, Hilton's boldly colored and lyrically exuberant paintings became increasingly abstract. Nonetheless, like the Americans of the Abstract Expressionist generation, whom he admired, he was not afraid to maintain discreet references to both landscape and figure.

All my thinking about art is haunted by a mystical belief that in its practice one is tapping sources of truth. If it were not that one caught, in this practice, glimpses of some certainties, one would not continue it.

The combination artist-picture is a total machine which is one of the vital antennae—an intuitional one—which man uses in the exploration of his environment.

The painter today is like the ancient alchemists: he is concerned not so much with visible reality as with reality *tout court*. His pictures are not a picture of the world but an attempt to change it.

At heart everyone knows that beneath the everyday appearance of things are hidden truths which intuition alone can grasp. Today, when everything is put in question, man is trying again to orientate himself, to give himself a direction, to reestablish laws based on absolute truths. In crucial moments in the history of man such as we are living through today there is no excuse for fooling around.

I see art as an instrument of truth, or it is nothing.

It may be thought that technique which has been built up for the purposes of figurative art ceases to apply where nonfiguration is concerned. But I think that the figurative parts of pictures are not, in a final analysis, what the picture is really concerned with. It follows that the technique has been built up not so much for the purposes of representing the visible world as for being an instrument capable of embodying men's inner truths. Abstraction has been due not so much to a positive thing but to the absence of a valid image.

Abstraction in itself is nothing. It is only a step toward a new sort of figuration, that is, one which is more true. However beautiful they may be, one can no longer depict women as Titian did. Renoir in his last pictures had already greatly modified her shape. Today one sees people who are changing abstraction into landscape (the easiest to do). For an abstract painter there are two ways out or on: he must give up painting and take to architecture, or he must reinvent figuration.

Now that we have conquered new plastic ground during the last fifty years, there is no reason why images should not return to painting without fear of repeating what has already been done.   *[1961]*

DAVID HOCKNEY

(1937–)

Hockney has been called the wunderkind of British art, having won an international reputation while still a student at the Royal College in 1962. His whimsical figurative paintings are sometimes related to Pop Art, but he rejects the label. He has also made photomontages and theater sets. His motifs are often derived from the rather high-style life he observes as he travels about—life around Hollywood swimming pools for instance—but he also works with such intimate and thoroughly conventional subjects as still life.

I can say that my primary interest is in pictures of all kinds—paintings, drawings, photographs, prints, etc., but best of all I like handmade pictures; consequently, I paint them myself. They always have a subject and a little bit of form. Balancing the two makes me, I suppose, a traditional painter. I am in complete sympathy with W. H. Auden's lines:

> To me, art's subject is the human play
> And landscape but a background to a torso.
> Cézanne's apples I would give away
> For a small Goya or a Daumier.

[1975]

PHILLIP KING

(1934–)

King's experiments with materials such as fiberglass and mesh wire led him in the mid-1960s into a fresh, somewhat Surrealist idiom that was often described as enigmatic or bizarre. His use of rare configurations and shapes, such as the cone he describes below, distinguished him from the burgeoning school of welders following in his teacher Caro's wake.

Why the preoccupation with a cone shape?

First of all I started making elements stand up by their mutual pressure at the top, thus forming a triangle. This seemed a way of getting out of the standing piling-up idea, without losing anything. In an attempt to make mass less a question of weight in the material, I started using the split cone, and the elements became sheets in the shape of semi-cones. More recently, I have come to use the cone more because it is such an extremely stable shape, that has maximum mass for its volume and can allow maximum maneuverability in an effort to make mass controllable in terms of shape, volume, surface, color, contour, space. The cone as something earthbound was important to me. I suppose it's the equivalent of trying to use very heavy steel or stone to make something very light—purely in shape terms. Surface is more fundamental to the structuring of the shape in the cone than it is the cube or other shapes.   *[1975]*

R. B.   K I T A J
(1932–   )

In the mid-1950s the American-born Kitaj came to England to study and remained long enough to become identified as a major figure in the British Pop Art movement. However, Kitaj's sources were always in intellectual history, and his interests moved toward ethical and political statements conveyed by means of a deceptively illustrative technique.

To my way of thinking art-things put people *in mind, aspire* beyond them-selves. Some very wide, even great themes or motives like questions probing at the difficulties of dealing with each other day in and day out, the games people play, and . . . at a remove—the moving injustice in societies . . . these . . . *are* of *moment* . . . art-thing *will* touch down in those places because *they* will touch art . . . these motives are inevitable—like death is inevitable and *that* sure as hell touches art like when it does, art stops . . . and if you can accept that death touches art and that art is touched by suchlike external fundament then you won't feel at home with the trivial dream that an art may be willed into freedom from external interference. If death is inevitable so are those issues which will raise compassion and shame, and shame has been called by those who ought to know—a revolutionary sentiment . . . bringing it and what gives rise to shame well toward an art which we have not even begun to glimpse, so intent are we on our freedom to fashion things which will turn on themselves.

Whatever looms in the offing, in the night of our art . . . the broad day of it now registers only vestigial change. Those deep skills of imagination, by which insight, idea, and action get into art may wait upon a stage of belief which is not given to our time. We may just be *beyond repair* . . . and so as long as we remain unable to effect what Wallace Stevens called "an abstraction blooded, as a man by thought" . . . our art will gibber before a reality too great, appalled with perception, when like *we* fail though meaning persists.

In an epoch of lethal, enforced pace and of reflective imagination an art prompted by occasion in the world sounds a warning but remains by nature more speculative than in contention. There are times and places where one rushes in to the defense of a modernism which commands an irritation so intense because one knows the temptations, but those moments now lie thin on the ground for me. There will always be skylarks; even a few nightingales. But arts are not only the human equivalent of the song of singing birds.

[1967]

RICHARD LONG

(1945–   )

Long executed his first landscape piece in 1967 and since then has been one of the most prominent so-called earthwork artists in the international context. His pronounced lyricism and principled approach to nature (never violating it) distinguish his work.

My art is about working in the wide
world, wherever, on the surface of the earth.

My art has the themes of materials, ideas,
movement, time. The beauty of objects, thoughts, places
and actions.

My work is about my senses, my instinct, my own scale
and my own physical commitment.

My work is real, not illusory or conceptual.
It is about real stones, real time, real actions.

My work is not urban, nor is it romantic.
It is the laying down of modern ideas in
the only practical places to take them.
The natural world sustains the industrial world.
I use the world as I find it.

My art can be remote or very public,
all the work and all the places being equal.

My work is visible or invisible. It can be an
object (to possess) or an idea carried out and equally
shared by anyone who knows about it.

My photographs are facts which bring the
right accessibility to remote, lonely
or otherwise unrecognizable works. Some sculptures
are seen by few people, but can be known about by many.

My outdoor sculptures and walking locations
are not subject to possession and ownership. I like the fact
that roads and mountains are common, public land.

My outdoor sculptures are places.
The material and the idea are of the place;
sculpture and place are one and the same.
The place is as far as the eye can see from the
sculpture. The place for a sculpture is found
by walking. Some works are a succession
of particular places along a walk, e.g.,
Milestones. In this work the walking,
the places, and the stones all have equal importance.

My talent as an artist is to walk across
a moor, or place a stone on the ground.

My stones are like grains of sand in
the space of the landscape.   *[1980]*

KENNETH MARTIN

(1905–1984)

*In his maturity, toward 1950, Kenneth Martin formulated a firm Constructivist
aesthetic, related to the mathematical theories of Max Bill and the American Charles
Biederman. His great versatility, demonstrated in constructions, paintings, prints,
and sculptures, as well as in unique mobiles, puts him in the forefront of the postwar
British group, including Adrian Heath, Anthony Hill, and Victor Pasmore, that
revitalized the nonobjective tradition of the prewar years.*

Construction stems from within. The work is the product of inner necessity
and is created through an inner logic, i.e., a developing logic within the
work that results in form. Works of art are made of feeling, concept, and
material. These three can be constructed together by a logic inherent within
them and their relationship. The end will be an expressive form dependent
on the power of the artist.

A construction can be of any material with which it is possible to do that
operation and can be in any possible dimension. Material and dimension
(choice and development) are governed by the practical and the aesthetic.

Being the opposite of abstraction, construction begins in the most primitive manner, but it is dangerous for the artist to fall in love with primitivism.
The elementary methods of construction are related to the elements of life,
the forces of life. An example can be a band ornament drawn linear on the
plane, which can be simple, subtle, and dramatic, which can be directly
related to life in its modulations and inevitability. Life is variable and
inevitable, recurrent and developable. For the individual it is essentially
tragic.

Or to restart rather differently.

An event or a series of events may be ordered by a rhythm. The same
event can be repeated varying its temporal or spatial position. An event can
be inverted and take on a new, strange character. A whole system can be
changed by inversions. Events and systems of events considered plastically
with equivalance between tangible and intangible elements can become an
expressive structure. Events are changed or rhythmically related by means
of kinetics. The primitive forces of kinetics are universal, they are within
us and without. Therefore, through their use it is possible to express life.
However construction must start with the simplest and most practical means
and to avoid confusion aim at the simplest results. The method is empirical
and moves from ignorance to knowledge.   *[1964]*

EDUARDO PAOLOZZI

(1924–)

*Born in Edinburgh of Italian parents, Paolozzi studied art in England and spent
two crucial years—1947–1949—in Paris, where he discovered the work of Dubuffet
and postwar Surrealism. On his return to England he began to develop an art of
collage, using printed sources, particularly from popular magazines and newspapers.
Paolozzi's later work, widely considered a seminal influence in the Pop Art movement,
developed out of these collages and out of his cast bronze sculptures made up of found
parts.*

Key phrases, like key sculpture, take time to make. The arrival at a plastic
iconography is just as difficult as a language. A few sculptures per year can
alter other plastic values. A few key statements can have a similar effect.

It is my opinion that to talk of Art or, to be specific, modern sculpture,
requires a special language:

Avoid using worn clichés, the words that can't even indicate or scratch at
the hundred hidden meanings in objects and structures.

My own reading or source material is largely that of previous art works,

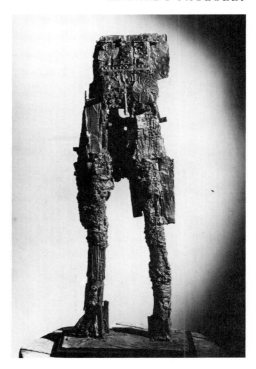

EDUARDO PAOLOZZI *Box Headed Figure*. 1957. Bronze. 48″ high.

technical magazines, and books, a world of intricate problems and a lucid language.

Experiment, discipline seem to find their own system. Rational order in the technological world can be as fascinating as the fetishes of a Congo witch doctor.

The multi-evocative image demands a prose lyrical style at least. Anyway, an object which suggests a number of things might be described by the spectator in that order.

Certain expressions are affected by developments such as "as far as the eye can see."

Symbols can be interpreted in different ways.

The Watch as a calculating machine or jewel, a Door as a panel or an art object, the Skull as a death symbol in the West, or symbol for moon in the East, Camera as luxury or necessity. Acid etched, copper plated, dipped in liquid solder, the printed circuit, intricate, complex, evocative, as pretty as a Fabergé jewel.

Modern polyethylene toys, due to the combination of plastic injection methods and steel dies, have a microscopic precision impossible to the handcraftsman of the past.

Giant machines with automatic brains are at this moment stamping out blanks and precision objects, components for other brains which will govern other machines.

Here is a list of objects which are used in my work, that is to say, pressed into a slab of clay in different formations. This forms an exact impression (in the negative of course) and from this a store of design sheets can be built up. They range from extremely mechanical shapes to resembling pieces of bark.

Metamorphosis of Rubbish
• Dismembered lock
• Toy frog
• Rubber dragon
• Toy camera
• Assorted wheels and electrical parts
• Clock parts
• Broken comb
• Bent fork
• Various unidentified found objects
• Parts of a radio
• Old RAF bomb sight
• Shaped pieces of wood
• Natural objects such as pieces of bark
• Gramophone parts
• Model automobiles
• Reject die castings from factory tip sites
Car wrecking yards as hunting grounds

At the elbow, in wax form: a Directory of Masks, sheets of an Alphabet of Elements awaiting assembly: boxlike Legs tube Arms, square Heads, copper Words, Wheels like eyes for symbols
  Grammar of Forms neo-geometric
  Encyclopedia of Forms including non-Face
  Elements at the ready
  Dictionary of Design Elements

My preoccupation or obsession with metamorphosis of the figure:
  That is a Cracked Column resembling a Petrified Tower
  Disintegrating Figure with a Shattered Head
  A Cracked Tower like a Shattered Figure
  The Metamorphosis of a Column into a Figure
  Into a Tower A maze of Parts and Persons like an avant-garde Power Plant   *[1958]*

VICTOR PASMORE

(1908–   )

Pasmore was one of the founders of the realist Euston Road School in the late 1930s, but, like Kenneth Martin, converted to pure abstraction in the late 1940s, and became a prominent leader in the nonobjective revival during the 1950s.

In spite of his dependence on freedom the visual artist has been led to the abstract not through a desire to increase his freedom of expression, but to deepen the reality of his work. This desire requires an approach which, superficially, is the reverse of traditional naturalism: it means that the artist must change his center of gravity from outside the object of inspection to inside it. But, to begin at the center of things and not from a point outside them means thinking in terms of universals rather than of particulars. This distinction is important because so much that goes under the name of abstract is, in reality, only a transitional stage where optical representation has been denuded of its particular content. But the particular cannot be torn from the visual world without a weakening of experience. Thus Abstract Expressionism and abstract impressionism, as ends in themselves, are a negative development. Properly speaking the abstract is a medium, not of the sensible, but of the intelligible and intuitive world; hence it must necessarily function in terms of universals. This does not mean that the individual and particular are denied in the abstract. On the contrary, the very fact that the form of the work must be determined by individual sensibility and present itself in terms of shape and substance means that it must express itself as a particular. Abstract art, therefore, approaches the particular by way of the universal—the reverse of naturalist art, yet at the same time a development of it.   *[1957]*

BRIDGET LOUISE RILEY

(1931–)

A graduate of the Royal College of Art, Riley earned international renown during the 1960s for her meticulous illusionistic abstractions that drew upon principles derived from optics. She was one of the prime painters of the so-called Op Art movement, and was often compared to the French artist Victor Vasarely, whose illusionistic paintings of geometric forms often depended on optical tricks.

My paintings are not concerned with the romantic legacy of Expressionism, nor with fantasies, concepts, or symbols.

I draw from nature, I work with nature, although in completely new terms. For me nature is not landscape, but the dynamism of visual forces— an event rather than an appearance—these forces can only be tackled by treating color and form as ultimate identities, freeing them from all descriptive or functional roles.

The context of painting provides an arena in which to tap these visual energies—to unlock their true potential and latent characteristics. Once released they have to be organized in new pictorial terms, every bit as much, though quite differently, as when painting nature in landscape or still life.

The new motif determines the size, the proportion, even the "way up" of the painting just as old natural motif determined these factors before. In working on a painting I choose a small group of colors and juxtapose them in different sequences, to provide various relationships and to precipitate color reactions. These color *events* are delicate and elusive, they have to be organized to make them more *present*—more *there* more *real*. I take for example three colors, say magenta, ochre, and turquoise plus black and white, a situation which then triggers off airy iridescent bursts of color.

I choose a form and a structure in which to repeat these color clouds, to accumulate them, to mass them until each painted unit is submerged in a visual rhythm which, in turn, collectively generates a shimmering colored haze. This luminous substance is completely meshed with the actual colored surface and together they provide the experience of the painting. *[c. 1981]*

WILLIAM TUCKER *Rim.* 1981.
Wood model for steel. 14' diameter.

WILLIAM TUCKER

(1935–)

One of Anthony Caro's students, Tucker brought to sculpture a searching intelligence and an understanding of the historical sweep of modern sculptural history. His work from the mid-1960s demonstrated a firm commitment to modernism, coupled with an audacity in choice of materials (timber beams, fiberglass, steel, plaster), and a will toward monumentality.

Sculpture is subject to gravity and revealed by light. Here is the primary condition. Gravity governs sculpture's existence in itself, light discloses sculpture to us. Sculpture's constancy, in time and in space, springs from its fundamental availability to perception. That is, sculpture, however extended, must have a physical boundary: its effect on perception must in the last reckoning derive from the knowledge that the sculpture is not the world, but is a part of it, even if from a certain aspect no boundary is visible. Equally sculpture's effect on perception rests on the knowledge that the boundary is stable: or at least has a sufficient ground of stability that the work's given character is not negated by its own movement exceeding the spectator's conceptual grasp.

The "free-standing" of sculpture must be understood in the light of these primary conditions. "Free," as wholly exposed to our perception, in light; "standing," as withstanding the pull of the earth. We perhaps take the free-standing of sculpture too much for granted, not realizing how recently it was regained for us (by Rodin and Degas), how infrequently it has obtained within the European tradition, and how it is a quality that has to be recovered in each sculpture as it is made even, or especially, now.

The pressure on sculpture to adopt the painting-directed role of relief has been enormous throughout the modern period, whether the ground of relief has been the wall or the floor, or recently the surface of landscape itself. In each case the condition of gravity is ignored, and sculpture is reduced to a more available, more "present," but in fact hollow and perverse surrogate-painting. (Only David Smith of the great modern sculptors accepted painting's planar directive and turned it to sculpture's profound advantage, giving sculpture a new order of depth and transparency.)

Sculpture's free-standing is thus more than a neutral description: it is an aspiration. To stand free, for sculpture, demands a positive acceptance and understanding of its condition; and it follows that a free sculpture will remain inconvenient, obtrusive—a challenge to facile and conventional views of history and aesthetic.   *[1975]*

JOHN WALKER

(1939–   )

Walker studied at the Birmingham College of Art from 1955 to 1960, and soon after became known for the adventurous paintings in which he took inspiration from the work of the American Abstract Expressionists. He works large, often troweling on both paint and gesso, and using collage elements. Although his work is largely abstract in character, Walker often introduces a recognizable motif or symbol.

I didn't want to get into some kind of geometric game-playing. That is not real painting. Take Vermeer's *View of Delft*, one is constantly persuaded by the illusion. You look four miles deep into it and the wonderful thing is that you are constantly brought flicking back to the surface. There's a conversation going on which builds up the tension. All great painting has it, the conversation between the illusion and the surface. That's where the energy is. . . .

I think painting is a big thing not a small thing, not a reductive thing; if

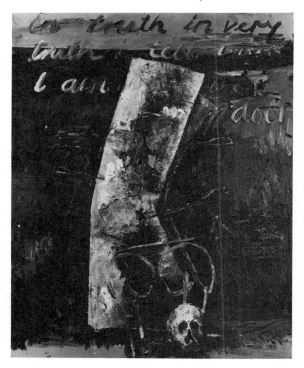

JOHN WALKER *Form and Skull I.* 1983.
Oil on canvas. 85¼ x 67¼".

you look at a Rembrandt you feel that everything was available to him, if
he'd needed anything he would have had it to make a painting. I also feel
that about Goya. They select things, they take things out, they limit. But
you never feel that they aren't complete in themselves. With a lot of recent
painting you can't feel that anymore. It's been reduced to nothing. People
have been caught in that sort of trap . . . they've got interested in meagerness
and can't get out of it. . . .

I'm ambitious, in the way that Matisse said that it is the painter's job to
introduce new things into the world. It's important always to have that on
one's mind: you've got to put yourself in the position where that possibility
is there. I started collaging because I was shaken by two Matisse paintings
I saw in a traveling show from the Hermitage in Russia: one is a beautiful
dark blue-green painting, a portrait of his wife, and the other has a plant
stand with nasturtiums tumbling down, behind it a painting of the dance—
what struck me about these paintings, what really hit me, was the architecture of them, the idea of something built. They look built. . . . I guess it
seemed to me that that was what my art lacked at the time. The collage
was a deliberate attempt to literally build something.   *[1978]*

ISRAEL

YAACOV AGAM

(1928–)

Agam came to Paris in 1951 after having studied in Switzerland with the Bauhaus master Johannes Itten. His approach to art was based on the prewar principles evolved at the Bauhaus by Moholy-Nagy and Max Bill, but his experiments with movement and perceptual illusion brought him into a new configuration of artists in postwar France, among them Pol Bury and Victor Vasarely, intent on bringing kinetic elements to bear in a universal artistic language.

From my very first experiments, it has always been my intention to create a work of art existing beyond the visible, getting away from the image, which could only be grasped in stages, with the awareness that what one had there was but the appearance of a partial and dynamic revelation, and not the finalized perpetuation of an existing thing. My aim is to show the visible as possibility in a state of perpetual becoming.   *[1967]*

MORDECAI ARDON

(1896–)

Born in Poland, Ardon studied at the Bauhaus and emigrated to Palestine in 1933. He was one of Israel's most enthusiastic artists, throwing his energies into teaching, and becoming director of the Bezalel Academy, Israel's major art school, in 1940. His earlier landscapes in an Expressionist mode gave way to hectic, fantastic imagery after 1950.

Pictures are exhibited, dimensions are listed, signature and year of origin are noted; and now words stride forth . . . introduction, biography, criticism . . . leading the way out into the world, in the van of the canvases.

As it happens, however, the gates are barred and bolted as once upon a time, was the Quinta del Sordo.* . . . Not a whisper penetrates from the outside. . . . Deaf to mere words, Goya goads his pilgrims, clochards, beggars across dark chasms. . . . A goat? . . . ah, let it be a goat, then, if goat it be! What leaps to the eye is a demoniac black that pours in deepest

---

* Goya's house, known as "The House of the Deaf Man."

despair over the palette, midst torrents of gray and white and ochre. . . .

The gates are barred and bolted, but inside an old man whips forth a witches' sabbath from out the depths of his soul, as he cackles grimly. . . . Is it an indictment? Ah, no, bitter scorn that is the message!

These are scenarios of silent suffering . . . of yearnings and rebellions . . . of visions and dreams of color . . . color . . . color that screams from the palette in grief and desperation.

Words? What use are words?
Still, custom must have its due!
A bow to the Jodengracht!†
A bow to the Quinta del Sordo! *[1973]*

† Rembrandt's quarter of Amsterdam.

AVIGDOR ARIKHA

(1929–)

Arikha grew up on a kibbutz, and was trained in both Israel and Paris, where he spends most of his time now. He has worked in many media, from book illustration to stained glass. For a time he was an abstract painter, but around 1965 he began to concentrate on drawing from the figure. Since then his paintings and drawings have been interpretations of objects, interiors, and figures.

All that's visible around us is in itself inexpressible, whereas what's expressible is within us, in itself invisible. On the other hand, whereas the need to express seems to remain constant from generation to generation, the possibilities of expression seem to shrink. Entropy seems to govern the evolution of art the same way it governs everything else: we go from more to less. Painting from life again with such an awareness excludes therefore the concept of "realism" (which emerged as an antithesis to "idealism" governing both neoclassicism and romanticism during the nineteenth century).

These paintings are an attempt, a very cautious one, to try to paint again through the visible by the visible, through the equation of what's seizable with what's expressible. Hence the restriction to one thing at a time, not yielding to the temptation to paint more than the "less" to which we seem to be restricted. *[1971]*

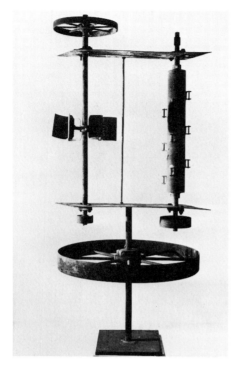

YEHIEL SHEMI   *New-York I* (second wall).
1975. Corten steel. 10 x 12'.

YEHIEL SHEMI

(1922–)

Born in Haifa, Shemi early settled on a kibbutz, where he developed his sculpture in a modern idiom, combining quasi-organic with abstract forms often composed of welded iron. In recent years, Shemi has made large abstract works combining both wood and steel elements.

Cézanne and the early Constructivists dictated new values loaded with new ways of expression and sensitivities which still have great influence on us and a meaning to modern art.

With no absolute scale of values against which art can be measured, the artist of today who forms his personal rules for his work is confronted again and again with the need to measure his work against values of the past.

Sculpture has freed itself from the need to fulfill social demands, and from the expectation of standing as a symbol. Thus, sculpture has contributed immensely to new explorations of materials, forms, and concepts, as well as to the understanding of today's art. It is the process, no less than the final statement, that characterizes the art of today. The more readable the process, the better it is. I start to work on a sculpture from the "beginning," from the element which should be loaded enough with ideas and possibilities. The meaning will arrive and reveal itself, and will bring the entire process to its final fulfillment and statement. It is the deep need for spiritual fulfillment which makes the role of art today vital.   *[1984]*

YEHESKIEL STREICHMAN

(1906–)

Born in Kovno, Lithuania, Streichman settled in Palestine in 1924, where he became a leading member of the avant-garde group New Horizon in Tel Aviv. This group was largely responsible for keeping an international viewpoint alive in the burgeoning state of Israel.

I do not think that I am influenced by any particular painting, but I am bound to a tradition. My painting stems from a long European lineage— Tiepolo, Fragonard, the *Nymphéas* of Monet. My generation of abstract painters has been generally nourished in Impressionism. My abstraction is a natural outcome of all these and of others. There is no returning: easel painting, as it is now, may disappear in the near future, but there is no way back to literary painting.

I consider myself an Israeli painter. The physical fact of Israel is the very source of my inspiration. I witnessed the revival of the Jewish State. My painting is clear, colorful, and joyous (not to be misconstrued to mean that the painter is happy). I reject the somber Jewish painting with its literary, religious, and philosophical symbols. I consider that the use of Jewish symbols is merely a way of exploiting sentiment. By this, I definitely affirm my Judaism. As a matter of fact, I am a Zionist painter. Israeli painting should be free, vibrant, rhythmic, and alive. I use light colors—pinks, yellows. I feel that I am an integral part in the rebuilding of Israel—not unlike a construction worker.   *[1964]*

YOSSEF ZARITSKY

(1891–)

Zaritsky was born in Kiev, and in 1923 emigrated to Israel, where his watercolor paintings quickly gained him a leading reputation. After founding the New Horizons group in 1948, Zaritsky gained an international renown on the strength of his large, lyrical abstractions. He is the foremost Israeli painter and has inspired many subsequent young artists.

To be a painter is more simple than you may think. To paint means to use oil paint, watercolors, brushes, pencils, papers, canvas, and such other things that enable the painter to make a world. Yet, it would not be true to say that the painter finds his painting in nature. What he sees before him is only the source or the rectangle of the paper or canvas. It is not through the observing eye that he is related to nature, but through the atmosphere. And the atmosphere is composed of one plane, which is the sky; another which is earth, and other planes between them. Painting is created only by someone born to be a painter. And if he was born to be one, what is he confronted by? He is confronted by the material of which the world is built.

Nobody is painting from nature. Whoever says he does is lying. Painting is painting and you cannot copy nature. Yet without nature there is no painting. Even abstract painting cannot exist without it.

Art is the one and only god we have and we cannot worship him partially.

The painter, in my opinion, serves only himself. And if what he is doing is true, then we have to see the beauty of the painting according to the systematical laying on of paints on canvas.   *[1984]*

ITALY

VALERIO ADAMI

(1935–)

Adami's use of flat rich color and simplified linear shapes led critics to lump him indiscriminately with the international Pop Art movement of the 1960s. His visual wit, however, and his tendency to allegory set him apart.

"It takes more than a key to open a door," said Wittgenstein, and this is as true for the creative process as for that accomplished by the spectator.

I would like my pictures to be seen in the same way as, according to McLuhan, a televised image is composed: as a result of three million stimulations per second. I think the spectator should relive, in his own way, the formative process which the image has followed. He should not find himself faced with a closed, immobile object. He should find himself implicated in something which is still in process of happening. The picture is a complex proposition in which anterior visual experiences form unpredictable combinations, the imagination creating incessantly new associations—one image expands into another and its original form is in continual transformation.

This is how I proceed when I am drawing. I place myself before a "fact"—an "interior with figures" for instance, and I think these as they are, that is to say I do not limit myself to looking at them; I think them as they are. And then, it is as though the image went on a journey, starting from its external appearance, through a new dimension—I become spectator and protagonist—and in my unconscious are then released certain associations, my hand following this private circuit organizes this material, giving a new and complex form to the objectivity from which I started. I try to record coldly. My hand should be a kind of seismograph giving body to the traces left by the circuit of the imagination. In looking at a thing one discovers there a whole internal stock-in-trade, and from these relations, at first unknown, spring alterations in the structures of forms. The work of art, therefore, expresses itself in a constant dialectical play which, through the painting, reaches the mind of whoever is looking at it, then, rebounding on to the picture, makes of it a veritable extension of the spectator.   *[1968]*

Drawing is a literary occupation. Etc. . . .

I would like it if they could use the words "prose" and "poetry" also in painting, and could define my work as painting in prose. The narrative élan is essential. But form modifies my convictions and my doubts, just as a curved or broken line inflects the discourse. Matter is vague and hypocritical. It is in exactitude that one best finds freedom.

All signs are in themselves definitions—to draw a fold, painting the anatomy of a body, an escape plan, a touch, etc. . . . other significations follow and precede the execution. . . .

We follow the line of a contour from its nervous system to the exaltation of the author. Thus geometry is a symbolic form. Truth and illusion are in accord.

The contour varies and the idea varies. When the form becomes clear it becomes an idea.

To become a metaphor is the intelligence of painting; form transforms itself like a phoenix.

The image reveals itself between the present and the past, between appearance and memory—there where the filigree is found.

Before a painting one must see something other than what one knows already. Associations and significances mingle together beyond the palette.

Everything is movement; in each painting is found the beginning of the next, and the finishing is a beginning, not an end.

The scene unfolds on the horizons limited by the frontiers of the painting and it is in this precise place that a strand of lines weaves itself in order to capture thoughts. The pencil explores far and wide, from top to bottom of the memory: that is how the hand writes involuntary confessions.   *[1984]*

ALBERTO BURRI

(1915–)

Burri, who had been a physician before the war, began painting while a prisoner of war in Texas in 1944. He returned to Italy after the war, and in 1948 had his first one-man exhibition. The works shown startled his contemporaries: paintings made of soaked rags and charred wood, and often colored in crimsons and blacks that carried undeniable associations with the carnage of war. His antitraditional way of working established him as one of the important artists in postwar Europe, and paved the way for later manifestations in Italy such as Arte Povera.

Words are no help to me when I try to speak about my painting.

It is an irreducible presence that refuses to be converted into any other form of expression.

It is a presence both imminent and active.

This is what it stands for: to exist so as to signify and to exist so as to paint.

My painting is a reality which is part of myself, a reality that I cannot reveal in words.

It would be easier for me to say what does *not* need to be painted, what does not pertain to painting, what I exclude from my work sometimes with deliberate violence, sometimes with satisfaction.

Were I master of an exact and less threadbare terminology, were I a marvelously alert and enlightened critic, I still could not verbally establish a close connection with my painting; my words would be marginal notes upon the truth within the canvas. For years pictures have led me, and my work is just a way of stimulating the drive.

I can only say this: painting for me is a freedom attained, constantly consolidated, vigilantly guarded so as to draw from it the power to paint more.   *[1955]*

ETTORE COLLA   *Solar workshop*. 1964.
Iron. 84″ high.

ETTORE COLLA

(1899–1968)

Colla turned to sculpture in 1947 and quickly became a leader in postwar Italian vanguard circles. His iron sculptures, assembled from found parts from both urban and rural contexts, are usually endowed with symbolic overtones.

Of this only have I always taken care, that my work should not escape from a rigorous discipline or from my direct control. Nothing, in all that I have produced, is left to chance and so resolved automatically; rather, it is governed by very precise canons in matters both technical and conceptual. I do not believe in an absolute automatism and I am sure it does not exist, just as, certainly, artists lacking the will to conceive their work, do not exist. The work of man and particularly of artistic man is solidly blocked by a creative will which, otherwise, could not be accepted.

Therefore, in those works in which the gestures of a mental eloquence meet, you must identify the will and also the possibility of conception in it.

It is illogical to suspect, after so many affirmations laboriously obtained, that a work could be born casually. At the most, some facts may play a part there, some chances, some coincidences, however, and they are always relative to the will and the ability of the artist. *[c. 1959]*

PIERO DORAZIO

(1927–)

A leader of the generation that came of age after the Second World War, Dorazio commenced with abstract reliefs and later turned to nonobjective paintings related to Bauhaus principles of color juxtaposition and shallow space. His writings in the early 1950s helped his generation to restore a knowledge of the modern tradition that had become obscured during the Fascist years.

Nonobjective painting and a new order were born when artists were more moved by facts and needs of the human spirit than by a sunset. This truth produced the conception and styles of Kandinsky and Boccioni, for example. Space is a continuous structure of energetic elements which can appear in different combinations, relationships, scale, and most important, color or light values. I would like not to reproduce but to reinvent the structure of light in a way pertinent to painting rather than to optics—a structure beyond the physical values of light, closer to the spiritual, closer to the instinct, to the unexplored world of the modern soul.

It is then no longer a question of fixing a moment of our fantastic life but to give a new dimension to fantasy. Our images cannot be symbols of the exterior world re-created by our fantasy and ordered in a preestablished space, they must be the vision of an existing, unseen reality. Unlike the nonobjective masters, from Kandinsky to Miró and Dubuffet, we cannot express an attitude of contemplation in front of something real or unreal. They express the condition of European civilization in the first half of the century, where man dominates and exploits any natural condition, leaving for himself any possibility of evasion he pleases. Their art means that everything is possible, that men can do everything with their technical ability as well as with their imagination. The Futurists, Klee, and Mondrian, each for different reasons, seem to me of more living actuality. But we have now a recent and already established tradition which proves once more that although the development of style and technique is important, it still is an elementary problem, a *conditio sine qua non* preceding the proper creative activity. Wols has exploded a grenade in the great secrecy. Pollock erased and painted the "nothing" to show us how it looks, how it is made, real, and complex. The result of such tradition is a great silence, the luminous silence of large expanses of color as in Newman and Rothko, or the classic serenity of masterful, decisive stokes as in Hartung, de Kooning, Motherwell, and Kline.   *[1961]*

LUCIO FONTANA

(1899–1968)

Painter, sculptor, ceramicist, light artist, and all-around innovator, Fontana was the earliest and most notable nonfigurative sculptor in Italy during the 1930s. During the war he returned to Argentina (where he had been born to Italian parents) and activated an avant-garde with his White Manifesto *in 1946. When he returned to Italy in 1947, he reiterated its principles in a group of manifestoes he called "Spazialismo": these proposed to incorporate radical scientific discoveries of the twentieth century into the general aesthetic.*

It is necessary to overturn and transform painting, sculpture, and poetry. A form of art is now demanded which is based on the necessity of this new vision. The baroque has guided us in this direction, in all its as yet unsurpassed grandeur, where the plastic form is inseparable from the notion of time, the images appear to abandon the plane and continue into space the movements they suggest. This conception arose from man's new idea of the existence of things: the physics of that period reveal for the first time the nature of dynamics. It is established that movement is an essential condition of matter as a beginning of the conception of the universe. At this point of evolution the requirements of movement were so powerful that the plastic arts were unable to respond; whilst music took on this evolution the plastic arts evolved into a neoclassicism, that dangerous bog in the history of art. Nevertheless, the movement was irresistible and in time the Impressionists sacrificed the design of the composition to color-light. Futurism eliminates some of the elements, others lose their importance and are subordinated to feeling. Futurism adopts movements as its principle and sole aim. The development of a battle into space, the basic forms of continuity into space initiate the only and really great evolution of contemporary art (plastic dynamism). The spatialists go beyond this idea; neither painting nor sculpture, but "forms, color, sound, through space." Whether fully conscious or otherwise in this research, the artists could not have reached their aim had they not had available new technical means and new substances. This justifies the evolution of the means in art. The triumph of the photogram for instance is a definite sign of a more dynamic attitude. Glad of this transformation in the nature of man, we abandon the habit of forms in known art and we face the development of an art based on the unity of time and space. Existence, nature, matter are one perfect unity and they develop in time and space. Movement, the property of evolution and of development, is the basic condition of matter; this in fact now exists in movement and in other forms: its development is eternal: the new art integrated through the hand-in-hand development of the phenomena of color and sound. The subconscious, where all the images and perception of meaning reside, adopts the essence and form of these images. The subconscious molds the individual; it completes and transforms him, giving him the guidance which it receives from the world and which he from time to time adopts. Society tends to avoid the separation between the two forces in order to unite them in one single major form, modern science works on the gradual integration between its elements. From this new state of consciousness there arises an integral art where the being takes charge and shows itself in its totality.

[1946]

MEXICO

GUNTHER GERZSO

(1915–)

Although Gerzso was born in Mexico, he spent his early youth in Europe, returning to Mexico only in 1942. His early paintings were marked by his encounter with Surrealists such as Wolfgang Paalen and Leonora Carrington who had taken refuge in Mexico during the war. During the early 1950s Gerzso began a series of abstract paintings which incorporated allusions to pre-Columbian art. Later, he worked more austerely with highly geometric conformations and cold but highly luminous colors. He is Mexico's foremost abstract painter.

In painting, as in all the arts, one has to give one's self, and by doing so one shares the human condition with others, and that is the important thing. I am very much taken by landscapes. Whether my paintings evoke Mexican or Greek landscapes, or, as in the case of my recent acrylics, the urban landscape, the emotion behind them remains basically unchanged. They are my expression of a person living today.

I have no theories on how to go about painting a picture and I am frequently surprised at analyses of my paintings. Many people say I am an abstract painter. Actually, I think my paintings are very realistic. They are real because they express very accurately what I am all about, and in doing so they are to some degree about everybody else.

Creation enables the artist to keep his unconscious world under control,

GUNTHER GERZSO   *Morada Antigua.* 1964. Oil on canvas. 23⅝ x 28¾".

to cope with his inner problems. Thus the artist must find an image of his very own with which to express his emotion. The emotional content of my paintings is always the same, and each painting is only a variation of that emotion.

Of course I am influenced, like all artists. My influences are mainly from Cubism, Surrealism, and pre-Columbian art. I think I use the forms of this continent from its earliest times to the present, but I express them with Western European means, as most Latin American artists do.

Am I a Latin American artist? What is my identity? These questions greatly perturb me at times and produce a kind of crisis in my thinking about my painting and myself. But, from one point of view at least, I consider that the accumulated influences, both of the European continent and this, have enriched my capacity as an artist and, therefore, to find a label for what I am is really immaterial.   *[1983]*

MATHIAS GOERITZ

(1915–)

In 1949 the German-born Goeritz arrived in Mexico. He immediately stirred con-
troversy by attacking both the static situation of the arts there, and the heroes of the
mural movement of the prewar years. Goeritz's combination of architectural, sculp-
tural, and painterly effects in single monumental works won him international fame
in later years, and he is considered one of Mexico's most influential vanguard artists.
His description below refers to one of the very first environmental sculptures in the
Western hemisphere.

In the El Eco experiment, integration was not planned. There was no
intention of putting paintings or sculptures on the building as is done with
movie posters or with carpets hanging from palace balconies, but the architectural space had to be understood as a big sculptural element without
falling into Gaudi's romanticism or empty German and Italian neoclassicism.
Sculpture, like my *Serpent* of the patio, had to become an almost functional,
architectural construction (with openings for the ballet) without losing its
value of sculpture and giving a sense of movement to the flat walls.

The building has almost no ninety-degree junctions. Some of the walls
are thin on one side and wider on the opposite side.

There is a search for that strange and almost imperceptible asymmetry
which one can observe in any face, any tree, any living being. There are no
gracious curves, no sharp vertexes. The construction was done at the site
itself, without precise plans. The architect, mason, and sculptor were one
and the same person.   *[1953]*

RUFINO TAMAYO

(1899–)

Tamayo rejected the grand ambitions of the previous generation of muralists but he
himself, a Zapotec Indian, drew upon Mexican traditions to develop an idiom un-
mistakably related to folk art.

Outside of Orozco, who never traveled, most of the artists involved on the
mural projects had studied or worked in Paris for years. When they returned,
because of the revolution, they and those of us at home were all trying to

liberate ourselves politically and economically. In that atmosphere the artists turned strongly nationalist. At that moment it was *necessary* for us to be very nationalist. That meant we could go back to our roots and absorb from them whatever we could. We had to become sure of ourselves. Before the revolution the Mexican government didn't really believe in Mexico's artists. They thought that because we had no experience we knew nothing, and therefore anything of quality could come only from foreigners.

The trouble was that the painters portrayed only a surface nationalism. They painted the facts of Mexico's history and culture, all leading to the facts of the revolution. But revolution is not a Mexican phenomenon. It happens all over the world. I'm not opposed in theory to what they did. It was natural for them. But I myself felt something beyond that. I was a rebel, not against the revolution, but against the Mexican mural movement which was conceived to celebrate it. It is impossible, I feel, in this time when communications are so open, to set out deliberately to make an art which is Mexican, or American, or Chinese, or Russian. I think in terms of universality. Art is a way of expression that has to be understood by everybody, everywhere. It grows out of the earth, the texture of our lives and our experiences. Maybe it was because the other painters were older than I that they were so concerned with the facts of the revolution. I wanted only to go back to our roots, our wonderful plastic tradition. The others were not concerned about this.   *[c. 1972]*

THE NETHERLANDS

AD DEKKERS

(1938–1974)

After graduating from the Academy of Art in Rotterdam in 1958, Dekkers developed a highly refined, geometric style in which he juxtaposed relief planes on polyester grounds, exploiting light reflection and intricate shadow patterns.

Mondrian and later van Doesburg greatly influenced the decisions I have taken with respect to my work. Not so much due to the primary use of color or the Utopian horizontal-vertical ideal of harmony, but rather due to their mentality and philosophy, which was directed toward ultimate purity in the use of visual means. This purity is still one of the most important points of departure in my work. Before Mondrian became important to me I had already, hesitantly, made a number of reliefs. Looking back I can say that I translated the principles of de Stijl into terms of space, because I could not reconcile myself to the fact that Mondrian's paintings had a spatial affect which is not realistically spatial.   *[n.d.]*

JAN DIBBETS   *Forest Piece.* 1969. White paint on trees.

JAN DIBBETS

(1941–   )

In the late 1960s Dibbets gave up painting in order to find a nontraditional means to express his relationship to nature. His works in outdoor situations were among the pioneer offerings of a tendency that was called either "Earth Art" or "Land Art." Certain of his ecological expressions are rendered in photomontages with drawing added, but others are ephemeral works on specific sites.

I thought that the lawn was really the most beautiful sculpture I could imagine. And so I started to use nature as visual material. My first projects were the *Grass Rhomboids*, rectangular sections of grass which I cut out and piled on top of each other. This was still related to the superposed painting: instead of paintings, I now piled up grass-sods. I realized that if you want to use nature, you have to derive the appropriate structure from nature too. This resulted in the *Grass-Roll*, actually the first proper grass sculpture.

Nature consists of a large number of ecological systems. For example: a tree needs a certain amount of space throughout its growth, and crowds out less healthy specimens of trees and plants. Natural selection takes place, which is why trees make a particular pattern in a wood. If the trunks of one kind of tree are painted white, this natural pattern becomes visible. The wood then becomes a big sculpture, and nature a work of art.   *[1969]*

LUCEBERT

(1924–   )

Draftsman, poet, storyteller, and painter, Lucebert was affiliated with the generation of young artists, including Karel Appel and Corneille, who, after the Second World War, developed Expressionist figurative or semi-figurative idioms. He participated in the COBRA exhibitions in Amsterdam, but was never a member of any group.

I think art *can* speak for itself. I enjoy reading well-written biographies of artists, because a lot of weird and amusing characters have climbed Parnassus, but it's sheer nonsense to think that biographies can give you more insight into the work of the artists concerned. At most the description of good times and bad merely confirms what the artworks themselves had already told you long ago and much more clearly. It's extraordinary, for instance, that some abstract artists in the first half of this century were motivated by Marxism, and others by theosophy or some related religious-mystical philosophy. But the artworks themselves do not in any way reveal the irreconcilable oppositions that exist between these two ideologies. There is a reason for everything, and artworks don't appear out of the blue. But the teleological idea that has been impressed on our minds makes us insist on seeing a function and purpose behind every explanation. Apparently a lot of people cannot cope with the thought that there are things and creatures that have no specific function at all, whose presence can elicit feelings of enjoyment and admiration precisely because of their irrelevance. Most modern artists want to be free from all restrictions as far as subject and style are concerned. This freedom was laboriously won by their predecessors at the expense perhaps of direct intelligibility, but it has yielded an unprecedented wealth of pluriformity and self-expression.   *[1974]*

JAN SCHOONHOVEN

(1914–)

Schoonhoven was among those Dutch artists who retrieved the nonobjective, geometric tradition after the Second World War, experimenting in both sculpture and painting. His pristine papier-mâché relief paintings and his white drawings with their delicately scored lines won him an international reputation.

"Weltanschauung" is a vague term; I don't know much about it. Things are really quite simple. Carpenters used to make things as straight as possible. On paper I aim at harmony. I want certain things in a drawing to cancel others out. Where stripes meet, a diagonal enters from the other side, as a counterweight. Things may look perfectly chaotic, but there's always a balance. I'm always busy making things cancel each other out. That's the way I like to talk too, have one statement cancel the previous one.

My drawings have been described as anti-Fascist, because the stripes are more or less similar, without hierarchy. But you might equally well say that they are lined up and that I lined them up. Fascism is the reaction. There's none of that in Mondrian's work. The revolutionary aspect comes from society. Art is not in itself social. It depends on the period. Modern art is connected with the working-class revolution. There is a connection, but not a direct one. Modern art can make a contribution. There is also an aspect of general pleasure. Capitalists like modern art too. This indicates a broken existence. Music is more for the privileged class than for the socially deprived. It seems more normal to like modern music and at the same time to adopt a social-critical attitude. The connection is there. Man should be regarded as a total being. Art *can* have a social effect. There wouldn't be any society without art, it's part of human nature. It doesn't have a direct effect on the revolutionary struggle, though. However, everything the human mind does provide fertile soil for Marxism.   *[1975]*

CAREL VISSER

(1928–)

Freely working with varied materials, including rope and leather, Visser has produced an oeuvre of highly original sculpture ranging from almost classical neoplastic forms to Surrealist fantasies. He is an accomplished welder and ironworker, as well as an inspired draftsman.

At a given moment in life, you can choose to build on your accomplishments and extend the positions you hold. But you can also choose for adventure. You choose either for what exists and should survive, or for what doesn't exist but may come, whatever it is. In my work I go against what exists and choose for what doesn't exist yet. I can't imagine getting up in the morning full of enthusiasm to make something that I already made the day before. I just couldn't do that to myself. That's why it's good to question the things you're sure about and to relativize your own work.   *[1980]*

POLAND

TADEUSZ KANTOR

(1915–)

Kantor studied at the Kracówo Academy of Art and began as a Surrealist painter. In the 1950s, he moved toward an expressive abstraction, and was soon making objects that were wrapped and tied, suggesting sinister situations with oblique references to the war years. At the same time he was active as a theater director, and extended his visual theories to set and costume design. He continues to work in his Cricot Theater in Kracówo, and to make poems, stories, and drawings.

In artistic development there are frequent moments when the vital creative act degenerates into a pursuit of a convention, when a work of art no longer involves any risk, adventure, revolt, or uncertainty and becomes respectable and well established in its seriousness, dignity, and prestige.

When this happens, the wisest thing to do is to leave the recognized stage and to shift to disinterested activities, on the verge of the ridiculous and shameful, deserving scorn and doomed to neglect. Instinctively, I gave all my attention, and very soon all my passion, to objects of the "lower rank" that normally pass unnoticed, are skipped over, forgotten, and then simply dumped off. I started to collect my own notes, sketches, scraps of paper, hasty records of the "urgent" matters, those early discoveries when nothing is known for certain yet, when the "arrangements" are still under way and it doesn't even occur to make things that are "ready" for consumption, varnished, openly demonstrating the perfection of the work and its maker. . . .

The imagination was suddenly no longer a store of materials for constructing and executing pictures, but a space into which objects from my own past were falling, in the shape of wrecks or shams, but also not my own, strange, trite, schematic, accidental, mixed with important ones, valuable and negligible, facts, persons, letters, prescriptions, addresses, traces, dates, appointments. It was an inventory without any timing, hierarchy, or location. Personally, I was in the midst of all this, without any definite role.

Such an adjustment of my own ambition to "create" near the zero point automatically brought about an essential shift in my attitude toward the past, with its relics and claims, as well as toward the object. For the aim was not to repeat it, but to recapture!   *[1963]*

PORTUGAL

MARIA ELENA VIEIRA DA SILVA

(1908–   )

Vieira da Silva established her reputation on an international scale only after the Second World War, when her compositions, with their deeply veering perspective lines, were exhibited in Paris and elsewhere.

We are talked to about reality. Everything amazes me, and I paint my amazement which is at the same time wonder, terror, laughter. I would exclude none of my amazement. My desire is to make pictures with many different things, with every contradiction, with the unexpected. I would like to become so agile, so sure of my movements, and of my voice, that nothing could escape me, neither the buoyancy of the birds, the weight of the stones, nor the glow of metal. I would like to observe attentively the strings that pull people forward or hold them back. One should go everywhere, dance, play music, sing, fly, plunge into the depths of the sea, watch lovers, enter factories and hospitals, know by heart many poems, the *code civil,* and the history of nations. But, alas, painting is long, and the days are short.

When I am before my painting and palette, there is a constant effort; a little more white, a little more green, it is too cold, too warm, lines that ascend, that descend, that meet, that part. This means so much in painting and so little in words.

I believe that it is by adding one small brushstroke after the other, toiling like the bee, that a picture is made. A painting must have its heart, its nervous system, its bones and its circulation. In its movements it should be like a person and have the tempo of a person's movements. Looking at it one should feel opposite a being that will keep one company, that will tell one tales, that will give one assurance. For a painting is not excape; it should be a friend who speaks to you, who discovers the hidden treasures within you and around you.   *[1955]*

SPAIN

RAFAEL CANOGAR

(1934–)

Canogar was an original member of the El Paso group, founded in 1957 by young Spanish artists chafing under Franco's rule and eager to reflect postwar European tendencies in their paintings. He gradually modified his extremely tormented abstract style, and in the mid-1960s human figures and political motifs began to emerge openly in his work.

After passing through the first step—logical in the circumstances in which we painters found ourselves in Madrid—I feel the need to draw nearer to reality with a more calm spirit. I'm seeking a formal-informal synthesis, an equilibrium between form and material. I work with a primary informal material, tortured and organic—whose antecedents are possibly in the baroque—which construes and organizes itself into a latent geometry. . . . Expansion-contention, two elemental forces that I'm interested in investigating. *[1962]*

EDUARDO CHILLIDA

(1924–)

Trained as an architect, Chillida turned to sculpture during the late 1940s, retrieving the tradition of the wrought-iron folk sculptors who had influenced both Gargallo and González in the pre–World War II period. His work in the 1950s grew increasingly monumental, and was characterized by its unusual curving forms in obdurate materials, giving it a lyrical character that distinguished it from other nonobjective sculptures of the period.

A piece of iron is an idea in itself, a powerful and unyielding object. I must gain complete mastery over it, and force it to take on the tension which I feel within myself, evolving a theme from dynamism. Sometimes the iron refuses to give in. But when I eventually reach my goal I always know; the individual fragments crystallize with a sudden shock and form a whole. Nothing can now separate the space from the form which encircles it.

Sculpture is a function of space. I am not concerned with the space which lies outside the form, which surrounds the volume and in which the shapes

EDUARDO CHILLIDA   *Iru Burni* (also titled *Space Modulation IV*). 1966. Iron.
22⅝ x 21¼ x 37⅜".

dwell, but with the space actually created by the shapes, which dwells in them and is all the more effective when it works in secret. I might perhaps compare it to the life-giving breath which causes the form to swell up and contract and makes visible that inner psychic space which is hidden from the outside world. To me this space is not something abstract, but forms a reality as concrete as the reality of the volumes which enclose it. It must be as tangible as the form in which it is revealed, for it has a character of its own. It sets in motion the matter which encloses it; it determines its proportions and scans and regulates its rhythms. It must find a corresponding echo in us and it must possess a kind of spiritual dimension. In the same way, any room I live in, for however brief a period, must harmonize with an ideal pattern which corresponds to my actions and which also governs them. Some rooms are suffocating—one is stifled by them, one feels physically unwell; this type of room is uninhabitable. The same is true of sculpture. I am always searching for a space which conforms with the dynamic image of which I spoke earlier. Volumes exist only in relation to this unseen element; the essence of a sculpture must make its presence felt and transpose its inner harmony to the world of externals.

Form is the product of unceasing and ever-renewed efforts. A single wave means nothing; but one wave follows another and the arrival of each one presupposes the arrival of the next—and of all those to come. Without the steady force of water the single wave would collapse and dissolve. Together they form a single huge entity. No one would think of singling out a note from a symphony. Each note owes its existence to the whole movement of the music; it swells, the individual notes are superimposed one on the other, and then it finally dies away. Sculpture and music exist in the same harmonious and ever developing space. The volume of musical sound fills the silence with tension; similarly there could be no volume in sculpture without the emptiness of space. In the void the form can continue to vibrate beyond its own limits.

The artist's attitude to his work is like a spiral. That's why I have so often harked back to a spiral in my sculptures. A spiral is the geometric representation of a movement which only seems to swerve away from its target so that it can encircle in its detours and curves all conceivable possibilities inherent in a spatial figure. In this figure there is an alternation between emptiness and mass, which are bound to a common axis. It reminds me of the way in which a bird of prey circles its hunting ground. My spiral lies at the heart of the volume, in the vacuum in which the soul of the work crystallizes, the invisible center of its evolution.   *[c. 1965]*

ANTONIO SAURA

(1930–   )

Saura's first influence derived from a brief stay in Paris in 1953, where he encountered the Surrealist group around André Breton. Returning to Spain in 1955, he developed an expressionist abstract style that eventually included figurative elements. He was an important founder of the El Paso group in 1957. The manifesto of the group stated that the art produced by these young artists would not be valid unless it contained "an inquietude coinciding with the signs of the epoch" and unless the artist "assumes his social and spiritual responsibility." The manifesto was a clear declaration against Franco, and Saura's subsequent painting, often evoking death and crucifixion, was, and is, anti-Fascist in character.

What interests me is matter, convulsed under the will to action; the biological dynamic that from a paroxysmic work surges from ecstasy; the "maelstrom"; the centrifugal or centripetal force of a passionate creation in which each painting is a living organism that evolves according to its own determinism; the inclusion of the first expression of the furious gesture in a new plastic structure. . . .

Beyond useless discussions of figurative or abstract art, nonfigurative or

concrete art, beyond all purist preconceptions, fantastic, aesthetic or theoretical, is the imperious necessity to shout, to express oneself as one is,
making ours all the energetic possibilities of the universe.   *[1958]*

A N T O N I   T À P I E S

(1923–   )

*Born in Barcelona, Tàpies was deeply affected by the tragedy of the Spanish Civil
War. When he took up painting after studying law in the late 1940s, he first used a
Surrealist vocabulary to express his view of public events. Later, he experimented
with informal procedures and unusual materials, such as heavy layers of paint
adulterated with sand, plaster, and all sorts of debris. He felt that in this way he
could infuse his material with his vision of the human events that engender tragedy.*

Then came "the time of solitude." In my little bedroom-studio my own
forty days in the wilderness began—a wilderness of which I still do not
know if it will ever come to an end. . . . One day I tried to attain this
silence directly with greater resignation, giving myself up to the fatality that
governs all profound struggle. . . . Suddenly, as if I had passed through the
looking glass, a whole new perspective opened up before me as if to tell the
innermost secrets of things. A whole new geography lit my way from one
surprise to the next. [Quoting the Tao te Ching he continues:] "Emerging
into dust lies beneath our profound identity, by which I mean the inner
profundity between man and nature."   *[1969]*

Outworn forms cannot contribute contemporary ideas. If the forms are
incapable of wounding the society that receives them, of irritating it, of
slanting it toward meditation . . . if they are not a revulsion, then they are
not a genuine work of art. . . . The viewer has to feel obliged to make an
examination of conscience and to readjust his former conceptions. The artist
has to make him understand that his world was too narrow, has to open up
new perspectives to him. To do this is a task for the humanist.   *[c. 1970]*

The artist will always be part of life and change. His task, in my view, is
not purely receptive. He is not, as some say, a simple reflection of his time.
I am more inclined to believe that the role of the artist can be an active one
and that with others he has it in his hands to modify our concept of reality.
. . . He is neither a humble servant nor absolute monarch, he is an intermediary, a vehicle for nature. It is not to be wondered at, in an age and a
country like ours in which the human drama has become so acute and so
violently to the fore, that at times all good measure seems to have been lost.

It is not strange therefore that I always like to add, he is a vehicle certainly, but one that conveys the variable concept man forms of his own nature.

[1974]

SWEDEN

OLLE BAERTLING

(1911–1981)

Born in Sweden, Baertling drew his artistic inspiration from Mondrian and Léger, developing a severe geometric style in both painting and sculpture.

Art for me has always been abstract motion.

Abstract motion excels over physical or naturalistic motion in its speed and feeling of exhaltation.

Everything is motion, everything moves. There is no fixed point in the universe. But whereas such motion is physical, abstract motion is in tune with human thought.

Thoughts can cross centuries, millennia, from the ancient Egyptians to the present in a flash.

Such motion arises and is perceived with abstract means.

Art is research into the unknown, adding a little to the fund built up by earlier generations. This is the task of the artist.

Employing new materials does not amount to a regeneration. What must be renewed is the expression, the language of art. Materials are just the means and should not take up any room in the artistic expression.

The external work simply houses the expression, the artist's work, which should always dwell in the world of the spirit.   *[1974]*

CARL FREDRIK REUTERSWÄRD
(1934–)

*A Swedish-born artist residing in Switzerland, Reuterswärd extends the Dada atti-
tudes of Marcel Duchamp, subjecting various modern institutions, including the art
world, to inventive, searing laughter. His constructions and drawings often deal with
ridiculous aspects of modern life, above all the use of money. He has also been the
foremost experimenter with laser beam and holographic art, using it both in his
installations and in theater sets.*

My works and activities can be seen as a circus performance; at best you
conceive the whole by means of a lot of different appearances.

But in order to understand the man behind, the audience itself must also
perform. It does so through a number of deputy clowns, who in the intervals
play the most cheap and superficial jokes on the spectators.

It may seem true if you say that I represent an uncommitted highbrow
culture. The real fragment of highbrow culture, the poet Arthur Rimbaud,
once wrote about a being who exclaimed: "I am a Roquefort cheese!" I
agree. I feel I represent *an interior* of such a cheese; a mold culture.

Rinds of Cheddar cheese have critically regarded my one-man collective,
my cultivation of myself under the glass cover. They have noted that I sell
myself on the cheese market and they have regarded me as standing in the
centre of the bourgeois cheeseboard. To that extent the Cheddar rinds are
right.

However, I am not just a lump of cottage cheese or a Swiss cheese with
holes in it. Mold can become medicine and it is not only the burgeois who
need penicillin! This is where I can say goodbye to highbrow culture. For
why cannot deliveries of antibiotics, e.g., in the form of an ironic and
affirmative—not scornful—cheerfulness, be an attitude toward a crude and
unsound society? Who can determine *how* one is committed; as grated cheese
or as a cheese-hopper? Au gratin or as whey?

If there is to be taste in dogma—then I have none.

In French the word *elegance* also means purity and simplicity. The child's
toys often have pure, bright colors, just like the adult's playing cards or
billiard balls. In my game with the spectator I consider it important that
the legibility in my works, the clarity, is as distinct as possible.

You should not have to hesitate two seconds as to whether it is the ace or
the two of spades you see. If you are anxious to have a joke rightly understood, you take pains about your enunciation. Clarity has also to do with
time. I want my pictures to be capable of being grasped quickly and with

precision, rather like a jazz tune or fireworks. But there is no reason why you should not take another look, to play it over or to set light to it again.

Retake, repetition, is a basic element of my pictures. The idea is that the viewer himself retakes or breaks the contact with the picture.   *[1978]*

SWITZERLAND

MAX BILL

(1908–   )

Bill studied at the Dessau Bauhaus, where he assimilated the ideas of functionalism prevalent there, and went on to become Switzerland's most distinguished nonobjective artist. His approach to art, based on an almost religious belief in the beauties of mathematics, was widely diffused in South America, Italy, and Germany, where, in 1951, he became the director of the School of Art and Design at Ulm.

I am convinced it is possible to evolve a new form of art in which the artist's work could be founded to quite a substantial degree on a mathematical line of approach to its content. This proposal has, of course, aroused the most vehement opposition. It is objected that art has nothing to do with mathematics; that mathematics, besides being by its very nature as dry as dust and as unemotional, is a branch of speculative thought and as such in direct antithesis to those emotive values inherent in aesthetics; and finally that anything approaching ratiocination is repugnant, indeed positively injurious to art, which is purely a matter of feeling. Yet art plainly calls for both feeling and reasoning. In support of this assertion the familiar example of Johann Sebastian Bach may be credited; for Bach employed mathematical formulas to fashion the raw material known to us as sound into the exquisite harmonies of his sublime fugues. And it is worth mentioning that, although mathematics had by then fallen into disuse for composition in both his own and the other arts, mathematical and theological books stood side by side on the shelves of his library.

It is mankind's ability to reason which makes it possible to coordinate emotional values in such a way that what we call art ensues. Now in every picture the basis of its composition is geometry or in other words the means of determining the mutual relatonship of its component parts either on plane or in space. Thus, just as mathematics provides us with a primary method of cognition, and can therefore enable us to apprehend our physical surroundings, so, too, some of its basic elements will furnish us with laws to appraise the interactions of separate objects, or groups of objects, one to another. . . .

In one of these recently conquered domains the artist is now free to exploit the untapped resources of that vast new field of inspiration I have described with the means our age vouchsafes him and in a spirit proper to its genius. And despite the fact the basis of this Mathematical Approach to Art is in reason, its dynamic content is able to launch us on astral flights which soar into unknown and still uncharted regions of the imagination.   *[1948]*

JEAN TINGUELY

(1925–)

Educated in his native Switzerland, Tinguely settled in Paris in 1953, where he quickly became one of the most noted experimenters with kinetic sculpture. His sculptures, often composed of found parts and detritus from junkyards, are generally set in motion by simple machines. They are programmed to perform such tasks as painting, making sounds, or destroying themselves, and are often infused with an element of wild humor. Tinguely's irony places him in the tradition of Duchamp and the early modernists, whose sallies against machine culture often incorporated images of machines.

MODERN ART: PLAYING—IRON—SUFFERING—COOKING—FILING—EXHIBITING—DRILLING—SCORCHING—POLISHING—BURNING OFF—LAUGHING—SETTING UP—SELLING—SWEARING—PULLING DOWN—WELDING—PACKING—MOUNTING—REMOVING—ETC.

The relationship of art and play: play is art—consequently I play. I play furiously. All machines are art. Even old, abandoned, rusty machines for sifting stones. (Is it okay to "write" for the N.Z.?)* (So: art is the distortion of an unendurable reality. I correct the vision of reality that strikes me in the everyday world. Art is correction, modification of a situation, art is communication, connection— . . . only . . . well? Art is social, self-sufficient, and total (does Rüdlinger† agree?).

Techniques: the materials of the modern work of art: whisky—aluminum—nuts—sausage—salad—petrol—Sugus [soft candy]—complexes—money—screws—pastries—engines.

REVOLUTION IS ART

The most glorious function of art is assassination (if an artist languishes in wealth for years—he will pay for his insolence). Art is techniques (e.g.,

* *National Zeitung*, the Basel newspaper.
† Curator of the Basel art museum.

watercolor). Techniques are so mystical: if I wanted to understand an electric motor I would go to a fortune-teller.

Anyway, is art so modern?

Art is as modern—as modern as, e.g., Giotto's team painting, which was several centuries ahead of the cinema and comics.

Limits of modern art: art is total and limitless, and not always identifiable, thanks partly to the permanent shortcomings of art criticism (which is effective only when it is negative—when it is positive it is usually misleading, unreadable, and boring).

Art is total, because it can be "made" from stone and oil, wood and iron, air and energy, from gouache and canvas and situations—from imagination and obstinacy, from boredom, from intelligence, from paste and wire or opposition or with a camera. And think: a beautiful oil refinery or your Johanniterbrücke [St John's Bridge], which are supposed to be solely functional, are important additions to modern art.

So, art is also: the achievements of engineers and technicians, even if they express themselves unconsciously or purely functionally. Art is everything. (Do you think art ought to be made only by "artists"?) And: art is everywhere—at my grandmother's—in the most incredible kitsch or under a rotten plank.

Art is movement

Because everything moves

Because everything etc.—

Or Laotse: Softness will always overcome hardness—for the tongue, which is soft, lasts—the teeth, which are hard, break.

and definitive is in any case provisional.

and chaos is order

NONETHELESS I AM—IN DESPAIR

After all, I am one individual, imprisoned in myself, hanged and condemned to solitary in my own ego for life. And if I want to make an immediate getaway from this dreadful situation, today for instance: I would love to decorate the windows of [a department] store. I would build a really marvelous machine, something like a scorpion, a proud, black monster—and there would be a conveyor which would bring two or three thousand teapots a day to the machine with mechanical reliability, complete regularity (one every eighty centimeters) and whoops and crash, the teapots would be neatly destroyed, annihilated, for weeks on end (until the shop was bankrupt). And there would be a man in the window as well, an old Chinese, who would sweep up the bits and tip them tidily through a slot in the wall at one side, put there specially for the purpose: How does an artist make contact with the public?

Nonsense is a dimension that irony can be built into. Nonsense is a poetic element à la Nutcracker. Much freedom and the *acte gratuit* are made possible via nonsense—it's like oil really!—for instance, it introduces both the provocative and the Sisyphean side of man into my constructions. Or: it is easier to address the unconscious with nonsense (Is that true?) So nonsense can be useful and consequently make sense.

Art is nonsense and—like everything—not senseless.   *[1967]*

UNITED STATES

J O S E F   A L B E R S

(1888–1976)

From his days at the Bauhaus in 1920–1933, Albers preserved strict attitudes toward painting. When he came to America in the mid-1930s, he dedicated himself to teaching his principles, first at Black Mountain College in North Carolina and later at Yale University. His work became severely restricted to variations on the most natural form he could find, the square, which, by subtle combinations of color, he was able to animate. His notion of color, developed into a lengthy treatise, is briefly described below.

They are juxtaposed for various and changing visual effects. They are to challenge or to echo each other, to support or oppose one another. The contacts, respectively boundaries, between them may vary from soft to hard touches, may mean pull and push besides clashes, but also embracing, intersecting, penetrating.

Despite an even and most opaque application, the colors will appear above or below each other, in front or behind, or side by side on the same level. They correspond in concord as well as in discord, which happens between both, groups and singles.

Such action, reaction, interaction—or interdependence—is sought in order to make obvious how colors influence and change each other: that the same color, for instance—with different grounds or neighbors—looks different. But also, that different colors can be made to look alike.

It is to show that three colors can be read as four, and similarly three colors as two, and also four as two.

Such color deceptions prove that we see colors almost never unrelated to each other and therefore unchanged; that color is changing continually: with changing light, with changing shape and placement, and with quantity which denotes either amount (a real extension) or number (recurrence). And just as influential are changes in perception depending on changes of mood, and consequently of receptiveness.

All this will make aware of an exciting discrepancy between physical fact and psychic effect of color.   *[1962]*

CARL ANDRE
(1935–)

In 1966, in a controversial exhibition at the Jewish Museum in New York called "Primary Structures," Andre exhibited a row of 139 firebricks as an illustration of what he called a mathematical principle. After that, this witty practitioner of minimal, conceptual art installations was hailed as an innovator. His ground-level works never fail to stir controversy. Andre probably has a greater affinity with Duchampian irony than with minimalist sobriety.

There is no symbolic content to my work. It is not like a chemical formula but like a chemical reaction. A good work of art, once it is offered in display and shown to other people, is a social fact.

The art of association is when the image is associated with things other than what the artwork itself is. Art of isolation has its own focus with a minimum association with things not itself. The idea is the exact opposite of multi-media communication. My work is the exact opposite of the art of association. I try to reduce the image-making function of my work to the least degree.

My works are in constant state of change. I'm not interested in reaching an ideal state with my works. As people walk on them, as the steel rusts, as the brick crumbles, as the materials weather, the work becomes its own record of everything that's happened to it.

I think it is futile for an artist to try to create an environment, because you have an environment around you all the time. An astronaut who slips out of his capsule in space has lost his environment, any living organism has an environment. A place is an area within an environment which has been altered in such a way as to make the general environment more conspicuous.

Every thing is an environment, but a place is related particularly to both
the general qualities of the environment and the particular qualities of the
work which has been done.

Place is a pedestal for the rest of the world.   *[1968]*

WILLIAM BAZIOTES

(1912–1963)

*Baziotes, of all the Abstract Expressionist group, was most closely related to Surrealist
sources. His soft, aquatic, horizonless imagery reflected a preoccupation with the
atmosphere of dreams. His participation in discussions with other painters in New
York in the 1940s left a strong imprint on him, and he has described the spirit of the
time in the statement below.*

Inspiration comes to me unexpectedly, never by virtue of deliberate stimu-
lation, never by sitting in a chair: it always happens in front of the easel.

What impressions, events, moods, set off a painting? Man—the tragicomic
in man. Man, the ape and evolution. The fear in man. Man's duality. Pierrot.
The faces of the matadors. And landscape—the sadness of autumn. Winter
as in Brueghel's hunting scene. The feeling of love in spring. The night.
The moon. And animals—the rhinoceros, a dangerous clown. The power
of the fighting bulls of Spain. The age of the dinosaurs and great bird-
lizards flying overhead. And finally, old photographs—people, interiors, and
scenes from the nineteenth century. Old houses of America. History of the
Civil War and the bad men of the Old West. . . .

Contact with other artists has always been of great importance to me.
When the artists I know best used to meet ten or twelve years ago, the talk
was mostly of ideas in painting. There was an unconscious collaboration
between artists. Whether you agreed or disagreed was of no consequence.
It was exciting and you were compelled to paint over your head. You had
to stay on a high level or drown. If your painting was criticized adversely,
you either imitated someone to give it importance, or you simply suffered
and painted harder to make your feelings on canvas convincing.

At the time, Mondrian, Duchamp, and Max Ernst were here. Later Miró
came. It was wonderful to see how they conducted themselves as artists
outside their studios, what their manners and attitudes were toward specific
situations, how they lived, how they believed in and practiced their uniqueness, how they never spoke of ideas but only of the things they loved.

I remember Mondrian at a party, dancing the lindy, on and on for hours and hours. Duchamp, and his kindness and interest towards young American painters. Max Ernst, describing in loving detail the snake dances of the Hopi Indians, Miró, unveiling the mural in his studio, watching for the reaction of the onlookers, walking rapidly and excitedly all over the place, upset and very nervous.

I do not feel alone. There is always unconscious collaboration among artists. The painter who imagines himself a Robinson Crusoe is either a primitive or a fool. The common goal is difficult to describe, but I do know it is not a certain universal subject matter. However, in the best practitioners of abstract painting, I sense the goal when I see the artist has had the courage to live in his time and in his own fashion. And when he has courage, there is *style* in his work. The subject matter in his work can be the tremors of an unstable world, or the joy of a summer day. Both are equally valid. Each artist must follow his own star.

[1954]

ROMARE BEARDEN
(1914—)

A semi-abstract painter well-schooled in the French tradition, Bearden turned to his experience as a black Southerner in the late 1950s and, in a series of montages, introduced narrative elements. Later, he combined fragments of photographs with paintings in a significant series on ritual, alluding to the fusion of African with American sources. Many consider him the foremost black painter in America.

I did the new work out of a response and need to redefine the image of man in the terms of the Negro experience I know best. I felt that the Negro was becoming too much of an abstraction, rather than the reality that art can give a subject. James Baldwin and other intellectuals were defining the Negro sociologically, but not artistically. What I've attempted to do is establish a world through art in which the validity of my Negro experience could live and make its own logic. . . . The medium I used was chosen intentionally because assemblage forges a variety of contrary images into one unified expression.

[1968]

I think a quality of artificiality must be retained in a work of art, since, after all, the reality of art is not to be confused with that of the outer world. Art, it must be remembered, is artifice, or a creative undertaking, the primary function of which is to add to our existing conception of reality. Moreover, such devices of artificiality as distortion of scale and proportion, and abstract coloration, are the very means through which I try to achieve a more personal expression than I sense in the realistic or conventionally focused photograph.

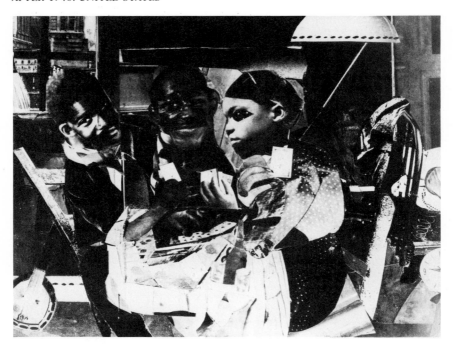

ROMARE BEARDEN   *Evening, 9:10, 461 Lenox Avenue.* 1964.
Collage. 8½ x 11".

The initial public reaction to my work has generally been one of shock, which appears to rise out of a confrontation with subject matter unfamiliar to most persons. In spite of this, it is not my aim to paint about the Negro in America in terms of propaganda. It is precisely my awareness of the distortions required of the polemicist that has caused me to paint the life of my people as I know it—as passionately and dispassionately as Brueghel painted the life of the Flemish people of his day. One can draw many social analogies from the great works of Brueghel—as I have no doubt one can draw from mine—my intention, however, is to reveal through pictorial complexities the richness of a life I know.

I am afraid, despite my intentions, that in some instances commentators have tended to overemphasize what they believe to be the social elements in my work. But while my response to certain human elements is as obvious as it is inevitable, I am also pleased to note that upon reflection many persons have found that they were as much concerned with the aesthetic implications of my paintings as with, what may possibly be, my human compassion.   *[1969]*

PETER BLUME

(1906–)

During the late 1930s, Blume found a new way to offer social criticism by fusing Precisionist and Surrealist techniques. After the war, his work took on an Expressionist sobriety. His insistence on the narrative content of painting found little response during the 1940s, but was welcomed again after 1970.

Since I am concerned with the communication of ideas, I am not at all ashamed of "telling stories" in my paintings, because I consider this to be one of the primary functions of the plastic arts. Visual or pictorial images are as much a part of the material of a painter as the color, shapes, and forms he uses. They have, moreover, a unique quality which is as distinct from verbal language as the senses are from one another. They must be used plastically in order to evoke the "total image" which a painting is capable of.

Modern aesthetics has stripped painting of this quality almost with repugnance. Any sophisticate now knows there is no more devastating criticism of a picture than "illustrative" or "literary." Personally, I believe in expanding the range of experience in art rather than contracting it. I would like to see the quality of light, now almost lost, as Caravaggio developed it, integrated once more in painting. I would like to see illusion, illusion of space, texture, and reality, restored again as another one of the mysteries in the art of painting, which makes it really unique. On the critical level I would like to see a general reappraisal of values which would reduce the cult of primitivism and "innocence" to its proper perspective. Finally, I would like to see a fresh interest in the human gesture, with all its infinite variations and subtlety. This offers the most challenging material for the artist. Why not use it?   *[1963]*

ILYA BOLOTOWSKY

(1907–1980)

From the mid-1930s, Bolotowsky followed the principles of the de Stijl movement, although allowing himself variations and never creating a dogma. He was one of the few nonobjective artists who managed to hold their footing during the rush to Abstract Expressionism after the Second World War.

In the early forties I still used diagonals. A diagonal, of course, creates ambivalent depth—diagonal depth might go either back or forth. It's not like perspective which goes only one way. This ambivalence I discovered was antithetical to my style. Although I hated to give up diagonals, I had to give them up finally. Mondrian gave them up quite early in his career. Although he had used them very well, he had to give them up too. Glarner, on the other hand, rediscovered diagonals and he held on to them. We all solve our own practical problems. I had to give up diagonals because the space going back and forth was becoming too violent. The diagonal space was getting in the way of the tension on the flat surface. You cannot get an absolute flatness in painting because of the interplay of the colors, the way they feel to us. But you can achieve relative flatness, within which the colors and the proportions might push back and forth creating an extra tension. This tense flatness must not destroy the overall flat tension, which, to my mind, in two-dimensional painting is the most important thing. Now of course, in a different style, it's a different story.   *[1974]*

LOUISE BOURGEOIS *Blind Man's Buff.* 1984.
Marble. 36½ x 35 x 25".

LOUISE BOURGEOIS

(1911–   )

Born in France, Bourgeois emigrated to America in 1938. She devoted herself to sculpture beginning in the late 1940s, and was known for her carved wood, painted, totemlike shapes arranged in free-standing ensembles to resemble crowds. Her free approach to the problems of sculpture led her to be associated with the Abstract Expressionists, who generally agreed that the subject of a work of art would find its material expression quite naturally and was of primary importance even in seemingly abstract works.

Several years ago I called a sculpture *One and Others.* This might be the title of many since then: the relation of one person to his surroundings is a continuing preoccupation. It can be casual or close; simple or involved; subtle or blunt. It can be painful or pleasant. Most of all it can be real or imaginary. This is the soil from which all my work grows. The problems of realization—technical, and even formal and aesthetic—are secondary; they come afterward and they can be solved.   *[1983]*

C H R I S T O (Christo Jaracheff)

(1935–)

A naturalized American born in Bulgaria, Christo has specialized in spectacular
public events, such as wrapping up buildings, installing hundreds of oil drums in
public spaces, and extending miles and miles of fabric fence on the Pacific coast.
Christo's events usually engage the entire community and are meant to both provoke
and entertain.

Our perception of art is basically Victorian. The object, the commodity as
a work of art is a completely recent perception, and of course this became
more and more evident—perhaps I now talk like a Marxist—with the advance of capitalist society and industrial society, when you have the family,
the molecule of husband, wife, and children, an apartment, and have the
commodity, transportation, goods that you can move out fast with yourself.

And of course relating the value of art in terms of a commodity object is
important. The most important part is really the driving energy for the
physical object. If the physical object is not the ultimate end, we never
arrive at this fantastic power of the project. . . .

What is important with the *Running Fence* or the *Reichstag* or the *Valley*
Curtain—they are outside of that art system, and they are thrown directly
into the everyday life of the country, of the community, of politicians, of
the army, of circulation on streets and highways. And of course that is like
teasing the system, you know, and the system responds very seriously, and
that became the humor of the project, because when the system responds
very seriously, we go to court and have these three judges discussing the
fence in court. Before the fence was built. . . .

Before, art was a much more fluid communication—I always think that
art in the tenth century was much more democratic than it is today. In that
time nobody was involved with owning art because the people owned the
kings and the gods, and there was a complete link, like for them the kings
and gods were the same thing, and they were the direct link with art that
was real, existing.

But when art became a commodity and we started to own it and to have
it only for ourselves, that is when our monumentality started to be broken
into small pieces. We cannot have monumentality when we are involved
with a commodity, with transportation of goods and all these things, and
it's very sad to see that we are claiming that we are doing public art when
actually we do only garden objects and things of that kind around the city.
I don't know how long it'll take until our society understands that it's capable

of mobilizing energy, if you call it that, or wealth or money or power, so that that power can be used for irrational purposes. That's very important.

[1979]

WILLEM DE KOONING

(1904–   )

De Kooning's thorough training in Holland before his arrival in the United States in 1926 equipped him for the struggle to overcome the stale conventions of modern art. His work in the late 1940s struck an instant chord of innovation. His first one-man exhibition in 1948 was widely remarked for his use of free-flowing paint in broad, curving configurations that suggested an interpenetration of figure and ground. Many younger artists adapted de Kooning's large, painterly gestures and rich impastos, formulating the style that dominated the 1950s, Abstract Expressionism. It was largely on the basis of de Kooning's style that the critic Harold Rosenberg coined the phrase "Action Painting" to cover the work of the New York School in the 1940s and 1950s.

For the painter to come to the "abstract" or the "nothing," he needed many things. Those things were always things in life—a horse, a flower, a milk-maid, the light in a room through a window made of diamond shapes maybe, tables, chairs, and so forth. The painter, it is true, was not always completely free. The things were not always of his own choice, but because of that he often got some new ideas. Some painters liked to paint things already chosen by others, and after being abstract about them, were called classicists. Others wanted to select the things themselves and, after being abstract about them, were called romanticists. Of course, they got mixed up with one another a lot too. Anyhow, at that time, they were not abstract about something which was already abstract. They freed the shapes, the light, the color, the space, by putting them into concrete things in a given situation. They *did* think about the possibility that the things—the horse, the chair, the man— were abstractions, but they let that go, because if they kept thinking about it, they would have been led to give up painting altogether, and would probably have ended up in the philosopher's tower. When they got those strange, deep ideas, they got rid of them by painting a particular smile on one of the faces in the picture they were working on.

Kandinsky understood "form" as *a* form, like an object in the real world; and an object, he said, was a narrative—and so, of course, he disapproved of it. He wanted his "music without words." He wanted to be "simple as a child." He intended, with his "inner-self," to rid himself of "philosophical

WILLEM DE KOONING   *Woman.* 1950.
Oil on canvas. 64 x 46".

barricades" (he sat down and wrote something about all this). But in turn his own writing has become a philosphical barricade, even if it is a barricade full of holes. It offers a kind of Middle European idea of Buddhism or, anyhow, something too theosophic for me.

The sentiment of the Futurists was simpler. No space. Everything ought to keep on going! That's probably the reason they went themselves. Either a man was a machine or else a sacrifice to make machines with.

The moral attitude of Neoplasticism is very much like that of Constructivism, except that the Constructivists wanted to bring things out in the open and the Neoplasticists didn't want anything left over.

I have learned a lot from all of them and they have confused me plenty too. One thing is certain, they didn't give me my natural aptitude for drawing. I am completely weary of their ideas now.

Spiritually I am wherever my spirit allows me to be, and that is not necessarily in the future. I have no nostalgia, however. If I am confronted with one of those small Mesopotamian figures, I have no nostalgia for it but, instead, I may get into a state of anxiety. Art never seems to make me peaceful or pure. I always seem to be wrapped in the melodrama of vulgarity. I do not think of inside or outside—or of art in general—as a situation of comfort. I know there is a terrific idea there somewhere, but whenever I want to get into it, I get a feeling of apathy and want to lie down and go to sleep. Some painters, including myself, do not care what chair they are sitting on. It does not even have to be a comfortable one. They are too nervous to find out where they ought to sit. They do not want to "sit in style." Rather, they have found that painting—any kind of painting, any style of painting—to be painting at all, in fact—is a way of living today, a style of living so to speak. That is where the form of it lies. It is exactly in its uselessness that it is free. Those artists do not want to conform. They only want to be inspired.

The argument often used that science is really abstract, and that painting could be like music and, for this reason, that you cannot paint a man leaning against a lamppost, is utterly ridiculous. That space of science—the space of the physicists—I am truly bored with by now. Their lenses are so thick that, seen through them, the space gets more and more melancholy. There seems to be no end to the misery of the scientists' space. All that it contains is billions and billions of hunks of matter, hot or cold, floating around in darkness according to a great design of aimlessness. The stars *I* think about, if I could fly, I could reach in a few old-fashioned days. But physicists' stars I use as buttons, buttoning up curtains of emptiness. If I stretch my arms next to the rest of myself and wonder where my fingers are—that is all the space I need as a painter.

Personally, I do not need a movement. What was given to me, I take for granted. Of all movements, I like Cubism most. It had that wonderful unsure atmosphere of reflection—a poetic frame where something could be possible, where an artist could practice his intuition. It didn't want to get rid of what went before. Instead it added something to it. The parts that I can appreciate in other movements came out of Cubism. Cubism *became* a movement, it didn't set out to be one.   *[1951]*

RICHARD DIEBENKORN

(1922–)

Born in Portland, Oregon, Diebenkorn encountered the influence of Abstract Expressionism at the California School of Fine Arts, where Clyfford Still and occasionally Mark Rothko held forth. Until 1955 he worked in an abstract landscape idiom, then, for a few years, explored the human figure in various environments associated with

RICHARD DIEBENKORN   *Ocean Park #117*. 1979.
Oil on canvas. 45 x 45".

the Western landscape, but eventually returned to abstraction. His Ocean Park
*series, with its references to the high Western light and its calm planar abstraction,
won him a place as an American classic.*

All paintings start out of a mood, out of a relationship with things or people,
out of a complete visual impression. To call this expression abstract seems
to me often to confuse the issue. Abstract means literally to draw from or
separate. In this sense every artist is abstract . . . a realistic or nonobjective
approach makes no difference. The result is what counts. . . .

   A forceful quality in art, truly representative of our modern situation,
will rise above the labels of abstraction and realism . . . a painter is bound
to reflect himself and his times.   *[1957]*

JIM DINE

(1935–)

Out of a background of Happenings, Dine went into painting. At first he included real objects, such as chairs or hatchets which he affixed to his canvases, but later merely used images of mundane objects drawn from popular imagery. He was associated with Pop Art, although his own interests, he always insisted, lay elsewhere.

What is your attitude to Pop Art?

I don't feel very pure in that respect. I don't deal exclusively with the popular image. I'm more concerned with it as part of my landscape. I'm sure everyone has always been aware of that landscape, the artistic land-scape, the artist's vocabulary, the artist's dictionary.

Does that apply to the Abstract Expressionists?

I would think so—they have eyes, don't they? I think it's the same landscape only interpreted through another generation's eyes. I don't believe there was a sharp break and this is replacing Abstract Expressionism. I believe this is the natural course of things. I don't think it is exclusive or that the best painting is being done as a movement. . . . Pop Art is only one facet of my work. More than popular images I'm interested in personal images, in making paintings about my studio, my experience as a painter, about painting itself, about color charts, the palette, about elements of the realistic landscape—but used differently.   *[1963]*

Who are you, Jim Dine? What's your pitch?

I'm not a Pop artist. For me Pop never was. My pitch is that I'm turned on to the world.

Why do you say you're not a Pop artist?

Because I'm too subjective. Pop is concerned with exteriors. I'm concerned with interiors. When I use objects, I see them as a vocabulary of feelings. I can spend a lot of time with objects, and they leave me as satisfied as a good meal. I don't think Pop artists feel that way.   *[1966]*

MARK DI SUVERO

(1933–)

Born in Shanghai, Di Suvero came to the United States in 1941. He studied philosophy at the University of California at Berkeley. In 1957 he settled in New York, where he participated in the activities of the young avant-garde eager to break with sculptural tradition. He was soon creating large-scale works, often composed of found materials, sometimes incorporating motion. After 1971, in protest against the war in Vietnam, Di Suvero moved to Italy, where he remained until the end of the war, building huge sculptures throughout Europe. The works he has produced since the mid-1970s—powerful, monumental sculptures, with a simple, often rough-hewn character—have gained him a position as one of America's foremost sculptors.

Steel is very direct. Steel is very honest. You make a mistake, it tells you quick. It's the easiest. It's easier than wood. Wood has its own life, wants it own way, has its grain, and it's grown, suffered, and by the time you get it it has already been killed, and you're supposed to do something; and they have done great things with it, just incredible sculptures in wood. Steel is so much more protean. It has the capacity for many images. For years I tried to get the one image, you know, like Brancusi got into stone. I tried to get the one image out of steel. It's like trying for the one shape of water, and the water is our body, and a cell, and an iceberg, and a cloud.

I think we are deeply influenced by our methods, our tools are the way we work. Working with a crane, what the crane does, it literally turns everything into the same weight; that is, it is either capable of picking it or not, and when it is capable of picking it—it acts differently of course if it's fifteen tons or five tons, but essentially you don't feel it in your body—and so it gives you that dematerialized moment, and to offer that dematerialized moment to people in a piece of sculpture is essentially what I do.

We have seen sculpture grow in the last few years so that now a fifteen-foot piece might be considered normal for the Museum. But I think our dreams are grand and there is always that funny gap. And if there isn't that gap between our dream and what we can achieve, then we are flattened-out artists, we have become run over.

I have worked for about fifteen years in order to try to do a piece that would have that kind of really archaic Greek essentiality, and have motion and participation, where people could get into it kinesthetically so that even someone who was blind could feel it and understand it. There is a certain angle on a beam that you can make where everybody will climb up, and the relationship between them is only something like 40 degrees. Now you can choose it on the basis of expression, that angle, because you want to get a special kind of structure and an internal feeling to the person who is looking at it, offer a kind of horizontality or verticality or diagonal twists like that view from the airplane window when it's banking and you're looking down onto that jeweled web that nobody who lives in that town knows that they are making, and yet it is an incredible beauty and you try for that distortion or you try for letting people climb up or not. It works with many of these variables and part of it is where the piece is going to go.

I've finally arrived at an art that can be objective. I can say does it work or not, and if it doesn't work it folds over and is on the ground—it just goes back down and you know it doesn't work. It is such a relief to have left aesthetic choice behind, that kind of ego that says, "Well, that curve would satisfy me more than this curve." It's nice to leave that behind in order to find out that this works or this won't work. You get balance, rotation, and movement of tons—or you can even take a simple swinging bed—you think you can put it anywhere? You get twenty kids on it, that's a ton. A ton moving and you've got to be able to handle it. Fortunately, with these tools I can test it first and the test tells you—the crane never lies, pick it up, the center of gravity always goes underneath the point of suspension and if you have it rigged wrong it tells you real quick.

It is the re-formation of material, the transformation of material which is what all of art is about whether it comes out of a tube or a billet that they change into an I-beam, we re-form it to that moment where it does that tuning fork to our knowledge of form within.   *[1981]*

ÖYVIND FAHLSTRÖM

(1928–1976)

Swedish by birth, Fahlström came into prominence in New York, where he settled in 1961, as an innovative social critic. He used game theory and other techniques drawn from modern philosophy to produce an art sharply critical of public events such as the Cold War and the war in Vietnam. Sometimes he drew his subjects from the stylized comic strips which he set out in what could be described as picture puzzles, whose solution carried his message of dissent.

Art. Consider art as a way of experiencing a fusion of "pleasure" and "insight." Reach this by impurity, or multiplicity of levels, rather than by reduction. (The fallacy of some painting, music, etc.; satori by mere reduction. The fewer the factors, the more they have to be "right," "ultimate.")

Games. Seen either as realistic models (not descriptions) of a life-span, of the Cold War balance, of the double-code mechanism to push the bomb button—or as freely invented rule-structures.

Multiples. Painting, sculpture, etc., today represent the most archaic art medium, depending on feudal patrons who pay exorbitantly for uniqueness and fetish magic; the "spirit" of the artist as manifested in the traces of his brushwork or at least in his signature (Yvès Klein selling air against a signed receipt in 1958).

It is time to incorporate advances in technology to create mass-produced works of art, obtainable by rich or not rich. Works where the artist puts as much quality into the conception and the manufacturer as much quality into the production, as found in the best handmade works of art. The value of variable form: you will never have exactly the same piece as your neighbor.

Risk reforms. Attitude to society: not to take any of the existing systems for granted (capitalist, moderately socialized, or thoroughly socialized). Refuse to presume that "sharpness" of the opposite systems will mellow into a worthwhile in-between. Discuss and otherwise influence the authorities toward trying out certain new concepts.   *[1966]*

DAN FLAVIN

(1933–   )

Flavin took up where such Constructivists as Moholy-Nagy left off, producing an art entirely with light. His experiments with neon tubing were launched early in the 1960s and continue to this day.

In time, I came to these conclusions about what I had found in fluorescent light, and about what might be done with it plastically:

Now the entire spatial container and its parts—wall, floor, ceiling, could support this strip of light but would not restrict its act of light except to enfold it. Regard the light and you are fascinated—inhibited from grasping its limits at each end. While the tube itself has an actual length of eight feet, its shadow, cast by the supporting pan, has none but an illusion dissolving at its ends. This waning shadow cannot really be measured without resisting its visual effect and breaking the poetry.

Realizing this, I knew that the actual space of a room could be broken down and played with by planting illusions of real light (electric light) at crucial junctures in the room's composition.   *[1965]*

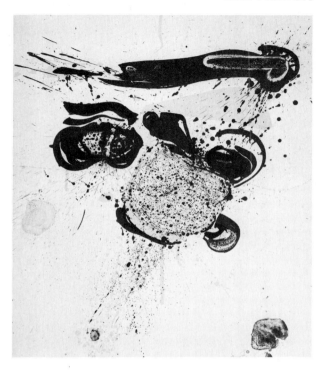

SAM FRANCIS   *Untitled (Blue over Yellow).* 1963.
Color lithograph. 23 x 19⅞".

SAM FRANCIS
(1923–   )

Francis was born and educated in California. During a long convalescence from an injury sustained in the air corps in the Second World War, he began to paint. Eventually, he went to Paris to study, and there, in 1952, he had his first one-man show. He was already at that time identified with the Art Informel movement in Paris, which, in turn, was associated with American Abstract Expressionism. Under the influence of Oriental art—especially that of Japan, where he frequently traveled— he began to incorporate large white spaces into his dappled, undifferentiated canvases with their oceanic references. He lives and works both in Tokyo and in Santa Monica, California.

What we want is to make something that fills utterly the sight and can't be used to make life only bearable; if the painting till now was a way of making bearable the sight of the unbearable, the visible sumptuous, then let's now strip away . . . all that.

These paintings lie under the cloud that soared over the inlaid sea.

Do you still lie dreaming under that huge canvas? Complete vision abandons the three-times-divided soul and its vapors; it is the cloud come over the inlaid sea. You can't interpret the dream of the canvas for this dream is at the end of the hunt on the heavenly mountain—where nothing remains but the phoenix caught in the midst of lovely blueness.   *[1959]*

I live in a paradise of hellish blue balls—merely floating, everything floats, everything floats—where I carry this unique mathematics of my imagination through the succession of days toward a nameless tomorrow. What a delight as if I were lighting the way with my own eyes against my will and knowing that I'd rather have paneless windows for eyes.

So I continue to make my machines of strokes, dabs, and splashes and indulge in my dialectic of eros—objectively for myself and subjectively in the eyes of the audience.   *[1975]*

LEON GOLUB

(1922–   )

Although the strongest tendency during the late 1950s remained abstract, Golub made his mark by remaining faithful to a basically figurative, Expressionist idiom in which he responded to what he regarded as the more frightful public events of the century, including the war in Vietnam and, more recently, the terrors stalking Latin America.

My recent paintings can be viewed in various ways:

1. Man is seen as having undergone a holocaust or facing annihilation or mutation. The ambiguities of these huge forms indicate the stress of their vulnerability versus their capacities for endurance.

2. Man is seen in an heroic gesture of the very beauty and sensuous organic vitality of even fragmented forms. The enlarged carnal beauty of the fragment is contrasted to its pathos and monumentality.

3. These paintings attempt to reinstate a contemporary catharsis, that measure of man which is related to an existential knowledge of the human condition—a recognition that looks back to the symbolic incarnation of classic art.

4. The figures are implacable in their appearance and resistance, stance or stare. They are implacable in the compacted wearing down of surfaces and forms to simpler forms but with more complicated surfaces. They are implacable as they take on the resistance of stone as against the undulations of flesh. They are implacable as they know an absolute state of mind (on the edge of nothingness) just as they know a nearly absolute state of massiveness.   *[1959]*

ARSHILE GORKY *Portrait of Vartoosh.*
Mid-1930s. Oil on canvas. 20¼ x 15⅛".

ARSHILE GORKY
(1904–1948)

Gorky's encounter with European Surrealism during the 1930s enabled him to free himself from Cubist canons, and to infuse his abstractions with lyrical allusions to the myths of his childhood in Armenia. His letters to his sister and family attest to his nostalgia, but also to his view of the function of art, which he saw as discrete from social commentary or direct messages. Along with de Kooning and Pollock, Gorky was considered one of the strongest figures in the early years of Abstract Expressionism.

My dearest ones, the camera has rendered impotent any attempt to compete with it. This has to be accepted as a necessary and a scientific advance. What reason, therefore, remains to sit in realism's stagnation? Art is more than mere chronicle. It must mirror the intellect and the emotion, for anyone, even a commercial artist or illustrator, can portray realism. The mind's eye in its infinity of radiations and not optical vision of necessity holds the key to truth. It is left for the artist to forge the new metal, to resurrect his ancient role as the uncoverer and the interpreter, but never the recorder, of life's secrets.

Beloveds, the stuff of thought is the seed of the artist. Dreams form the bristles of the artist's brush. And, as the eye functions as the brain's sentry, I communicate my innermost perceptions through art, my worldview. In trying to probe beyond the ordinary and the known, I create an interior infinity. I probe within the finite's confines to create an infinity. Liver. Bones. Living rocks and living plants and animals. Living dreams.   *[1939]*

I like the heat, the tenderness, the edible, the lusciousness, the song of a single person, the bathtub full of water to bathe myself beneath the water. I like Uccello, Grünewald, Ingres, the drawings and sketches for paintings of Seurat, and that man Pablo Picasso.

I measure all things by weight.

I love my Mougouch [Gorky's wife]. What about papa Cézanne! I hate things that are not like me and all the things I haven't got are God to me.

Permit me—

I like the wheatfields, the plough, the apricots, the shape of apricots, those flirts of the sun. And bread above all. . . .

About 194 feet away from our house on the road to the spring, my father had a little garden with a few apple trees which had retired from giving fruit. There was a ground constantly in shade where grew incalculable amounts of wild carrots, and porcupines had made their nests. There was a blue rock half buried in the black earth with a few patches of moss placed here and there like fallen clouds. But from where came all the shadows in constant battle like the lancers of Paolo Uccello's painting? This garden was identified as the Garden of Wish Fulfillment and often I had seen my mother and other village women opening their bosoms and taking their soft and dependent breasts in their hands to rub them on the rock. Above all this stood an enormous tree all bleached under the sun, the rain, the cold, and deprived of leaves. This was the Holy Tree. I myself don't know why this tree was holy but I had witnessed many people, whoever did pass by, that would tear voluntarily a strip of their clothes and attach this to the tree. Thus through many years of the same act, like a veritable parade of banners under the pressure of wind all these personal inscriptions of signatures, very softly to my innocent ear used to give echo to the sh-h-h-sh-h of silver leaves of the poplars.   *[1942]*

Surrealism is academic art under disguise and anti-aesthetic and suspicious of excellence and largely in opposition to modern art. Its claim of liberation is really restrictive because of its narrow rigidity. To its adherents the tradition of art and its quality mean little. They are drunk with psychiatric spontaneity and inexplicable dreams. These Surrealists. These people are haltingly entertaining. We do not think alike since their views on life differ so vastly from mine and we are naturally of opposite backgrounds. Their ideas are quite strange and somewhat flippant, almost playful. Really they are not as earnest about painting as I should like artists to be. Art must always remain earnest. Perhaps it is because I am an Armenian and they are not. Art must be serious, no sarcasm, comedy. One does not laugh at a loved one.

Beloveds, art is never play. They feel it is play and they are players, not artists, as I view art. Nonsense. Art must remain structure and plasticity, otherwise it can be reduced to an unconscious game in which anyone can play irrespective of credentials and quality. Art can remain marvelous when not conquered by frivolity. It is not new things that are important, but new ways of expressing universals in the tongue of modern times. The deification of novelty robs art of its painstakingly acquired aesthetics and becomes rather the preserve of pedestrian businessmen. The tradition of art is the grand group dance of beauty and pathos in which the many individual centuries join hands in the effort and thereby communicate their particular contributions to the whole event just as in our dances of Van. They can however be rendered inadequate if the linking hands are broken. For this reason I feel that tradition, namely the related ages of the past and present, is so important for art. The soloist can emerge only after having participated in the group dance.

[1947]

ADOLPH GOTTLIEB

(1903–1974)

Gottlieb and Mark Rothko were both very much interested in archaic art and mythology during the early 1940s. Gottlieb developed a scheme of compartmentalized compositions in which he placed signlike forms. These "pictographic" paintings won him acclaim and a prominent place in the Abstract Expressionist group.

I would start by having an arbitrary division of the canvas into rough rectangular areas, and with the process of free association I would put various images and symbols within these compartments. And it was irrational. There was no logical or rational design in the placing of these. It was purely following an impulse, which was irrational, trying to use the method of free association. And then when all of these images and symbols were combined, they could not be read like a rebus. There was no direct connection one to the other. And, however, by the strange juxtapositions that occurred, a new kind of significance stemmed from this juxtaposition.

I don't want to give the impression that I was trying to convey some kind of literary message. I wasn't a writer, I was a painter. I was really trying to make paintings. Actually, I was involved with pictorial problems, such as the type of space I was using. I was trying to flatten out space. There was an article written in a magazine at the time that said Gottlieb kills space. Well, I was trying to kill space. That is, I was trying to kill the old three dimensional deep space, which may have been valid for the representation of actual objects and figures, but for what I was painting, that kind of space wasn't the right space. So I had to try to invent some other kind of pictorial space, which I did with this method of using lines that went out at the edges of the canvas and that formed these rectangular frames. So that it was a continuous space and the paintings had no definite focal point. If there was a focal point, there were, I would say, numerous focal points, which were distributed as I chose. And this was, I think, a painterly problem primarily. It was not an attempt to translate a literary message into a pictorial form.

There's a tremendous difference between my recent things and the pictographs. The pictographs were all-over paintings. There was no beginning, and no end, no definite focal point. However, when I broke away from that aspect of my work and got into the imaginary landscapes and into what people call the bursts I was working with definite focal points. By focal point I mean a point within the rectangle of the canvas to which one's eye is drawn. In portraits, for example, the focal point is the head. So instead of numerous focal points as in my pictographs I used only one or two. And that's the great difference in what I was doing before and what I have been doing since the late fifties. It's a different spatial concept, and naturally, the forms are different. Well, the space was determined by the forms. The character of the forms required a different kind of space, pictorial space, which is to say a flat space.   *[1967]*

PHILIP GUSTON

(1913–1980)

Guston came to the United States at the age of three from Canada. He was educated in Los Angeles, where he completed neither high school nor his subsequent course at the Otis Art Institute. Despite this, he was one of the most cultivated figures in the New York School, having made exhaustive studies of the history of painting, in both Italy and Mexico. He worked in a socially committed representational idiom during the 1930s and in a softer lyrical vein in the 1940s; in the 1950s, he developed an abstract mode that coincided with Abstract Expressionist ideals. In the late 1960s Guston startled his admirers by turning to large, satirical narrative paintings in which memories of the Ku Klux Klan and the Holocaust were generalized. During his last years Guston painted allegories expressing pessimistic, almost eschatological thoughts about the human condition.

P H I L I P   G U S T O N   *The Magnet.* 1975. Oil on canvas. 67½ x 80″.

In my experience a painting is not made with colors and paint at all. I don't know what a painting is; who knows what sets off even the desire to paint? It might be things, thoughts, a memory, sensations, which have *nothing* to do directly with painting itself. They can come from anything and any-where, a trifle, some detail observed, wondered about, and naturally from the previous painting. The painting is not on a surface, but on a plane which is imagined. It moves in a mind. It is not there physically at all. It is an illusion, a piece of magic, so what you see is not what you see. I suppose the same thing was true in the Renaissance.

The strange and the familiar, the everyday, can live together in a painting. I enjoy having a subject to paint. But it's not very controllable, in fact totally uncontrollable, because meaning keeps shifting and so does the structure. In this necessary engagement images appear, then as quickly disappear. Failures are always around, waiting. It has always been mystifying to me, why, on a lucky day, the images do take hold, grip, and there is no urge to clear it off. This temporary satisfaction, very temporary, is always a surprise to me. Then a sort of chronic restlessness enters the studio and you begin again.

Of the two writers that I've admired the most for years, Franz Kafka and Isaac Babel, Isaac Babel gave a lovely, ironic speech to the Soviet Writers Union. It was 1934. He ended his talk with the following remark. "The party and the government have given us everything, but have deprived us of one privilege. A very important privilege, comrades, has been taken away from you. That of writing badly." Isn't that beautiful? Where am I? Doesn't anyone want to paint badly?

I think that probably the most potent desire for a painter, an image-maker, is to see it. To see what the mind can think and imagine, to realize it for onself, through oneself, as concretely as possible. I think that's the most powerful and at the same time the most archaic urge that has endured for about twenty-five thousand years. In about 1961 or 1962 the urge for images became so powerful that I started a whole series of dark pictures, mostly just black-and-white. They were conceived as heads and objects.

I think in my studies and broodings about the art of the past my greatest ideal is Chinese painting, especially Sung painting dating from about the tenth or eleventh century. Sung period training involves doing something thousands and thousands of times—bamboo shoots and birds—until someone else does it, not you, and the rhythm moves through you. I think that is what the Zen Buddhists called "satori" and I have had it happen to me. It is a double activity, when you know and don't know, and it shouldn't really be talked about. So I work toward that moment and if a year or two later I look at some of the work I've done and try to start judging it, I find it's impossible. You can't judge it because it was felt.

What measure is there, other than the fact that at *one* point in your life you trusted a feeling. You have to trust that feeling and then continue, trusting yourself. And it works in a reverse way. I know that I started similar things in the past, twenty to twenty-five years ago, and would then scrape them out. I remember the pictures I scraped out very well, in fact some of them are sharper in my mind than the ones that remained. Well then, I would subsequently ask myself, "Why did I scrape them out?" Well, I wasn't ready to accept it, that's the only answer. This leads me to another point; it doesn't occur to many viewers that the artist often has difficulty accepting the painting himself. You can't assume that I gloried in it, or celebrated it. I didn't. I'm a night painter, so when I come into the studio the next morning the delirium is over. I know I won't remember detail, but I will remember the feeling of the whole thing. I come into the studio very fearfully, I creep in to see what happened the night before. And the feeling is one of, "My God, did I do *that?*" That is about the only measure I have. The kind of shaking, trembling of . . . "That's me? I did that?" But most of the time, we're carpenters, we build and build, and add and prepare and when you drag yourself into the studio, you say, "Oh, that's what I did. It's horrible. All of it has to go." This is one of the last minute touches.

Often at the moment you're playing your last card and are ready to give up, another kind of awareness enters and you work with that moment. But you can't force that moment either. You truly have to have given up. And then something happens. *[1978]*

HANS HAACKE

(1936–)

Born in Cologne, Haacke studied art in Kassel and in 1963 emigrated to the United States. His works of the mid-1960s were largely devoted to environmental art, using earth, air, and electrical devices. After 1968, Haacke turned toward an art that would propound a critique of society, often attacking the politics of the art world. His work has been called "conceptual," but in fact moves outside of any specific movements.

What is considered beautiful depends on who you are talking to. The way one looks at and talks about what is considered aesthetic or art at any given time is quite relative. It is generally based on the shared attitudes of the culture to which the viewer belongs, and in particular is determined by those who wield the cultural power in that population. To a certain degree even our sensory and psychic apparatus seems to be influenced by culturally acquired habits.

Any product or activity designed to communicate feelings and ideas—and artworks certainly belong to that category—performs a social function and is therefore implicitly, if not explicitly, also of political import. What I am saying here is obviously not new. I believe it is generally accepted in the social sciences. The theorizing about culture among critics and producers, more so in Europe than here, seems to be moving in that direction, too. . . .

What distinguishes formalist work and criticism is the exclusive attention that is paid to the presumably pure structural qualities of the respective medium, without regard to and usually rejecting any content. But there just is no structural element absolutely immune to signification and history. The meanings, no matter if they are acknowledged or not, have had ideological import. The denial of their existence does not obliterate them and the denial by itself is ideologically quite significant.

If a critical appraisal of this old-time religion got hold, it could eventually have economic consequences for its adherent. But besides these varied interests, there is also a large segment of society which very deeply hopes that art is different, that art is produced, promoted, and consumed in a totally disinterested fashion. The liberal myth has it that beauty is ideologically neutral. . . .

HANS HAACKE *Seurat's "Les Poseuses" (Small Version) 1888–1975.* 1975. One of fourteen panels and a color reproduction of Seurat's "Les Poseuses."

The formalist ghettoization of art turns art into a socially irrelevant phenomenon, and consequently it deepens the alienation between high culture and contemporary life. When one examines it in those terms, I believe one will find that for the individual practitioner as much as on societal level the formalist approach may lead to very serious psychological problems. Politically it has become a proponent of the status quo.   *[1978]*

DAVID HARE

(1917–)

An early adherent of the Surrealist movement in the United States, Hare developed his sculpture on Surrealist principles, finding strange associations in his welded metal forms and exploiting them.

I believe that in order to avoid copying nature and at the same time keep the strongest connection with reality it is necessary to break up reality and recombine it, creating different relations which will take the place of relations destroyed. These should be relations of memory and association. If you make a child and locomotive you might make the engine even larger than it should be. This would not be only a change in volume relation but in memory relation. When one is small, a locomotive is very big. Perhaps you remember especially the wheels, and perhaps the way you remember them is not at all like wheels. If you make them as you remember, and you are lucky to have had the same memory as the observer, he will say, "Why that is more locomotive than a locomotive," and you will have created not just a locomotive but what a locomotive means to a man. There is a great difference.

I should like to be able to use motion in such a way as to give another dimension to sculpture. Not a material or visual dimension but a purely mental one. If you say, "a road of white asphalt," it leaves one with a strange feeling. If you paint a road of white asphalt it is not white asphalt, it is merely a white road. The impossible does not take place in the world of vision. Asphalt can only be white in the mind. Perhaps it would be possible to create these same unsettling sensations in sculpture by the use of motion. Movement only exists at the actual point of motion and yet this movement can be continued in the mind to complete a form which could not possibly exist in reality.

If one is to devise new frameworks and relations with which to build a reality they must be objective. To this end it is necessary to make the generic and not the particular figure. One may recognize Man, Woman, House, etc., but it is impossible to be objective about the particular. Reality exists not in the individual object but somewhere in the mind as it moves from one object to another. And so I feel that sculptors should present reality not as an object which might exist by itself in the closet, but as the relations between that object and the observer.   *[1946]*

AL HELD

(1928–   )

After his student years in Paris from 1949 to 1952, Held returned to the United States, where he developed a painting style that combined Abstract Expressionist heavy impastos with geometric imagery. During the 1960s his work slowly changed, and from around 1970, Held began to paint lean-surfaced, linear abstract works in which dazzling perspectives and effects of trompe l'oeil suggested cosmic scenography.

I fundamentally believe that modernism is a radical, new language, but I think it is a young, new language. What I set out to do is expand the vocabulary of what modernist painting could be. It's the only way to revitalize modernism, to keep it going as a growing language. . . . These paintings are a reflection of the attempt to break down the shoulds and should nots.

I think one characteristic of all the paintings is the optimism and hope. I think of myself as a Utopian—it's not the nineteenth-century Utopianism of perfection—but one living in the twentieth century who has to somehow deal with the reality of things. I think there are other people who in the act of making paintings are really talking about the despair of things, the impossibility of continuing in this chaotic, mad situation. At this point, I think that the only way out of the maze, so to speak, is not to somehow take the maze and straighten it out into a straight line, but to be able to somehow go through the maze without feeling that it's endangering. It may add an enlightening or freedom-giving aspect to our lives. *[1983]*

E V A   H E S S E

(1936–1970)

Hesse developed complicated techniques, using rubber, plaster, and synthetic materials, in order to find a sculptural idiom that relinquished volume and gravity. Her fragile-seeming sequences, often in regular rhythms, were sometimes suspended, producing effects that were far more complex than those of others working in a modular idiom.

irregular, edges, six to seven feet long.
textures coarse, rough, changing.
see through, non see through, consistent, inconsistent.
enclosed tightly by glass like encasement just hanging there.
then more, others. will they hang there in the same way?
try a continuous flowing one.
try some random closely spaced.
try some distant far spaced.
they are tight and formal but very ethereal. sensitive. fragile.
see through mostly.
not painting, not sculpture. it's there though.
I remember I wanted to get to non art, non connotive,
non anthropomorphic, non geometric, non, nothing,
everything, but of another kind, vision, sort.
from a total other reference point. is it possible?

I have learned anything is possible. I know that.
that vision or concept will come through total risk,
freedom, discipline.
I will do it.

[1969]

HANS HOFMANN

(1880–1966)

When Hans Hofmann settled in the United States in 1930, he brought with him a thorough acquaintance with all the major tendencies in modern European art. These he transmitted to countless students, first in California, then New York, including many second-generation Abstract Expressionists. His own works—exuberant abstractions in varying degrees of Expressionism—became known only toward the end of the 1940s.

Basically I hate categorical labels. As a young artist I already was very clear about this—that "objectification" is not the final aim of art. For there are greater things than the object. The greatest thing is the human mind. I must insist that there is immense confusion in the attitudes that make art opinion. Now I have to state a terrible truth—that no one can give a correct explanation of what art really is.

There is definitely, however, an abstract art. Not everything that sails under the name "abstract" is actually abstract. The word's meaning is too loosely considered these days. What goes on in abstract art is the proclaiming of aesthetic principles. As time went on, in figurative painting the aesthetic basis of creation was almost completely lost. It is in our own time that we have become aware of pure aesthetic considerations. Art never can be imitation. But let's go further. Art is not only the eye; it is not the result of intellectual considerations. Art is strictly bound to inherent laws dictated by the medium in which it comes to expression. In other words, painting is painting, sculpture is sculpture, architecture is architecture. All these arts have their own intrinsic qualities. . . .

What do I mean by "aesthetic"? I'll give you an example. Take a line. Now a line can have millions of variations—thin, thick, short, long, sinuous, staccato; but heretofore a line always represented something else. Today it is the line for itself, and that's what I mean by the aesthetic experience. The same is true of color—color as an expresssive force in itself, as a language in itself. Both Kandinsky and Klee were among the first to realize this. In my work I have further tried to clarify the same idea. These examples of line, of color that I've mentioned are merely samples. The new outlook makes us understand that nature is not limited to the objects we see—but that everything in nature offers the possibility of creative transformation, depending of course on the sensibility of the artist. . . .

My paintings are always images of my whole psychic makeup. You cannot deny yourself. You ask, am I painting myself? I'd be a swindler if I did otherwise. I'd be denying my existence as an artist. I've also been asked, what do you want to convey? And I say, nothing but my own nature. How can one paint anything else? You can't deny your nature, but as an artist neither can you be dependent on your daily moods, because once involved in your work you very quickly forget your troubles. Least of all can you think of yourself, for then it all becomes too personal. I can't understand how anyone is able to paint without optimism. Despite the general pessimistic attitude in the world today, I am nothing but an optimist.   *[1960]*

ROBERT IRWIN

(1928–   )

With his "disc paintings" exhibited in 1968, Irwin fulfilled his need to create a perceptual effect of extreme immateriality. These acrylic discs were illuminated from four directions to produce haloed effects. Irwin's experiments with light were the most lyrical among those put forward under the "minimal" rubric.

I started out with Abstract Expressionism as a point of belief, and at one point, looking at my paintings, found too many arbitrary things in them, too many things that had no reason for being. I began to question the depth of the act—and myself.

Every element has its imagery; it also has its physicality. It can be dealt with on both levels. I took the history of modern art a step further away from imagery and tried to deal with it solely in terms of its physicality. When you consider that we have very image-focused eyes, this is very difficult. (Intellect is a system of focus.) So I got into what some referred to as a "less is more" thing, which is not really true at all; I was just trying to eliminate imagery in favor of physicality. The thing was to *maximize* the physicality while *minimizing* the imagery; so to someone oriented to look for imagery it would seem less. At this time my ability to separate the two was also very limited.

What I really wanted to do was paint a painting without a "mark" at all, but I had no way of conceiving that at the time, except just to leave the mark out, with a plain canvas. As an idea it seemed closer to what I was moving toward, but Yves Klein had already done so as an idea about the same time. But "idea" is the abstraction I was trying to move away from.

I ended up with two lines on a seven-foot-square canvas. I was interested in their physicality, not the idea. That physicality is not transferable abstractly and the only way you can deal with it is by being in its presence. That was the beginning. . . .

What I do now is come unprepared, no material, no presuppositions, the less I think I know the better. What I try to do is deal directly with the situation at hand. Not to change the environment to an "ideal" in some wholesale way but to begin using those givens that are already unique to the situation. What comes out of it may make you more aware of things that have been going on all along, simply ignored because of conditioning. For example, an empty room is not empty except of that abstraction for content. If you were to take all the events taking place in that empty room and commit them to a painting you would most certainly have a work at least as complicated as, say, a Mondrian. I felt it was reasonable to consider the possibility that the implication in Mondrian for perception would apply equally in the world. Now, by your individual participation in these situations, you may become a party to this extended view and structure for yourself a "new state of real," but it is you that does it, not me, and the individual responsibility to reason your own world view is the root implication in modern art. *[1976]*

JASPER JOHNS
(1930–)

Born in Georgia and raised in South Carolina, Johns served in the army and then settled in New York in 1952. In 1958 he exhibited his series of paintings of flags and targets, images he used for their "pre-formed, conventional, depersonalized" aspect. Later, Johns, like Robert Rauschenberg, incorporated real objects in his work. Both artists reacted against the philosophic assertions of the Abstract Expressionists and, in returning to identifiable imagery, opened the possibility of Pop Art.

Sometimes I see it and then paint it. Other times I paint it and then see it. Both are impure situations, and I prefer neither.

At every point in nature there is something to see. My work contains similar possibilities for the changing focus of the eye.

Three academic ideas which have been of interest to me are what a teacher of mine (speaking of Cézanne and Cubism) called "the rotating point of view" (Larry Rivers recently pointed to a black rectangle, two or three feet away from where he had been looking in a painting, and said " . . . like there's something happening over there too."); Marcel Duchamp's suggestion "to reach the Impossibility of sufficient memory to transfer from one like

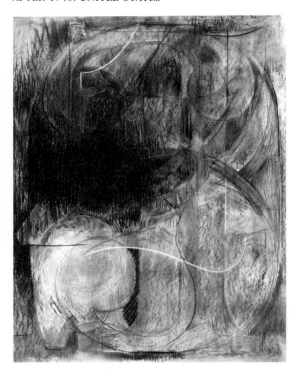

JASPER JOHNS   *0 Through 9.* 1961.
Charcoal on paper. 54 x 45".

object to another the memory imprint"; and Leonardo's idea ("Therefore, O painter, do not surround your bodies with lines . . .") that the boundary of a body is neither a part of the enclosed body nor a part of the surrounding atmosphere.

Generally, I am opposed to painting which is concerned with conceptions of simplicity. Everything looks very busy to me.   *[1959]*

DONALD JUDD

(1928–   )

Judd had his first one-man show in 1964 and was soon regarded as a forceful protagonist in the drive toward a "minimal art." His sculpture was austere and radically simplified, in keeping with his belief that the older forms of "relational" composition were exhausted.

In earlier art the complexity was displayed and built the quality. In recent painting the complexity was in the format and the few main shapes, which had been made according to various interests and problems. A painting by Newman is finally no simpler than one by Cézanne. In the three-dimensional work the whole thing is made according to complex purposes, and these are not scattered but asserted by one form. It isn't necessary for a work to have a lot of things to look at, to compare, to analyze one by one, to contemplate. The thing as a whole, its quality as a whole, is what is interesting. The main things are alone and are more intense, clear, and powerful. They are not diluted by an inherited format, variations of a form, mild contrasts, and connecting parts and areas. European art had to represent a space and its contents as well as have sufficient unity and aesthetic interest. Abstract painting before 1946 and most subsequent painting kept the representational subordination of the whole to its parts. Sculpture still does. In the new work the shape, image, color, and surface are single and not partial and scattered. There aren't any neutral or moderate areas or parts, any connections or transitional areas.   *[1965]*

ALLAN KAPROW
(1927–)

In the late 1950s, Kaprow began to compose "environments" from perishable materials through which the spectator could move. He then moved into the quasi-theatrical events that came to be called "Happenings." His exclusive concern with Happenings conferred on him the title of originator, although other artists such as Claes Oldenburg, Robert Whitman, and Jim Dine were composing Happenings during the same period.

A Happening is an assemblage of events performed or perceived in more than one time and place. Its material environments may be constructed, taken over directly from what is available, or altered slightly; just as its activities may be invented or commonplace. A Happening, unlike a stage play, may occur at a supermarket, driving along a highway, under a pile of rags, and in a friend's kitchen, either at once or sequentially. If sequentially, time may extend to more than a year. The Happening is performed according to plan but without rehearsal, audience, or repetition. It is art but seems closer to life.   *[1966]*

I was interested in the ideas of Kurt Schwitters. He actually conceived Happenings but never did them. His writings about possible activities are almost like pre-Happenings. Yet, the most important influence during the course of my studying Dada was Duchamp, because of what he *didn't* do.

After the big glass piece, he deliberately stoppped making art objects in favor of little (ready-made) hints to the effect that you could pick up art anywhere, if that's what you wanted. In other words, he implied that the whole business of art is quite arbitrary. I was hoping at the time I went to college, to be a professional philosopher, and Duchamp struck me as essentially a philosopher. I think my only abiding interest in art is philosophical, and thus media and techniques then were of only passing fascination. Schwitters and Duchamp had lively minds.

An Environment is literally a surrounding to be entered into. Environments have tended to be handmade, built-up affairs, exhibited in studios and galleries. Their early forms in the late fifties had the feel of Abstract Expressionism: lots of junk, lights, recorded noises, loosely hung together, and somewhat difficult to enter and walk or crawl through. Lately, the forms are close to the cooler styles of Pop and Primary Art. And as a result they are easier to negotiate, and induce a sense of detachment in the entrant. They will prove most interesting when they are made away from galleries: in the woods, along a highway, in a stone quarry, at the edge of an airport.

[1967]

ELLSWORTH KELLY

(1923–)

Kelly returned to America in 1954 from his studies in France with a vocabulary of elementary forms, often purely rectangular but occasionally curvilinear, that he arrayed in perfectly flat sequences of color. During the late 1950s he was among the most noted of the so-called Hard Edge painters.

When I was younger, I spent a great deal of time looking at the old masters in museums. When I was in the army, I had the librarian get the Phaidon books on Rembrandt, Donatello, Van Gogh. I liked Donatello very much at that time, in 1946. After that, it was artists like Max Beckmann, Picasso, Klee, and Matisse. But I didn't really feel close to American painting until I came back from Europe in 1954.

I'm not interested in edges. I'm interested in the mass and color, the black and white. The edges happen because the forms get as quiet as they can be. I want the masses to perform. When I work with forms and colors, I get the edge. . . . In my work, it is impossible to separate the edges from the mass and color.

I like to work from things that I see whether they're man-made or natural or a combination of the two. Once in a while I work directly from something I've seen, but not very often now. A lot of the earlier pictures were paintings of things I'd seen, like a window, or a fragment of a piece of architecture, or someone's legs; or sometimes the space between things, or just how the shadows of an object would look. The things I'm interested in have always been there. The idea of the shadow of a natural object has always existed, like the shadow of the pyramids and the pyramids, or a rock and its shadow and the separation of the rock and the shadow; I'm not interested in the texture of the rock, or that it is a rock but in the mass of it, and its shadow.

[1963]

ED KIENHOLZ *Barney's Beanery.* 1965. Mixed media with light, sound, and scent. 99⅝ x 263¾ x 74¾".

ED KIENHOLZ

(1927–   )

Like George Segal, Kienholz developed a sculptural idiom based on tableaux taken from real life. However, Kienholz's vision was a mixture of cruel fantasy and social commentary, and he used found objects as well as constructed ones to suggest a sordid reality.

I mostly think of my work as the spoor of an animal that goes through the forest and makes a thought trail, and the viewer is the hunter who comes and follows the trail. At one point I as the trail-maker disappear. The viewer then is confronted with a dilemma of ideas and direction. The possibilities are then to push on further by questions and answers to a new place that I can't even imagine or turn back to an old, safe place. But even the decision is direction. I like this because as I make the trail I'm making my own way and I'm finding my own forms and solutions for me. I like to think of it as so.

I really begin to understand any society by going through its junk stores and flea markets. It is a form of education and historical orientation for me. I can see the results of ideas in what is thrown away by a culture. *[1977]*

FREDERICK KIESLER

(1896–1965)

Kiesler brought from his native Vienna, in 1926, a well-founded reputation as an innovative sculptor, architect, and aesthetic provocateur. In the United States he worked on unorthodox sculptures—hybrids between architecture and sculpture—that sometimes evolved into structures such as his "Endless House," and on a series of fantastic landscapes, as well as on designs for theaters and art galleries.

The artist creator has always been in search of the basic laws of the world he lives in. He tries to express the unknown *with* the known, contrary to the scientist, who tries to find the unknown *in* the known.

He has become aware of the forces which hold planets, suns, and stardust in set relations to each other so that, even when orbiting, they do not lose their family relationships. The continuity of this correlation is never interrupted. . . .

In my galaxies the paintings are also set at different distances from the wall, protruding or receding. Naturally they have no isolating frames, since the exact interval-space between them makes frames superfluous. The total space of the wall or room-space provides a framing in depth—in fact, a three-dimensional frame without end. These galaxies, although they start from a minimum of three units and expand to as many as nineteen, were only an attempt at endlessness within the enclosure of a room. But I think they could, with careful nurturing, be added to *until the power of the inner magnetism* is exhausted. And if they actually end (physically), their capacity to inspiring continuity would still be great, in that the observer could go on adding more and more units according to his own imagination. He would then be extending the new magnetic field derived from the existing nucleus of the original concept. *[1964]*

FRANZ KLINE   *Ink Drawing*. 1959. Ink on paper.
11 x 8½".

FRANZ KLINE

(1910–1962)

Kline spent three years in London at an academic art school, returning to the United States in 1935. There, he painted scenes of city life and occasional satiric crowd scenes for several years. A friend of most of the leading Abstract Expressionists, above all Jackson Pollock and Willem de Kooning, Kline moved into abstraction only toward 1950. His large black-and-white paintings, with their veering, swiftly plunging broad strokes, were later widely acclaimed for their autographic character.

Somebody will say I have a black-and-white style, or a calligraphic style, but I never started out with that being consciously a style or attitude about painting. Sometimes you do have a definite idea about what you're doing— and at other times it all just seems to disappear. I don't feel mine is the most modern, contemporary, beyond-the-pale, *gone* kind of painting. But then, I don't have that kind of fuck-the-past attitude. I have very strong feelings about individual paintings and painters past and present.

Now, Bonnard at times seems styleless. Someone said of him that he had the rare ability to forget from one day to another what he had done. He added the next day's experience to it, like a child following a balloon. He painted the particular scene itself: in form, the woman can't quite get out of the bathtub. And he's a real colorist. The particular scene itself? Matisse wouldn't let that happen, he didn't let himself get too entranced with anything.

If you're a painter, you're not alone. There's no way to be alone. You think and you care and you're with all the people who care, including the young people who don't know they do yet. Tomlin in his late paintings knew this. Jackson always knew it: that if you meant it enough when you did it, it will mean that much. It's like Caruso and Bjoerling. Bjoerling sounds like Caruso, but if you think of Caruso and McCormack you think of being in the world as you are. Bjoerling sounded like Caruso, but it turned out to be handsome. Bradley Tomlin didn't. Unless . . . Hell, if you look at all the painting in the world today it will probably all turn out to be handsome, I don't know.

The nature of anguish is translated into different forms. What has happened is that we're not through the analytical period of learning what motivates things. If you can figure out the motivation, it's supposed to be all right. But when things are "beside themselves" what matters is the care these things are given by someone. It's assumed that to read something requires an ability beyond that of a handwriting expert, but if someone throws something on a canvas it doesn't require any more care than if someone says, "I don't give a damn."

Like with Jackson: you don't paint the way someone, by observing your life, thinks you *have* to paint, you paint the way you have to in order to *give*, that's life itself, and someone will look and say it is the product of knowing, but it has nothing to do with knowing, it has to do with giving. The question about knowing will naturally be wrong. When you've finished giving, the look surprises you as well as anyone else.   *[1958]*

SOL LeWITT

(1928–   )

In 1965, LeWitt had his first exhibition, in which he presented works based on his theory that a work of art could be entirely dependent on the mental processes of its conception. Soon his aluminum structures covered with baked enamel—airy and full of visual conundrums—gained him an international reputation as a leader of the conceptual art movement.

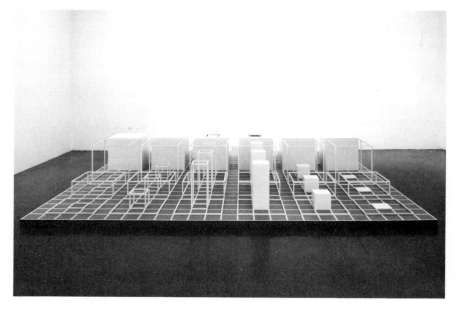

S O L   L E W I T T   *Serial Project No. 1 (ABCD)*. 1966.
Baked enamel on aluminum. 20 x 13'7 x 13'7".

. . . I will refer to the kind of art in which I am involved as conceptual art. In conceptual art the idea or concept is the most important aspect of the work. When an artist uses a conceptual form of art, it means that all of the planning and decisions are made beforehand and the execution is a perfunctory affair. The idea becomes a machine that makes the art. This kind of art is not theoretical or illustrative of theories; it is intuitive, it is involved with all types of mental processes, and it is purposeless. It is usually free from the dependence on the skill of the artist as a craftsman. It is the objective of the artist who is concerned with conceptual art to make his work mentally interesting to the spectator, and therefore usually he would want it to become emotionally dry. There is no reason to suppose, however, that the conceptual artist is out to bore the viewer. It is only the expectation of an emotional kick, to which one conditioned to expressionist art is accustomed, that would deter the viewer from perceiving this art.

. . . Conceptual art is not necessarily logical. The logic of a piece or series of pieces is a device that is used at times, only to be ruined. Logic may be used to camouflage the real intent of the artist, to lull the viewer into the belief that he understands the work, or to infer a paradoxical situation (such as logic vs. illogic). Some ideas are logical in conception and illogical perceptually. The ideas need not be complex. Most ideas that are successful are ludicrously simple. Successful ideas generally have the appearance of simplicity because they seem inevitable. In terms of ideas the artist is free even to surprise himself. Ideas are discovered by intuition.

What the work of art looks like isn't too important. It has to look like something if it has physical form. No matter what form it may finally have it must begin with an idea. It is the process of conception and realization with which the artist is concerned. Once given physical reality by the artist the work is open to the perception of all, including the artist. (I use the word *perception* to mean the apprehension of the sense data, the objective understanding of the idea, and simultaneously a subjective interpretation of both.) The work of art can be perceived only after it is completed.

. . . If the artist carries through his idea and makes it into visible form, then all the steps in the process are of importance. The idea itself, even if not made visual, is as much a work of art as any finished product. All intervening steps—scribbles, sketches, drawings, failed works, models, studies, thoughts, conversations—are of interest. Those that show the thought process of the artist are sometimes more interesting than the final product.

[1967]

ROY LICHTENSTEIN

(1923–   )

While working as a commercial artist in the early 1950s, Lichtenstein began painting in a humorous, Expressionist vein. Toward 1957, he shifted ground and shocked his viewers with his adaptation of the printing techniques of newspapers, particularly comic strips. Later, he turned his attention to other subjects, such as the early history of modern art, satirizing its shibboleths in a style derived from printed sources. In the process he became one of the most celebrated artists associated with the Pop Art movement of the early 1960s.

What is Pop Art?

I don't know—the use of commercial art as subject matter in painting, I suppose. It was hard to get a painting that was despicable enough so that no one would hang it—everybody was hanging everything. It was almost acceptable to hang a dripping paint rag, everybody was accustomed to this. The one thing everyone hated was commercial art; apparently they didn't hate that enough either.

Is Pop Art despicable?

That doesn't sound so good, does it? Well, it *is* an involvement with what I think to be the most brazen and threatening characteristics of our culture, things we hate but which are also powerful in their impingement on us. I think art since Cézanne has become extremely romantic and unrealistic, feeding on art; it is Utopian. It has had less and less to do with the world, it looks inward—neo-Zen and all that. This is not so much a criticism as an obvious observation. Outside is the world; it's there. Pop Art looks out into the world; it appears to accept its environment, which is not good or bad, but different—another state of mind.

Are you anti-experimental?

I think so, and anti-contemplative, anti-nuance, anti-getting-away-from-the-tyranny-of-the-rectangle, anti-movement and -light, anti-mystery, anti-paint-quality, anti-Zen, and anti all of those brilliant ideas of preceding movements which everyone understands so thoroughly.

We like to think of industrialization as being despicable. I don't really know what to make of it. There's something terribly brittle about it. I suppose I would still prefer to sit under a tree with a picnic basket rather than under a gas pump, but signs and comic strips are interesting as subject matter. There are certain things that are usable, forceful, and vital about commercial art. We're using those things—but we're not really advocating stupidity, international teen-agerism, and terrorism.   *[1963]*

R I C H A R D   L I N D N E R

(1901–1978)

German-born, Lindner fled Nazi Germany in 1933 for France, and arrived in the United States in 1941. His first American exhibition in 1954 included many paintings of children depicted as small, distorted adults in a style related to between-the-wars German New Objectivity. By the late 1950s Lindner had incorporated motifs from New York City life, hardened his contours, and introduced certain local effects, such as the neon-lighted emporiums of Times Square. These practices sometimes led his viewers to associate him with the Pop Artists, although Lindner did not share their preoccupation with the popular media and remained aesthetically faithful to his German sources.

Subject matter for me is always a man, a woman, a child, and a dog. Dogs, like children, are the real grown-ups. And dogs and their owners have always amused me. The other day I was in an elevator and there was an old lady holding a poodle. She said to it, "Say hello to the nice gentleman!" Anyway, I never use a model. Models disturb me. They want to talk, and I don't like that. I never do color sketches. I do color on the canvas. About color: I have always felt that in order to be a good painter one should be color-blind, because color doesn't have to be seen. It needs only to be felt. When I told that to some of my students, they thought I was crazy!

Anyway, my paintings have a lot to do with balance and composition. I like structure. As for the women in my paintings, you have only to look at my wife to know that the women I paint are not at all my type. Sometimes the women are very big for reasons of pictorial balance. But, of course, those women have haunted me. Still, I have never really been hurt by a woman. All my women have stayed friends. No. I'm not in the least attracted to the kind of women I paint. However, I think that one must deal with one's complexes. . . .

But, you know, my work is really a reflection of Germany of the twenties. It was the only time the Germans were any good. On the other hand, my creative nourishment comes from New York, and from pictures I see in American magazines or on television. America is really a fantastic place!

I admire the Pop artists—Warhol and Lichtenstein and Oldenburg—but I'm not one of them—never was. My real influences have been Giotto and Piero della Francesca, timeless and ageless artists. I look at them all the time! And I hope that something of their strength has come into my pictures. Basically it's what I'm aiming for—that kind of structural solidity . . . that kind of power!   *[1978]*

It is all awareness of reality.

In a chinese vase we can see all that the artist rejected in order to have as close an approximation as possible to his response to reality. We can feel as he felt looking at his work. The same response is made continually over a thousand years. Proving its reality. That is what art is about.

There is no such thing as "contemerary" art. Any material may be used but the theme is the same and the response is the same for all art work.

I want to emphasize the fact that we all have the same experience and the same conserm, but the artist must know exactly what the experience is. He must pursue the truth relentlessly. Once he sees this fact his feet are on the path. If you want to know the truth you will know it.

The manipulation of materials in art work is a result of this state of mind. The artist works by awareness of his own state of mind

AGNES MARTIN

(1912–)

Born in Canada, Martin came to the United States in 1932 to attend Columbia University and then settled in the Southwest. After producing a body of lyrical abstractions relating to the New Mexico desert in the late 1940s, Martin moved back to New York in the early 1950s. There, she reduced her pictorial vocabulary in order to express intuitions of a rhythmic universe in an almost musical sequence of recessive, often white forms. Her work since the mid-1950s has increasingly reflected her experience of light and color in the New Mexico desert, to which she returned in 1967.

ROBERT MORRIS

(1931–   )

During the mid-1960s a number of artists in New York were engaged in reducing the terms of their art to a primary condition of simplicity. Morris, one of the most articulate and intellectual among them, developed a theory of perception that justified his reduction of his early sculptures into completely self-contained "gestalts" that could be seized immediately, in their entirety, without subordinate relationships.

. . . The simpler regular and irregular [polyhedrons] maintain the maximum resistance to being confronted as objects with separate parts. They seem to present lines of fracture by which they could divide for easy part-to-part relationships to be established. I term these simple rectangular and irregular polyhedrons "unitary" forms. Sculpture involving unitary forms, being bound together as it is with a kind of energy provided by the gestalt, often elicits the complaint among critics that such works are beyond analysis.

Characteristic of a gestalt is that once it is established all the information about it, qua gestalt, is exhausted. (One does not, for example, seek the gestalt of a gestalt.) Furthermore, once it is established it does not disintegrate. One is then both free of the shape and bound to it. Free or released because of the exhaustion of information about it, as shape, and bound to it because it remains constant and indivisible.

Simplicity of shape does not necessarily equate with simplicity of experience. Unitary forms do not reduce relationships. They order them. If the predominant, hieratic nature of the unitary form functions as a constant, all those particularizing relations of scale, proportion, etc., are not thereby canceled. Rather they are bound more cohesively and indivisibly together. The magnification of this single most important sculptural value, shape, together with greater unification and integration of every other essential sculptural value makes on the one hand, the multipart, inflected formats of past sculpture extraneous, and on the other, establishes both a new limit and a new freedom for sculpture.   *[1966]*

ROBERT MOTHERWELL   *Nip and Tuck.* 1984.
Collage and acrylic on canvas panel. 40 x 30″.

ROBERT MOTHERWELL

(1915–   )

After growing up and attending college in California, Motherwell traveled in Europe and then, in 1940, settled permanently in New York. His association with émigré European artists such as Max Ernst and the Chilean Matta spurred him to experiment in the Surrealist idiom. In 1944 he had his first one-man show at Peggy Guggenheim's Art of This Century Gallery, showing paintings and collages. Thereafter, Motherwell articulated the views of the Abstract Expressionist generation in his writings as well as in activities as editor, spokesman, and friend of the New York School painters. Motherwell is best known for his extended series of meditations on the Spanish Civil War, the Elegy to the Spanish Republic, *and for his large, free-form abstractions, but he has also produced a large oeuvre of collages and prints.*

I believe that the New York School, like other schools of what is called modern art, has as part of its background of thought those fragments of felt thought which, taken as a whole, we call the "symbolist" aesthetic, in modern French poetry—whose formulation began with Edgar Allan Poe and Charles Baudelaire and reached its climax in France during the decade 1885–1895, though its influence has extended into our own time, in the persons of a number of poets, of many Occidental countries, Valéry, Yeats, Joyce, Rilke, Lorca, Apollinaire, Eliot, and cummings, among others. The influence of the symbolist aesthetic is a proposition that is perhaps impossible to demonstrate, and, if it represents a truth, represents a truth of which, I am sure, many members of the New York School are unaware: perhaps the best evidence would be if, in thinking of that background of thought, the character of the paintings as they were viewed became more clear. My emphasis here is that modern art, of which the New York School is a part, has a history.   *[n.d.]*

An odd contradiction, if the layman were correct in his unconscious assumption that an artist begins with reality and ends with art: the converse is true—to the degree that this dichotomy has any truth—the artist begins with art, and through it arrives at reality. If one were to ask such-and-such a painter what he felt about anything, his just response—though he seldom makes it—would be to paint it, and in painting it, to find out. . . . It could be that, in trying to paint it, he finds that he cannot, that something else keeps appearing on the canvas; that is, in regard to this thing under discussion, he finds that he has no real feelings at all.   *[n.d.]*

That painting and sculpture are not skills that can be taught in reference to preestablished criteria, whether academic or modern, but a process, whose content is found, subtle, and deeply felt; that no true artist ends with the style that he expected to have when he began, any more than anyone's life unrolls in the particular manner that one expected when young; that it is only by giving oneself up completely to the painting medium that one finds oneself and one's own style; that it is only someone who himself is engaged in this process who is likely to be able to "read" the truest works of a period when they first appear—such is the experience of the School of New York.
[1951]

The ancient Chinese painters, who did all the writing about art in China and almost gave the word to the wordless, used to say that no truth is true that is not subtle. I mean the same thing when I say that the criterion of truth for me is adequacy; truth is not a property of reality—reality just is what it is, whatever it is, just as yellow is yellow, and neither true nor false; truth is a property of symbolizations of reality, not reality itself. Truth exists for men alone, because men alone symbolize. From this point of view, works of art are true or false (as well as beautiful or ugly, and good or evil), as with propositions and mathematical formulas. This point of view enforces upon you the obligation to be very accurate in ascertaining what a work of art is really symbolizing.   *[1954]*

Generally, I use few colors: yellow ochre, vermilion, orange, cadmium green, ultramarine blue. Mainly, I use each color as simply symbolic: ochre for the earth, green for the grass, blue for the sky and sea. I guess that black and white, which I use most often, tend to be the protagonists. . . . I often begin to paint on the floor. The paint often drips too much when the painting is upright. One can control the paint better when the canvas is lying down flat, and at the same time there is a less restricted view. I can walk around it, for example. I tend to the plane surface, and miraculously, the three-dimensional space takes care of itself. I finish the painting upright, right-side up! Physical limitations restrict us all. I would paint much larger if it wouldn't be such an enormous project to move and to store canvases. As it is, I restrict myself to a maximum of eighteen feet. I tend to be excited with either a tiny, or a very large format. It's the format, not the subject that determines a lot in the painting. I don't like to use the usual "easel-size" canvas; a different size, greater or smaller, sharpens one's sense of space. Thus, easel size has always been more "difficult" for me. (But my collages are easel size, probably because of the scale of the "found" elements.) I don't exploit so-called accidents in painting. I accept them if they seem appropriate. There is no such thing as an "accident" really; it is a kind of casualness: it happened, so let it be, so to speak. One doesn't want a picture to look "made," like an automobile or a loaf of bread in waxed paper. Precision belongs to the world of machinery—which has its own forms of the beautiful. One admires Léger. But machinery created with brush and paint is ridiculous, all the same. . . . I agree with Renoir, who loved everything hand-made.   *[1963]*

REUBEN NAKIAN

(1897–)

During the late 1940s Nakian experimented with a free, Expressionist way of composing sculptures with chicken-wire armatures covered with soaked burlap. He also made swift, baroquely scored terra-cotta sketches that aligned him with the Abstract Expressionist spirit, although his themes were drawn largely from classical mythology.

The [Metropolitan] Museum was a continental university for me—a gold mine for young students. They were in plaster—no matter, form is form be it mud or marble. In those days the attendance was not too much—better for studying. A great museum will civilize you more than a dozen universities. Art should seep into your pores by contact. A museum of plaster casts should be reestablished. This generation flies off from Picasso and falls flat on its face—instead of fledging from the pedestals of the past.

Art is born out of art. Cézanne said he'd hoped to be able to add a link to the chain. Cézanne was a true oracle—not ambiguous like the Delphian. Art should be aristocratic, elegant, with gardens and beautiful costumes, and horses and people speaking a clear and cultivated language. Like Goya and Frans Hals—aristocrats to their fingertips.

One of the wonderful things about being a sculptor is that after forty years of training I can appreciate old works so keenly; I can understand a little piece—a fragment—and reconstruct an entire figure. But I never "use" art history. I refer to it for subject matter and enjoy it for its ideas.

I look more to painting than to sculpture for concepts, for grandeur, in other words, for Art. There's no one to help in sculpture.

The great tragedy today is the death of Europe—it was born and died.

I think Ingres has the edge over Delacroix, form is greater than color.

Art is becoming more difficult—so much has already been done. The first artists were like divers who just had to go a few yards offshore to bring back a new shell. The next ones had to go further and further—now you have to swim ten miles out, almost killing yourself. A new sculpture is like a strange thing fought from the sea.   *[1958]*

LOUISE NEVELSON

(1900–)

During the 1950s Nevelson began to exhibit ensembles of wood sculptures painted black and arranged to relate a poetic theme. She later used found parts such as table legs or discarded wood radio cases to assemble boxed images that she then arranged in walls, often painted a uniform soot-black. These were celebrated as environmental sculptures, winning her worldwide attention.

Another thing about creation is that every day it is like it gave birth, and it's always kind of an innocent and refreshing. So it's always virginal to me, and it's always a surprise. I feel in principle or in the deep relationship of the vision and the object and the subject that there is a *unity* and that is *fresh* constantly. You make a living thing through your livingness. You move, you live, you breathe, so it enters . . . enters . . . enters. Each piece seems to have a life of its own. Every little piece or every big piece that I make becomes a very living thing to me, very living. I could make a million pieces; the next piece gives me a whole new thing. It is a new center. Life in total at that particular time. And that's why it's right. That reaffirms my life.

Now in the reality that I built for myself, what did I do? I took one tone. I gave the work order; I neutralized it by one tone. One of the reasons I originally started with black was to see the forms more clearly. Black seemed the strongest and clearest. But then somehow as I worked and worked and worked . . . it pleased me. You see, one thing about my way of thinking— I didn't want it to be sculpture and I didn't want it to be painting. I didn't want to make something. I think it's stupid to want to make anything. Why make anything? You know, there's an awful lot of crap on this earth and we don't want to fill it with any more. Let the air breathe. But—the thing is that it's something *beyond* that we make. My work has never been black to me to begin with. I never think of it that way. I don't make sculpture and it isn't black and it isn't wood or anything, because I wanted something else. I wanted an essence.

I have given shadow a form. And I gave reflection a form. I used glass for reflections, then I used mirror. Now we know that shadow and reflection, in a way, have a form—but not really an architectural or sculptural form. But one can do that. So I consider that I am an architect of shadow, and I'm an architect of reflection. Those are titles I gave to myself.   *[1976]*

BARNETT NEWMAN

(1905–1970)

The combative attempt to free themselves from subordination to European ideas led the Abstract Expressionists into considerable verbalization. Newman was one of the most articulate in the group and often set out to clarify its aims and to demonstrate the originality of the Americans after the Second World War. His own work—vast fields of flat color divided by narrow vertical bands—was considered innovative, and provided the model for many of the so-called Color Field painters.

If we could describe the art of this, the first half of the twentieth century, in a sentence, it would read as the search for something to paint; just as, were we to do the same for modern art as a whole, it must read as the critical preoccupation of artists with solving the *technical* problems of the painting medium.

   Here is the dividing line in the history of art! Whereas every serious artist throughout history has had to solve the problems of his medium, it has always been personal, a problem of talent. It was not until the Impressionists that a group of artists set themselves a communal task—the exploration of a technical problem together. With them, talent became axiomatic. What to do with it? That has become the earmark of modern art movements. This critical reevaluation of the artist's role, this refusal to continue blindly the ritual of what art professors like to call tradition, has become a dividing line in art that is sharp indeed. For were all knowledge, written and oral, of the dates of production of those great works that make up the art treasury of

Western Europe to be lost (let us hope the work is not) all of them, from Veronese to Delacroix would become a dateless jumble. No man could trace its chronological progress with accuracy, so unified is its general appearance. Were this jumble, however, to include the work of anybody after Courbet, beginning with the Impressionists, it would segregate itself at once. For good or bad, Impressionism has given art an unmistakably different look.

The artist today has more feeling and consequently more understanding for a Marquesas Island fetish than for the Greek figure. This is a curious paradox when we consider that we, as the products of Western European culture, have been brought up within the framework of Greek aesthetic standards—the tradition of the Greek style—and have had no intimate contact with the primitive way of life. All we concretely know of the primitive life are its art objects. Its culture patterns are not normally experienced, certainly not easily. Yet these art objects excite us and we feel a bond of understanding with the primitive artist's intentions, problems, and sensibility, whereas the Grecian form is so foreign to our present aesthetic interests that it virtually has no inspirational use. One might say that it has lost its culture factor. . . .

The Surrealists have been the only ones who have made a serious and vigorous attempt to revive Greek plasticity and sensibility, within a context of tragic subject matter. Inevitably they had to go outside the Greek sphere to achieve their tragic content; to give up the Greek hope. De Chirico could only use the Grecian form to express his yearning for his lost Greece. He degenerated into inanities as soon as he tried to say more than his despair. The Surrealists who followed were able to continue where de Chirico ended but only by moving away from the Greek into the fantastic world of the Oceanic magic-makers. They were able to maintain the highly polished surface of the Greek form but they found that this form was barren of the tragic subject they sought, and they had to assume the subject matter of the primitive world to express their Freudian terror, in order to reach what they thought this terror represented—the higher reality of tragedy. In other words, to express the tragic concept they sought they had to go beyond the forgotten to the unfamiliar.   *[c. 1944]*

ISAMU NOGUCHI

(1904–   )

After an apprenticeship to Brancusi during the late 1920s, Noguchi abandoned representational sculpture, beginning to work with jointed slabs of sheet metal and marble held by gravity alone. His interest in organic form was matched by his great

ISAMU NOGUCHI   *The Self.* 1957. Iron.
33⅞ x 8¼ x 9".

love for living rock, in which he carved monumental sculptures. In addition to set and costume designs for Martha Graham's modern dance theater, Noguchi extended his work to elaborate public projects—garden landscapes and sculptural ensembles covering many acres. These and other masterworks have marked him as one of the great creators of the twentieth century.

The essence of sculpture is for me the perception of space, the continuum of our existence. All dimensions are but measures of it, as in the relative perspective of our vision lie volume, line, point, giving shape, distance, proportion. Movement, light, and time itself are also qualities of space. Space is otherwise inconceivable. These are the essences of sculpture and as our concepts of them change so must our sculpture change.

Since our experiences of space are, however, limited to momentary segments of time, growth must be the core of existence. We are reborn, and so in art as in nature there is growth, by which I mean change attuned to the living. Thus growth can only be new, for awareness is the ever-changing adjustment of the human psyche to chaos. If I say that growth is the constant transfusion of human meaning into the encroaching void, then how great is our need today when our knowledge of the universe has filled space with energy, driving us toward a greater chaos and new equilibriums.

I say it is the sculptor who orders and animates space, gives it meaning.

[1946]

CLAES OLDENBURG

(1929–)

Along with Allan Kaprow, Jim Dine, and Robert Whitman, Oldenburg entered the public art scene as a maker of Happenings and environments. He then made a satiric group of popular objects (such as hamburgers) blown up to gigantic scale, and went on to create a humorous idiom in sculpture by fashioning "soft objects" in sewn, stuffed vinyl. A leader of the Pop movement, Oldenburg is a major American satirical artist whose projects extend considerably beyond the Pop program, often hinting at a critique of social and political injustice.

. . . My work makes a great demand on a collector. I have tried to make it in every way so that anyone who comes into contact with it is greatly inconvenienced. That is to say, made aware of its existence, and of my principles.

The cloth work is decidedly "sculptural" . . . by which I mean that it emphasizes masses, simple and articulated. It deemphasizes color. What the period of "sculptural" painting has left is the fluidity of the surface, which in these works is actual—that is because they are sculpture, the unillusory, tangible realm. . . . The dynamic element here is flaccidity where in the paint it was the paint action and the sparkle of light . . . that is, the tendency of a hard material actually to be soft not look soft (so it is a concretization or a naïve translation of painting).

. . . Gravity is my favorite form creator. *[1966]*

I use naive imitation. This is not because I have no imagination or because I wish to say something about the everyday world. I imitate 1. objects and 2. created objects, for example signs. Objects made without the intention of making "art" and which naïvely contain a functional contemporary magic. I try to carry these even further through my own naïveté, which is not artificial. Further, i.e., charge them more intensely, elaborate their reference. I do not try to make "art" out of them. This must be understood. I imitate these because I want people to get accustomed to recognizing the power of objects, a didactic aim. If I alter, which I do usually, I do not alter for "art" and I do not alter to express myself, I alter to unfold the object, and to add to it other object-qualities, forces. The object remains an object, only expanded and less specific.

This elevation of sensibility above bourgeois values, which is also a simplicity of return to truth and first principles, will (hopefully) destroy the notion of art and give the object back its power. Then the magic inherent in the universe will be restored and people will live in sympathetic religious exchange with the materials and objects surrounding them. . . .

My single-minded aim is to give existence to (my) fantasy. This means the creation of a parallel reality according to the rules of (my) fantasy.

I am compelled to do this to a greater degree than most painters.

This world cannot ever hope to really exist and so it exists entirely through illusion, but illusion is employed as subversively, as convincingly as possible. This critical moment is my act of seeing. The rest is the patient reconstruction of this hallucination and successive hallucinations which arise in the course of making.   *[1966]*

DENNIS OPPENHEIM

(1938–)

Oppenheim produced both earthworks and indoor installations beginning in 1968, working his way toward the gigantic fantasy machines that seem to relate to the machine aesthetic (and its ironic commentators) of the early part of the century.

In 1967, there was a lot of attention giving alternatives to the prevailing sculptural apparatus. Some of the alternatives to these conditions that existed then, namely minimalism, found themselves retreating further and further from the object. In other words, minimalism being the continued kind of stripping down of the emotional state and the supplanting of a cold kind of objective, logical handling of form and so as this kind of rationale continued, the stripping down left or departed from the object and began looking for a kind of extra object phenomena. Now, some of this extra object phenomena was manifested in terms of conceptual, within a conceptual framework, that is the thinking process kind of detached from the physical objectification of the work. . . . So, the site-markers' function is kind of conceptual methods of claiming, in this case, existing forms that were not made by the artist so, in this case, they are similar to the Duchampian found object.   *[1977]*

ROBERT RAUSCHENBERG *Drift*. 1956.
Combine painting. 56 x 43".

ROBERT RAUSCHENBERG

(1925–)

By the mid-1950s the Texas-born Rauschenberg was already notable for his new techniques of combining paint with real objects such as photographs, string, cups, and quilts to present vivid, kaleidoscopic images that frequently refer to topical events. He called these paintings "combines." Later, he developed silk-screen techniques and used frottage (the Surrealist technique of rubbing a surface to produce an image), thus opening the way to the use of a commercial imagery in Pop Art.

Any incentive to paint is as good as any other. There is no poor subject.

Painting is always strongest when in spite of composition, color, etc., it appears as a fact, or an inevitability, as opposed to a souvenir or arrangement.

Painting relates to both art and life. Neither can be made. (I try to act in that gap between the two.)

A pair of socks is no less suitable to make a painting with than wood, nails, turpentine, oil, and fabric.

A canvas is never empty.   *[1959]*

AD REINHARDT

(1913–1967)

An abstract geometric painter in the late 1930s and the 1940s, Reinhardt was already moving toward the austere, somewhat mystical paintings for which he gained fame in the mid-1950s—paintings that eventually eschewed all color but tones of black. Reinhardt was an associate of the Abstract Expressionists and spent considerable energy as a stringent critic of the burgeoning commercialism of the art world in the postwar years. His witty commentaries were couched in both written statements and cartoons.

Separation, in the past, of painting from walls and books, from architecture and sculpture, from poetry and theater, from religion, history, and nature, from decoration, documentation, and description, was achievement in awareness.

Separation, in history, of fine and liberal arts from labor and business, from trade skills and entertainment, from professions of pleasing and selling, was achievement in freedom.

Dumping together, in three American Fauve decades (social-real-surreal-abstract-expressionism) of painting with primitivity, suffering, propaganda, subconsciousness, pleasure, sadism, publicity, symbolism, poverty, spleen, practicality, solvency, life, love, hate, fate, folk, instruction, irrationality, action personality, and conspicuous patronization, was achievement in romancing.

Painting is special, separate, a matter of meditation and contemplation, for me, no physical action or social sport. "As much consciousness as possible." Clarity, completeness, quintessence, quiet. No noise, no schmutz, no schmerz, no Fauve schwarmerei. Perfection, passiveness, consonance, consummateness. No palpitations, no gesticulation, no grotesquerie. Spirituality, serenity, absoluteness, coherence. No automatism, no accident, no anxiety, no catharsis, no chance. Detachment, disinterestedness, thoughtfulness, transcendence. No humbugging, no buttonholing, no exploitation, no mixing things up. No lack of loftiness, no humorlessness.   *[1955]*

LARRY RIVERS

(1923–)

Rivers began as a professional jazz musician in the early 1940s, but soon switched to painting, studying with both Hans Hofmann and William Baziotes. The Abstract Expressionist loose-brush technique and fragmentary imagery served Rivers as a starting point for the art he began to exhibit in the mid-1950s. His larger works came to include both historical references and social criticisms.

In relation to the dominant interests of contemporary painting, the concern of the generation of painters a little older than myself and their followers, my work bears the stamp of a revolutionary, for these prevailing sentiments antagonize me and inspire me to do away with their effects. In relation to my own meanderings, disregarding what others do, feel, or think, my work at moments seems an attempt to solidify my identity with the "great" painters. I can only hope to be original with what they have given me.

My approach is of no importance. I mean this. Something exists before me in some manner and I determine the relationship between what I choose to see and what I take from the palette to the canvas. What *is* important is that the mind may make of it something crucial and arresting. At this point it is stupid to think the painter who paints looking at something is a lover of "things" and it is just as stupid to think nonrepresentational painters love "shapes" and hate "things." An artist is moved by himself and his anxiety about what he should do.   *[1956]*

JAMES ROSENQUIST

(1933–)

From his experience as a billboard painter Rosenquist derived a method of painting that quickly associated him with the Pop movement. His use of industrial techniques and imagery was imaginative, and also flexible enough for him to be able to include a note of social criticism in his huge mural-sized paintings.

I'm amazed and excited and fascinated about the way things are thrust at us, the way this invisible screen that's a couple of feet in front of our mind and our senses is attacked by radio and television and visual communications, through things larger than life, the impact of things thrown at us, at such a speed and with such a force that painting and the attitudes toward painting and communication through doing a painting now seem very old-fashioned. . . .

I think we have a free society, and the action that goes on in this free society allows encroachments, as a commercial society. So I geared myself, like an advertiser or a large company, to this visual inflation—in commercial advertising which is one of the foundations of our society. I'm living in it, and it has such impact and excitement in its means of imagery. Painting is probably more exciting than advertising—so why shouldn't it be done with that power and gusto, with that impact. I see very few paintings with the impact that I've felt, that I feel and try to do in my work. . . . My metaphor, if that is what you can call it, is my relations to the power of commercial advertising which is in turn related to our free society, the visual inflation which accompanies the money that produces box tops and space cadets.

When I use a combination of fragments of things, the fragments or objects or real things are caustic to one another, and the title is also caustic to the fragments. . . . The images are expendable, and the images are in the painting and therefore the painting is also expendable. I only hope for a colorful shoehorn to get the person off, to turn him on to his own feelings. . . .

I treat the billboard image as it is, so apart from nature. I paint it as a reproduction of other things; I try to get as far away from the nature as possible. *[1964]*

MARK ROTHKO

(1903–1970)

Born in Dvinsk, Russia, Rothko came to the United States at the age of ten and was educated first in Portland, Oregon, then for two years at Yale University, and during the 1920s, sporadically, at the Art Students' League. Beginning as a vaguely Expressionist, figurative painter, Rothko moved steadily toward a symbolic idiom in which he drew upon mythical themes during the late 1930s and early 1940s. He then began to eliminate even symbolic references. By 1947 he had arrived at the luminous reductions—simply divided canvases usually in glowing colors—for which he is celebrated. Rothko devoted the last years of his life to ensembles of paintings such as those in the Tate Gallery (originally designed for the Seagram Building in New York), the murals at Harvard, and the Houston Chapel, his crowning achievement. As one of the founders of the Abstract Expressionist school, Rothko played an important role, defending the right of a painter to explore spiritual themes in an abstract language.

Why the most gifted painters of our time should be preoccupied with the forms of the archaic and the myths from which they have stemmed, why Negro sculpture and archaic Greeks should have been catalyzers of our present-day art, we can leave to historians and psychologists. But the fact remains that our age [is] distinguished by its distortions, and everywhere the gifted men, whether they seat the model in their studio or seek the forms, all have distorted the present to conform with the forms of Nineveh, the Nile, or the Mesopotamian plain. . . . To say that the modern artist has been fascinated by the formal aspects of archaic art is not tenable. Any serious artist will agree that a form is significant insofar as it is expressive of that noble and austere formality which these archaic things possess. . . .

I am neither the first nor the last compelled irretrievably to deal with the chimeras that seem the most profound message of our time.

The real essence of great portraiture of all time is the artist's eternal interest in the human figure, character, and emotions—in short in the human drama. That Rembrandt expressed it by posing a sitter is irrelevant. We do not know the sitter but we are intensely aware of the drama. The archaic Greeks, on the other hand, used as their models the inner visions which they had of their gods. And in our day, our visions are the fulfillment of our own needs. . . . What is indicated here is that the artist's real model is an ideal which embraces all of human drama rather than the appearance of a particular individual.

Today the artist is no longer constrained by the limitation that all of man's experience is expressed by his outward appearance. Freed from the need of describing a particular person, the possibilities are endless. The whole of man's experience becomes his model, and in that sense it can be said that all of art is a portrait of an idea. . . .

If our titles recall the known myths of antiquity, we have used them again because they are the eternal symbols upon which we must fall back to express basic psychological ideas. They are the symbols of man's primitive fears and motivations, no matter in which land or what time, changing only in detail but never in substance. . . .

Our presentation of these myths, however, must be in our own terms which are at once more primitive and more modern than the myths themselves—more primitive because we seek the primeval and atavistic roots of the ideas rather than their graceful classical version; more modern than the myths themselves because we must redescribe their implications through our own experience. Those who think that the world of today is more gentle and graceful than the primeval and predatory passions from which these myths spring, are either not aware of reality or do not wish to see it in art. The myth holds us, therefore, not through its romantic flavor, not through the remembrance of the beauty of some bygone age, not through the possibilities of fantasy, but because it expresses to us something real and existing in ourselves, as it was to those who first stumbled upon the symbols to give them life.   *[1943]*

I insist upon the equal existence of the world engendered in the mind and the world engendered by God outside of it. If I have faltered in the use of familiar objects, it is because I refuse to mutilate their appearance for the sake of an action which they are too old to serve; or for which, perhaps, they had never been intended.

I love both the object and the dream far too much to have them effervesced into the insubstantiality of memory and hallucination. The abstract artist has given material existence to many unseen worlds and tempi. But I repudiate his denial of the anecdote just as I repudiate the denial of the material existence of the whole of reality. For art to me is an anecdote of the spirit, and the only means of making concrete the purpose of its varied quickness and stillness.

Rather be prodigal than niggardly I would sooner confer anthropomorphic attributes upon a stone, then dehumanize the slightest possibility of consciousness. *[1945]*

Pictures must be miraculous: the instant one is completed the intimacy between the creation and the creator is ended. He is an outsider. The picture must be for him, as for anyone experiencing it later, a revelation, an unexpected and unprecedented resolution of an eternally familiar need. *[1947]*

If I must place my trust somewhere, I would invest it in the psyche of sensitive observers who are free of the conventions of understanding. I would have no apprehension about the use they would make of these pictures for the needs of their own spirits. For if there is both need and spirit there is bound to be a real transaction. *[1954]*

GEORGE SEGAL

(1924–)

In the late 1950s Segal developed his unique technique for taking plaster casts from life. These he combined with real objects, making tableaux of real-life situations that introduced a completely new discourse in American sculpture.

I introduced a lot of realism into my work as a correction to certain excesses I noticed in abstract painting of the fifties. I considered it a healthy restorative to references that had become increasingly pale and tenuous—divorced from life experiences.

I love to watch people. I'm interested in their gestures and I'm interested in their experiences and mine. In the early years I spent a lot of time trying to look as bluntly as I could at people in their environments. Very often I saw them against garish light, illuminated signs. I saw them against visually vivid objects that were considered low class, anti-art, un-art, kitsch, disreputable, and I suppose this sculpture* is like some of those attitudes of that time.

Driving home from New York at two o'clock in the morning, as usual, I saw that scene—a fellow reaching up to pluck off the last letter from an illuminated sign and it was like seeing an exalted moment. It was like seeing an epiphany. But by the time I poked my wife and said, "Hey, look at that!" he was bending over and the scene looked totally different. I remembered the gesture of reaching upward and the man's body silhouetted against a wall of emanating light which appeared to dissolve his edges.

I was astounded at how intense these things seem. I was attracted to the fact that the plastic and the illuminated light were disreputable. I rebuilt those objects, emphasizing a set of formal qualities. I went to a sign shop and got the three-dimensional letters and electrified them myself. I built the wall to radiate fluorescent light. I bought plastic sheets, translucent white plastic. First I built a six-inch box and it wasn't deep enough, so I built a twelve-inch box and I got the light quality of the sign. I constructed the sign and got a fellow to pose the way I remembered. There was something about the formality, the proportions, and the qualities of emanating light that attracted me. I was composing with bits of real objects from the real world: the emanating light was real and it had an extraordinary set of associated, expressive qualities and the gesture of the man reaching upward had its own set of expressive qualities. It was like finding diamonds in the garbage.   *[1978]*

* His *Cinema* of 1963.

DAVID SMITH

(1906–1965)

During the 1930s, Smith began experimenting with welded metal techniques developed by the Spanish sculptor Julio González. His work rapidly evolved as he began to use found parts and assemble free-standing sculptures with specific symbolic associations. After the Second World War he was associated with the painters in the Abstract Expressionist group, but went on to produce a large oeuvre of extremely varied work. Smith is regarded as the most important sculptor of his generation within the New York School.

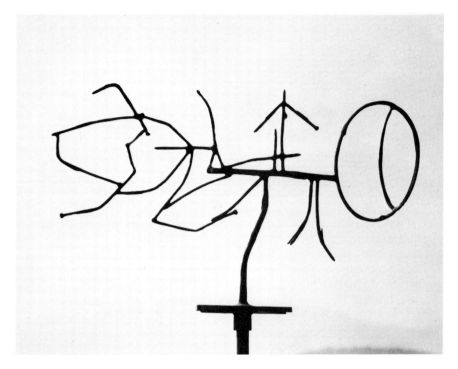

D A V I D S M I T H   *O Drawing.* 1957. Bronze. 31 x 50⅛ x 1½".

The artist has been the element of nature, and the arbiter of nature; he who has sat on a cloud and viewed it from afar, but at the same time has identified himself as one of nature's parts. The true artist views nature from his own time. The conflict with the audience is often one of time-nature regard rather than art. The hostile audience views nature in the rosy past. The artist views nature expertly before making his statement. The audience usually makes a prejudiced statement about nature before viewing it inexpertly. This makes a breach even before the mode of interpretation is considered. The artist's creative position to nature is much the same as that of primitive man. He does not take the scientific view of all important man and view nature as "it." He is the compassionate emotional man who is unquestioning, who accepts himself as a part of nature viewing nature as "thou."

I do not today recognize the lines drawn between painting and sculpture aesthetically. Practically, the law of gravity is involved, but the sculptor is no longer limited to marble, the monolithic concept, and classic fragments. His conception is as free as that of the painter. His wealth of response is as great as his draftsmanship. Plastically he is more related to pagan cultures with directives from Cubism and Constructivism. Modern tools and technics grant the expression of complete self-identity from origin of idea to material finish. His work can show who he is, what he stands for, with all the fluency he desires, for every step and stroke is his own. The stream of time and the flow of art make it plain that no matter what the sculptor's declaration or individual vision, he cannot conceive outside his time. His art conception takes place in dialectic order. The flow of art, the time of man still places him within his own period, out of which he cannot fly, and within which all other men exist. For no object he has seen, no fantasy he envisions, no world he knows is outside that of other men. No man has seen what another has not, or lacks the components and power to assemble. It is impossible to produce an unperceivable work. I believe only artists truly understand art, because art is best understood by following the visionary path of the creator who produces it. The Philistines will not attempt the projection. A work of art is produced by an expert. There must be expertness in its perception. There are degrees of expertness—some come close, some are on the fringe, some pretend; expertness naturally applies to both the artists creating and the audience response.

I was acquainted with metalworking before studying painting. When my painting developed into constructions leaving the canvas, I was then a sculptor, with no formal training in the sculpture tradition. When the constructions turned into metal—lead, brass, aluminum, combined with stone and coral in 1932—nothing technically was involved outside of factory knowledge. The equipment I use, my supply of material comes from factory study and duplicates as nearly as possible the production equipment used in making a locomotive. I have no aesthetic interest in tool marks or surface embroidery or molten puddles. My aim in material function is the same as in locomotive building: to arrive at a given functional form in the most efficient manner. The locomotive method bows to no accepted theory of fabrication. It utilizes the respective merits of casting, forging, riveting, arc and gas welding, brazing, silver soldering. It combines bolts, screws, shrink fits—all because of their respective efficiency in arriving at an object or form in function.

I do not work with a conscious and specific conviction about a piece of sculpture. It is always open to change and new association. It should be a celebration, one of surprise, not one rehearsed. The sculpture work is a statement of my identity. It is a part of my work stream, related to my past works, the three or four in process, and the work yet to come. In a sense it is never finished. Only the essence is stated, the key presented to the beholder for further travel. My belief in this direction is better stated by Picasso who once said, "A picture is not thought out and settled beforehand. While it is being done, it changes as one's thoughts change. And when it is finished it still goes on changing, according to the state of mind of whoever is looking at it. A picture lives a life like a living creature, undergoing the changes imposed on us by our own life from day to day. This is natural, as the picture lives only through the man who is looking at it." There is no conceptual difference between painting and sculpture. Both Picasso and Matisse are sculptors of great origins. The position of creating does not change for them just because the medium changes. *[1935]*

When I begin a sculpture I am not always sure how it is going to end. In a way it has a relationship to the work before, it is in continuity to the previous work—it often holds a promise or a gesture toward the one to follow.

I do not often follow its path from a previously conceived drawing. If I have a strong feeling about its start, I do not need to know its end, the battle for solution is the most important. If the end of the work seems too complete, and final, posing no question, I am apt to work back from the end, that in its finality it poses a question and not a solution. Sometimes when I start a sculpture, I begin with only a realized part, the rest is travel to be unfolded much in the order of a dream. The conflict for realization is what makes art, not its certainty, nor its technique or material. I do not look for total success. If a part is successful, the rest clumsy or incomplete, I can still call it finished, if I've said anything new by finding any relationship which I might call an origin. I will not change an error if it feels right, for the error is more human than perfection.

I make no claim for my work method over other media. It is not one of my private experience. It is one part of art that can definitely be taught or learned by the American aptitude for technics. A course in industrial high schools or an eight-week course in trade school suffices. The direct method, the part to the whole concept, quantity to quality, is not an exclusive approach, and does not exclude my use of other media.

A certain feeling for form will develop with technical skill, but imaginative form or aesthetic vision is not a guarantee for high technique. I have seen paper cut-outs that were finer art than piles of precious metals.

My own workshop is a small factory with the same make and quality tools used by production factories.

Art is a paradox that has no laws to bind it. Laws set can always be violated. That confuses the pragmatic mind. There may exist conventionalized terminologies and common designations for periods, but no rules bind, either to the material substances from which it is made or the mental process of its concept. It is created by man's imagination in relation to his time. When art exists, it becomes tradition. When it is created, it represents a unity that did not exist before.

I believe that my time is the most important in the world. That the art of my time is the most important art. That the art before my time has no immediate contribution to my aesthetics since that art is history explaining past behavior, but not necessarily offering solutions to my problems. Art is not divorced from life. It is dialectic. It is ever changing and in revolt to the past. It has existed from the minds of free men for less than a century. Prior to this the direction of art was dictated by minds other than the artist for exploitation and commercial use. That the freedom of man's mind to cele-brate his own feeling by a work of art parallels his social revolt from bondage. I believe that art is yet to be born and that freedom and equality are yet to be born.

If you ask me why I make sculpture, I must answer that it is my way of life, my balance, and my justification for being.

If you ask me for whom do I make art, I will say that it is for all who approach it without prejudice. My world, the objects I see are the same for all men of goodwill. The race for survival I share with all men who work for existence.   *[1952]*

TONY SMITH
(1912–1980)

Smith studied at the New Bauhaus in Chicago and then apprenticed himself to Frank Lloyd Wright. While he practiced architecture, until around 1960, Smith worked sporadically in painting and small sculptures. After 1960 he devoted himself entirely to sculpture. His extremely simple steel sculptures were large and commanding, earning him a prominent position in the so-called Minimal Art movement.

I'm interested in the inscrutability and the mysteriousness of the thing. Something obvious on the face of it (like a washing machine or a pump), is of no further interest. A Bennington earthenware jar, for instance, has subtlety of color, largeness of form, a general suggestion of substance, generosity, is calm and reassuring—qualities which take it beyond pure utility. It continues to nourish us time and time again. We can't see it in a second, we continue to read it. There is something absurd in the fact that you can go back to a cube in this same way. It doesn't seem to be an ordinary mechanical experience. When I start to design, it's almost always corny and then naturally moves toward economy.

I'm not aware of how light and shadow fall on my pieces. I'm just aware of basic form. I'm interested in the thing, not in the effects—pyramids are only geometry, not an effect.

We think in two dimensions—horizontally and vertically. Any angle off that is very hard to remember. For that reason I make models—drawings would be impossible.

I view art as something vast. I think highway systems fall down because they are not art. Art today is an art of postage stamps. I love the Secretariat

T O N Y   S M I T H   *#40, Free Ride.* 1962. Steel.
80 x 80 x 80".

Building of the UN, placed like a salute. In terms of scale, we have less art per square mile, per capita, then any society ever had. We are puny. In an English village there was always the cathedral. There is nothing to look at between the Bennington Monument and the George Washington Bridge. We now have stylization. In Hackensack a huge gas tank is all underground. I think of art in a public context and not in terms of mobility of works of art. Art is just there. I'm temperamentally more inclined to mural painting, especially that of the Mexican Orozco. I like the way a huge area holds on to a surface in the same way a state does on a map.   *[1966]*

ROBERT SMITHSON

(1938–1972)

In Robert Smithson's thoughtful analysis of tendencies in the mid-1960s, he identified the desire to reduce art to a minimum with the notion of "entropy." His own work, beginning with primary structures, moved out into the landscape, where he made memorable earthworks, one of the most celebrated being the 1970 Spiral Jetty.

Many architectural concepts found in science fiction have nothing to do with science or fiction, instead they suggest a kind of monumentality which has much in common with the aims of some of today's artists. I am thinking in particular of Donald Judd, Robert Morris, Sol LeWitt, Dan Flavin, and of certain artists in the "Park Place Group." The artists who build structured canvases and "wall size" paintings, such as Will Insley, Peter Hutchinson, and Frank Stella are more indirectly related. The chrome and plastic fabricators such as Paul Thek, Craig Kauffman, and Larry Bell are also relevant.

The works of many of these artists celebrate what Flavin called "inactive history" or what the physicist calls "entropy" or "energy-drain." They bring to mind the Ice Age rather than the Golden Age, and would most likely confirm Vladimir Nabokov's observation that, "The future is but the obsolete in reverse." In a rather roundabout way, many of the artists have provided a visible analog for the Second Law of Thermodynamics, which extrapolates the range of entropy by telling us energy is more easily lost than obtained, and that in the ultimate future the whole universe will burn out and be transformed into an all-encompassing sameness. . . .

Instead of causing us to remember the past like the old monuments, the new monuments seem to cause us to forget the future. Instead of being made of natural materials, such as marble, granite, or other kinds of rock, the new monuments are made of artificial materials, plastic, chrome, and electric light. They are not built for the ages, but rather against the ages. They are involved in a systematic reduction of time down to fractions of seconds, rather than in representing the long spaces of centuries. Both past and future are placed into an objective present. This kind of time has little or no space; it is stationary and without movement, it is going nowhere, it is anti-Newtonian, as well as being instant, and is against the wheels of the time-clock. . . .

This kind of nullification has re-created Kasimir Malevich's "nonobjective world," where there are no more "likenesses of reality, no idealistic images, nothing but a desert!" But for many of today's artists this "desert" is a "City of the Future" made of null structures and surfaces. This "City" performs no natural function, it simply exists between mind and matter, detached from both, representing neither. It is, in fact, devoid of all classical ideals of space and process. It is brought into focus by a strict condition of perception, rather than by any expressive or emotive means. Perception as a deprivation of action and reaction brings to the mind the desolate, but exquisite, surface-structures of the empty "box" or "lattice." As action decreases, the clarity of such surface-structures increases. This is evident in art when all representations of action pass into oblivion. At this stage, lethargy is elevated to the most glorious magnitude. . . .   *[1966]*

FRANK STELLA

(1936–)

Stella's determined rejection of illusionistic space in painting seemed, in the early 1960s, a radical departure. He was one of the foremost figures in a move away from Abstract Expressionism toward a cool, carefully reasoned approach to painting that sought to eliminate all but surface illusions. In later years Stella abandoned the rigid geometries of his original style in favor of hectic reliefs with swirling forms that still, in spite of the Expressionist abandon, seemed to retain their impersonality.

The painterly problems of what to put here and there and how to make it go with what was already there became more and more difficult and the solutions more and more unsatisfactory. Until finally it became obvious that there had to be a better way.

There were two problems which had to be faced. One was spatial and the other methodological. In the first case I had to do something about relational painting, i.e., the balancing of the various parts with and against each other. The obvious answer was symmetry—make it the same all over. The question still remained, though, of how to do this in depth. A symmetrical image or configuration placed on an open ground is not balanced out in the illusionistic space. The solution I arrived at—and there are probably quite a few, although I know of only one other, color density—forces illusionistic space out of the painting at a constant rate by using a regulated pattern. The remaining problem was simply to find a method of paint application which followed and complemented the design solution.

[1959–1960]

CLYFFORD STILL

(1904–1980)

Still's first one-man show—in 1946 at Peggy Guggenheim's Art of This Century Gallery, where Pollock and Rothko had shown before him—introduced New York to the large, heavily impastoed, darkly symbolic paintings for which he became famous. Still's attitude of total defiance toward all European modern conventions was expressed not only in his unorthodox work, but in his teaching at the California School of Fine Arts and in his written statements.

That pigment on canvas has a way of initiating conventional reactions for most people needs no reminder. Behind these reactions is a body of history matured into dogma, authority, tradition. The totalitarian hegemony of this tradition I despise, its presumptions I reject. Its security is an illusion, banal, and without courage. Its substance is but dust and filing cabinets. The homage paid to it is a celebration of death. We all bear the burden of this tradition on our backs but I cannot hold it a privilege to be a pallbearer of my spirit in its name.

From the most ancient times the artist has been expected to perpetuate the values of his contemporaries. The record is mainly one of frustration, sadism, superstition, and the will to power. What greatness of life crept into the story came from sources not yet fully understood, and the temples of art which burden the landscape of nearly every city are a tribute to the attempt to seize this elusive quality and stamp it out.

The anxious men find comfort in the confusion of those artists who would walk beside them. The values involved, however, permit no peace, and mutual resentment is deep when it is discovered that salvation cannot be bought.

We are now committed to an unqualified act, not illustrating outworn myths or contemporary alibis. One must accept total responsibility for what he executes. And the measure of his greatness will be in the depth of his insight and his courage in realizing his own vision.

Demands for communication are both presumptuous and irrelevant. The observer usually will see what his fears and hopes and learning teach him to see. But if he can escape these demands that hold up a mirror to himself, then perhaps some of the implications of the work may be felt. But whatever is seen or felt it should be remembered that for me these paintings had to be something else. It is the price one has to pay for clarity when one's means are honored only as an instrument of seduction or assault.   *[1952]*

M A R K   T O B E Y   *New York.* 1944.
Tempera on paperboard. 33 x 21".

M A R K   T O B E Y

(1890–1976)

Tobey's experiences in the Far East during the 1920s and 1930s led him to invent what he called his "white writing," a kind of calligraphic exploration of different levels in space. He felt his work reflected his beliefs as a member of the Baha'i faith by suggesting cosmic harmony and the oneness of the world. Tobey's abstractions were usually small in scale—a characteristic that distinguished him from the postwar Americans whose Abstract Expressionist paintings were often exceedingly large. He was, however, a seminal force in the evolution of American vanguard art, in which the use of linear masses in all-over compositions became widespread.

Line became dominant instead of mass but I still attempted to interpenetrate it with a spatial existence. "Writing" the painting, whether in color or neutral tones, became a necessity for me. I often thought of this way of working as a performance, since it had to be achieved all at once or not at all—the very opposite of building up as I had previously done.

While sitting on the floor of a room in Japan and looking out on a small garden with flowers blooming and dragonflies hovering in space, I sensed that this small world, almost underfoot, shall I say, had a validity all its own, but must be realized and appreciated from its own level in space. I suddenly felt I had too long been exclusively above my boots.

Earlier I got the idea of "writing" cities and city life. At last I had found a technical approach which enabled me to capture what specially interested me in the city—its lights—threading traffic—the river of humanity chartered and flowing through and around its self-imposed limitations, not unlike chlorophyll flowing through the canals of a leaf. Naturally I didn't consciously know what I was doing. The fact that I had to express things in this way often resulted in denying the way even while or after doing it, as there were no existing standards to give me support. I couldn't use much color, any more, I suppose, then the Cubists could in the first years of Cubism, for the problems were already complicated enough. Naturally color came back. During the forties and fifties my work varied from the use of a direct dynamic brush to the use of white dynamic flashes of line married to a geometry of space.

I have never wished to continue in any particular style. The path has been a zigzag—in and out of old cultures, seeking new horizons—mediating and reviewing for a better position to see. Subject matter has changed from the Middle West to the most microscopic worlds. On pavements and the bark of trees I have found whole worlds. I know very little about what generally is termed abstract. Pure abstraction for me would be a painting where one finds no correspondence to life—an impossibility for me. I have sought a unified world in my work and use a movable vortex to achieve it.

[1954]

JACK TWORKOV

(1900–1982)

Tworkov came to the United States from Poland at the age of thirteen and during the 1930s gained a reputation as a romantic, semi-abstract painter. During the Second World War he reconsidered his work and embarked on a more Expressionist path that brought him to recognition as one of the important members of the Abstract Expressionist group. In the early 1960s Tworkov became dissatisfied with the loose brushwork and free configurations in his work and developed a gridlike understructure based on elementary geometric figures.

Post–World War II painting in New York moved against two repressive experiences—the rhetoric of social realism, preached especially by the artists and ideologues on the arts projects of the thirties, and the hegemony of

Paris in modern art. The response was an art that stood against all formula, an art in which impulse, instinct, and the automatic, as guides to interior reality, were to usurp all forms of intellectualizing. I cannot remember any period in my life that so went to my head as 1949. It marked the foundation of the Artist's Club in New York and heralded a decade of painting as fruitful and revolutionary as the Impressionism of 1870.

But by the end of the fifties, I felt that the automatic aspect of Abstract Expressionist painting of the gestural variety, to which my painting was related, had reached a stage where its forms had become predictable and automatically repetitive. . . .

At the end of the fifties, I began to look around for more disciplined and contemplative forms. Although I've had practically no training in any branch of mathematics and little or no competence in any field of it, in 1965 I began to study elementary geometry and some aspects of the number system. I became fascinated with the little I learned and found in some aspects of the geometry of a rectangle a new starting point for composing a painting. An example of the kind of naïve question that was a starting point for me is the following: given any rectangle, what line can I draw that is not arbitrary but is determined by the rectangle? I soon arrived at an elementary system of measurements implicit in the geometry of the rectangle which became the basis for simple images that I had deliberately given a somewhat illusionistic cast. From then on, all my paintings began with carefully worked out drawings and measurements that I could repeat at will. But the actual painting I left to varieties of spontaneous brushing. What I wanted was a simple structure dependent on drawing as a base on which the brushing, spontaneous and pulsating, gave a beat to the painting somewhat analogous to the beat in music. I wanted, and I hope I arrived at, a painting style in which planning does not exclude intuitive and sometimes random play.

Above all else, I distinguish between painting and pictures (between Cézanne and Picasso). Where I have to choose between them, I choose painting. If I have to choose between painting and ideas—I choose painting; between painting and every form of theater—I choose painting.   *[1973]*

CHRISTOPHER WILMARTH
(1943–)

Raised in California, Wilmarth settled in New York as a student, where he witnessed the startling evolution from Abstract Expressionism to so-called minimalism in the 1960s. He began his own career with a rather severe, Constructivist approach, but soon veered toward lyrical expressions of his sense of vertical man in space. Known for

CHRISTOPHER WILMARTH   *Gnomon's Parade*
(Late). 1980. Glass and steel. 105 x 40½ x 30".

*his inventive sculptures combining plate glass and steel, Wilmarth has also excelled
in the art of illustration, with sculpture as well as with more traditional media. To
illustrate Mallarmé's sonnets, for example, he used blown glass and steel as well as
pastels and charcoal drawings.*

Light gains character as it touches the world; from what is lighted and who
is there to see. I associate the significant moments of my life with the
character of the light at the time. The universal implications of my original
experience have located in and become signified by kinds of light. My
sculptures are places to generate this experience compressed into light and
shadow and return them to the world as a physical poem.

Art exists for a reason. The reason is simple and often forgotten. Art is
man's attempt to communicate an understanding of life to man. To give in
a sculpture what I understand; to imbue concrete things with parallels to
human feelings; to do this in a real way; to be believable is my purpose.

In my attempt to make believable art I make sculptures in which the
forms seem to have evolved of themselves. They exist and imply change.
The personality of the piece is self-generated and not imposed in an illus-

trative way. It is not narrated. In their autonomy my sculptures are real. Certain formal limitations support this sense of self generation. The sculpture is given a first form which is finite. The finite is established by cutting the basic shape of the material with no sense of touch. The material is flat and the shapes are geometric. The memory of the first form is retained in the completed piece giving the sculpture a history. All subsequent working of the material is done with respect to the identity of the material, its first form, and to celebrate touch.

For years I have been concerned with the complex problem of implying the human presence in a nonobjective art. The concept of self-generated form approaches a solution in that the sculpture attains a living presence. The layering of material has organic implications but it was the feeling of people in places and the special energy certain places have long after the people have gone that provided insight into my concern with the figure. The configuration, scale, and proportion of place can evoke human presence. These are the places I speak of when I say my sculptures are places to generate experience. The feeling is intimate. You are acknowledged. *[1975]*

VENEZUELA

JESÚS RAFAEL SOTO

(1923–)

Soto had studied art in his native Venezuela before coming to Paris in 1950, where he undertook experiments with kinetic imagery. His large-scale, optically animated installations incorporated colored elements—standing or suspended—which created the illusion of motion. They established Soto as one of the most important international figures in the movement away from static painting and sculpture.

Penetrables, the new works placed on the floor, the integrations with the architecture, are, in essence, the result of all my earlier experiments. I have always worked in the spirit of a researcher wanting to make a discovery; just as my serial works led to the optical vibration of the painting, the superposition of works one upon another toward real movement, the explorations in the direction of a new language, model phrases, demonstrative elements, all led me toward pure abstraction. With my particular idea of the universal, there are no further limits: In principle, I could create a work which would stretch from Paris to Le Havre, or which would span the ocean—it would be the same process. Simply put, for a long while, I was only able to create small, laboratory-scale works. But for me, it's the same whether I do a painting which I would describe as a studio work, or a work of unlimited scale. I continue to experiment. I believe that art is a science, or a form of science.

The immaterial is the sensory reality of the universe. Art is the sensory knowledge of the immaterial. To become conscious of the immaterial in its state of pure structure, is to make the final leap toward the absolute.

I cannot conceive of art in any other sense, and as soon as you begin to think in this way, you come upon a fabulous world which has never been explored. That's why whenever I hear anyone say that abstract art is dead (a current view around 1950) I have to laugh.

I separate art and politics because I view politics as a series of transitory phases; if I submitted my work to politics, my art would lose whatever solidity it has. I would have to deviate from my speculative method. I would gradually have to abandon my experiments as an artist to political demands. I find it altogether normal that a politician should give priority to politics, but for me, an artist, my own priority is the domain of art.   *[1967]*

Since I am a firm believer in the Renaissance maxim "Truth is the daughter of Time," I regard much of the material in this book as a source for a later, more distanced view of twentieth-century art. The terminology itself is not seasoned, and often displays a tentativeness that I'm sure will be dispelled as the century draws to its close.

It is obvious that the twentieth century has been far more industrious about the business of inventing sobriquets than previous centuries, when such simple designations as "classical" and "romantic" or "baroque" could serve for decades. The reasons for the accelerated floriation of "isms" will also become more clear in future assessments. Moreover, since artists' talk about art is not always synchronous with intellectual currents of any given period, it will be apparent in future years that certain terms were less than satisfactory as descriptions of orders in the visual arts. I believe a close reading of the texts in this book will offer the reader clues about how to interpret the terminology, and more important, how to interpret the groupings of certain artists, both geographically and chronologically. Since most often the naming of movements is done by zealous critics rather than artists themselves, it behooves us to take cognizance of what artists say and pose it against the often hasty judgments of critics. The following list of terms, then, is meant to help the reader form an independent judgment and *not* to give definitive forms to things too close to us in history.

ABSTRACT EXPRESSIONISM   Term used to designate a group of American painters and sculptors who, during the Second World War, developed an independent view of the nature and meaning of their art. Although their works varied greatly, they generally believed that art was an expression of the individual psyche, that representational forms were not essential to project meaning, and that freedom from a priori conventions was implicit. Certain artists associated with the group emphasized the direct expression of gesture and brushwork (i.e., Jackson Pollock and Willem de Kooning) while others emphasized large surface, scale, and color values (i.e., Mark Rothko and Barnett Newman). Sculptors in the group—most notably David Smith—extended the implications of collage, assembling works from disparate units, usually working with welded metal. As a whole the group represented a point of view that was philosophically coherent but diverse stylistically.

ABSTRACTION-CRÉATION   A group formed in Paris in 1931 to foster the efforts of those who believed that pure abstraction, rather than abstraction visibly derived from nature, was the most progressive art of its time. Many members of the association worked with geometric elements, often echoing the principles of Piet Mondrian's and Theo van Doesburg's group, de Stijl. The association published an important international journal, *Abstraction-Création: Art Non-Figuratif*, from 1932 to 1936.

ACTION PAINTING   The American critic Harold Rosenberg used this term to describe the paintings of those among the Abstract Expressionists (such as de Kooning and Pollock) whose work emphasized the act itself of wielding a painting tool, revealing the energy of the rapid stroke and thereby reflecting the aesthetic belief that a painting included a visible account of the artist's process, his intimate experience, in its completion.

ART INFORMEL   A term used in Europe to distinguish artists who sought a psychological expression free from the restraints of formal picture-making. In general, Art Informel artists shared the assumptions of the American Abstract Expressionists in which the process of becoming is more important than the final product. Both groups were deeply imbued with the belief that the individual psyche harbors deep feelings that can be brought to the picture surface only by means of extremely free techniques, such as those suggested earlier by the Surrealists.

ART NOUVEAU   An international movement, originating in the late nineteenth century and lasting until the First World War, in which a new approach to design was advocated. Largely associated with the practical arts of architecture and the design of utilitarian objects, the movement is often perceived as having clarified modernism and introduced organic, ornamental style. Emphasizing the beauty of the curve, the Art Nouveau artists sought to combat the rampant eclecticism of nineteenth-century design. In painting, however, a more complex goal was implicit: to free painting from imitative realism. Art Nouveau became an opening wedge in the struggle to validate pure abstraction.

ARTE POVERA   Arte Povera was defined by the Italian critic Germano Celant in 1970: "Arte Povera expresses an approach to art which is basically anti-commercial, precarious, banal, and anti-formal, concerned primarily with the physical properties of the medium and the mutability of the materials." The artists Celant described generally eschewed both conventional painting on canvas and conventional free-standing sculpture, making hybrid works that partook of both but that were often composed with perishable materials such as ashes, leaves, and felt in theatrical arrangements. Some of their works were called "Installation Art."

BAUHAUS   Founded in Weimar, Germany, in 1919 by the German architect Walter Gropius, the Bauhaus was an art school that offered a new concept in the education of artists and architects based on Gropius's belief in the unity of the arts. By 1923, he addressed the question of mass production, advocating the application of high-level design principles to ordinary artifacts. The original staff included, among others, the outstanding painters Paul Klee and Wassily Kandinsky, the architect and furniture designer Marcel Breuer, and the designer Herbert Bayer. In 1925 the Bauhaus was moved to Dessau into buildings designed by Gropius and his students and staff. From 1925 to 1933—when the Nazis forced it to close—the Bauhaus exerted immense influence in architecture, design, theater, and the dissemination of the most avant-garde European ideas in the arts through its important publications.

DER BLAUE REITER (THE BLUE RIDER)   A group formed by Wassily Kandinsky in 1911 dedicated to the exhibition of advanced art from all over Europe and Russia. In 1912 Kandinsky and Franz Marc published a remarkable collection of essays and illustrations, "The Blue Rider Almanach," which included work by primitive artists, folk art, the art of children and of European avant-garde painters, as well as essays by Marc himself, the painter August Macke, and the composers Arnold Schoenberg and Theodor von Hartmann.

DIE BRÜCKE (THE BRIDGE)   A group of artists, most of whom had been architecture students, formed in 1905 in Dresden by Ernst Ludwig Kirchner, Erich Heckel, Fritz Bleyl, and Karl Schmidt-Rottluff, who intended to express an anti-bourgeois, socially progressive, and highly emotional attitude. Their works, and on occasion those of various other artists such as Emil Nolde, were exhibited together until around 1913. Their prints and paintings generally remained based on interpretations of landscapes and figures freely organized and often rendered in non-naturalistic color. The term *expressionism*, current before the First World War, was applied most often to the works of these artists.

CAMERA WORK   The title of a periodical founded in 1903 by the American photographer Alfred Stieglitz. Together with his gallery, "291," the magazine introduced major currents of European and American avant-garde art. Stieglitz was the first to show Henri Matisse, Francis Picabia, Pablo Picasso, Constantin Brancusi, and Georges Braque in America, and the first to show the Americans Marsden Hartley, Georgia O'Keeffe, Arthur Garfield Dove, and John Marin. *Camera Work* appeared from 1903 to 1917.

COBRA   An acronym for the cities Copenhagen, Brussels, and Amsterdam, chosen by the founding artists of the group—Asger Jorn, Karel Appel, Corneille, and Pierre Alechinsky—in 1948. Internationalist in perspective, these artists generally adhered to the figurative-expressionist tendency in the postwar Art Informel grouping, drawing their ideas from the earlier Surrealist and Expressionist phenomena.

CONCEPTUAL ART   A rather vague term used to designate works by artists who believe that the initial idea, however presented to the public, is the most important aspect of the work. The most frequent usages apply to works in which a written text is combined with a material object or image.

CONSTRUCTIVISM   A term engendering considerable controversy and often applied to deeply differing modes of art. In general the notion of constructing, with its implication of assembled, tectonic, and geometric configurations, underlies the term. Constructivism generally denies figurative imagery and often invokes mathematical principles. The term is most often applied to the Russian art movement founded in about 1913 by Vladimir Tatlin and spread by Naum Gabo and Antoine Pevsner.

CUBISM   A pejorative epithet coined on the occasion of a 1908 exhibition of the work of Georges Braque by a journalist referring to Braque's planar reductions—similar to those of Cézanne. Braque and Pablo Picasso were soon after dubbed Cubists, and their innovative approach to pictorial space and subject matter exercised vast influence on modern painting. By analyzing objects into their planar components and suggesting formal interactions on the entire picture surface, the Cubists formulated a new way of defining pictorial space.

DADA   The name was chosen randomly by a group of rebellious young artists from all over Europe sheltering in Zurich during the First World War. From 1915 on, leaders such as the artist Hans Arp, the poets Hugo Ball and Tristan Tzara, and the poet-musician Richard Huelsenbeck broadcast their anarchistic ideas. Dada quickly became an international movement that found adherents in Paris, Berlin, New York, and other capitals. Many participants saw their riotous poetry readings, randomly composed paintings, and absurdist plays as protest against the rational Western tradition that had culminated, they felt, in the horrors of the First World War. By 1923, the somewhat negative functions of Dada were superseded by Surrealism.

EARTH ART   During the late 1960s a number of sculptors began exploring ways to use large tracts of the actual landscape to form images. Sometimes literally moving earth and stone with modern machines—as in the case of Michael Heizer—and sometimes merely leaving marks on the landscape such as chalk lines or furrows, artists producing these works referred to them as "earthworks."

EL PASO   During the mid-1950s a number of Spnish artists and writers formed the El Paso group in Madrid as a means of bringing into the static Spanish culture fresh contemporary approaches to art, largely derived from France. Most of the artists identified closely with the Art Informel movement.

EUSTON ROAD SCHOOL   The name of an art school opened in London in 1937 which grouped painters such as William Coldstream and Victor Pasmore with others in a programmatic movement away from abstraction. Spurred by the economic failures throughout the Western world, its artists believed that art should reflect— and if possible change—the state of society.

EXPRESSIONISM   The term gained wide currency in the early part of the century to make a distinction between those painters—such as the Russian Wassily Kandinsky and the German Ernst Ludwig Kirchner—who felt their work expressed their inner feelings with direct emotional or intuitive means and those painters—such as the Cubists—who avoided violent color and emotive effects, fitting more nearly into an objective tradition often seen as classicism.

FAUVISM   A short-lived tendency in French painting in which Henri Matisse, André Derain, and Maurice Vlaminck (among others), working in the wake of Van Gogh and Gauguin, used brilliant color in broad impasto strokes to suggest the vitality and structure of their largely landscape motifs. The term was coined by a hostile critic: in French *fauves* means "wild beasts."

FUTURISM   A movement launched by the Italian poet Filippo Tommaso Marinetti, who published his Futurist manifesto in Paris in 1909. Adventurous artists, writers, poets, composers, and architects in Italy before the First World War flocked to Marinetti's banner, eager to proclaim the importance of new technology, new political ideologies, and new artistic styles to Italian culture, which they felt was mired in the heavy trappings of the past. The ideas set forth by such artists as Umberto Boccioni, Giacomo Balla, and Carlo Carrà, and by the composer Luigi Russolo and the architect Antonio Sant'Elia, had a broad influence throughout Europe and were of special importance to the Russian avant-garde on the eve of the First World War.

HAPPENINGS   A term used by the artist Allan Kaprow to describe the hybrid art forms of the 1960s in which visual artists extended their works into theatrical situations, often with spectator participation, and incorporated elements from painting, drawing, sculpture, dance, and film. Ephemerality and spontaneity were highly valued by Happenings artists such as Jim Dine, Robert Whitman, Claes Oldenburg, Robert Rauschenberg, and Red Grooms. Happenings had historical precedents in the early years of the Soviet Union and in the ideas of Marcel Duchamp and John Cage.

HARD EDGE PAINTING   Jules Langsner, a California critic, used the term in the late 1950s to distinguish the new nonobjective, geometrical painting from prewar varieties. Artists such as Ellsworth Kelly, he felt, had moved away from the dogmatic attitudes of artists such as Mondrian and van Doesburg, and were using broad, flat color planes and hard edges in a more open manner.

INSTALLATION ART   A rather loose term for works that appeared in the 1970s in which artists assembled elements of various materials in specific gallery or museum situations, intending to establish an environment rather than an isolated, single work of art.

KINETIC ART   Originally cited by Naum Gabo and Antoine Pevsner in their 1920 manifesto, the term was first used to describe works of art, particularly sculpture, in which moving parts are incorporated, powered either by motors or by natural forces as in the works of Alexander Calder. Later the term was extended to include works that induce optical illusion, as in the works of Jesús Rafael Soto or Yaacov Agam.

METAPHYSICAL SCHOOL (SCUOLA METAFISICA)   Metaphysical painting is mainly associated with the work of Giorgio de Chirico, who, early in the century, first showed his interest in eerie, strangely lighted effects that he felt expressed a meaning beyond that of ordinary reality. In 1917 he and Carlo Carrà talked about a "Metaphysical School," a loose group of artists who believed they could suggest such a mysterious and transcendent reality in figurative paintings. Briefly associated were Carrà, Giorgio Morandi, Mario Sironi, Filippo de Pisis, and others.

MEXICAN MURAL MOVEMENT   During the early 1920s the revolutionary Mexican government sponsored a vast program of education in which Mexican artists were enlisted to paint murals in public places. Strong figures such as David Alfaro Siqueiros, José Clemente Orozco, and Diego Rivera vigorously applied themselves to the art of the mural, covering the walls of countless Mexican public buildings with passionate accounts of Mexican history and revolutionary aspirations. Siqueiros's 1921 manifesto called for a monumental heroic art celebrating the culture of pre-Hispanic America.

MINIMAL ART   A term that came to be used in the late 1950s to distinguish a tendency among artists following the generation of Abstract Expressionists, and reacting against them by eschewing emotional effects and seeking to present an austere, stripped art whose components were often modular. The extreme simplicity of their works—in both painting and sculpture—derived not only from their compositional reductions but also from their use of unadorned surfaces and simple materials.

NEOPLASTICISM   Name given by Piet Mondrian to his newly formulated theory of art around 1917. The new plastic expression, he wrote, would ignore the particulars of appearance—natural form and color—in favor of the abstract form and color derived from straight lines and primary colors. He thought the unity of nature could be expressed through the precise use of the "two positions that form the right angle."

NEUE SACHLICHKEIT (NEW OBJECTIVITY)   A term used by the German critic G. F. Hartlaub in 1923 to describe the social realism of the works of such artists as George Grosz and Otto Dix, who cast a harsh and seemingly objective light on the society of Weimar Germany. They rejected the anarchic rebelliousness and individualism of the Dadaists, as well as the emotional excesses of the Expressionists.

NEW BAUHAUS   Founded by László Moholy-Nagy in Chicago in 1937, the school was modeled on the original Bauhaus, where he had taught from 1923 to 1928. It was one of the major sources of Bauhaus influence in the United States.

THE NEW YORK SCHOOL   One of the various names given to the group of artists who emerged during the Second World War, mostly in New York, also called Abstract Expressionists or Action Painters.

NOUVEAUX RÉALISTES   Artists grouped together by the French critic Pierre Restany whose "realism" consisted in their use of found materials and their rejection of conventional painting and sculpture formats. The chief artists associated with the group were Jean Tinguely, Yves Klein, Arman, and Martial Raysse.

PERFORMANCE ART   An extremely imprecise term used often to describe works by visual artists who draw upon several arts—such as dance, the theater, and sculpture—to make a work of hybrid character.

POP ART   A term coined by the British art critic Lawrence Alloway in the mid-1950s to describe the early work of such artists as Richard Hamilton and Eduardo Paolozzi, who were using "vernacular" culture and the products of the mass media as materials in their art. In America such artists as Andy Warhol and Roy Lichtenstein spearheaded the movement by using industrial products and techniques in their works and by elevating advertising, comic strips, and science fiction as appropriate subject matter in painting and sculpture.

PRECISIONIST MOVEMENT   During the 1920s, American artists such as Charles Sheeler, Charles Demuth, and Niles Spencer worked with Cubist principles to create a representational art that favored clean lines and functional subject matter (such as factories and barns) or urban vistas.

PRODUCTIVIST MOVEMENT   Derived from Vladimir Tatlin's 1920 manifesto, in which he advocated "production art" that would take into account new technological and industrial techniques and the skills of engineers to produce an art for the masses.

RAYONISM   In Russia around 1912, Mikhail Larionov formulated a theory of painting that drew upon Futurist ideas of dynamic force lines and semiscientific observations of the movement of light rays. Natalia Goncharova and Larionov himself became its best-known practitioners.

SECTION D'OR   An exhibition in Paris in 1912 and a publication that brought together such artists as Robert Delaunay, František Kupka, Jacques Villon, and several others, all of whom practiced variants of Cubism and were interested in the old mathematical idea of proportion called the Golden Section.

DE STIJL   Title of the magazine founded by Theo van Doesburg in 1917, which became the principal organ for the dissemination of Piet Mondrian's principles of painting, and of van Doesburg's and others' theories for the total revision of architectural principles.

DER STURM   Name of the journal founded by Herwarth Walden in 1910, and the gallery founded in 1912, in which works from all the major avant-garde movements of Europe—Cubism, Futurism, Orphism, and Expressionism—were exhibited and extensively discussed.

SUPREMATISM   Name given by Kasimir Malevich to his philosophy of art around 1915. Malevich and his followers advocated a nonobjective art that would express "pure feeling" and that, in its abstraction, would create a new spiritual dimension in art, independent of all "purpose" other than artistic.

SURREALISM   The word, coined by the poet Guillaume Apollinaire, was soon adopted by André Breton to describe the new approach to the arts that he had put forward around 1922, and that was eventually embraced by such writers as Paul Eluard, Louis Aragon, and Benjamin Peret, and such painters as Joan Miró, Man Ray, Alberto Giacometti, René Magritte, and Salvador Dalí. The philosophy of Surrealism was based on the new awareness of the subconscious heralded by Freud, and on the attempt to bring dream and reality to an existence on the same plane. Also important to the Surrealists was the commitment to radical political attitudes, opposing the capitalist structures that they felt had led to the carnage of the First World War.

SYMBOLISM   Used generally to characterize the work of artists and poets of the last decade of the nineteenth century, who had rebelled against the verism of both the naturalists and the Impressionists. The symbolists maintained, with the poet Stéphane Mallarmé, that oblique symbolic reference was the most profound. Among others, Gauguin and Odilon Redon advocated views that were called symbolist.

TACHISM   Term derived from the French word *tache* (stain or spot) to describe, in the mid-1950s, French lyrical painting of an abstract nature. Tachist works were sometimes related to those of the American Abstract Expressionists. The term *Tachism* was sometimes used interchangeably with Art Informel.

UNISM   Named by Władysław Strzeminski, Unism was a movement of several Polish artists in the mid-1920s who were seeking to go beyond Kasimir Malevich's principles to an art of all-over composition in which oppositions were minimal. Decades later, the American minimalists seemed to pose the same ideal.

VALORI PLASTICI   An important Italian art journal founded in 1918. In early issues, Giorgio de Chirico and Carlo Carrà defined Metaphysical painting; later issues sounded the call for a return to Italian classicism. During the 1920s, after the review had ceased to exist, many artists who had been exposed to *Valori Plastici* in Europe and even the United States were influenced to shift their focus away from Cubism and abstraction toward a new figurative expression.

VORTICISM   A term used by Ezra Pound in 1913 and enthusiastically adopted by the painter and writer Percy Wyndham Lewis in 1914 to characterize a motley group of British artists who, like him, had been influenced by both Italian Futurism and French Cubism.

WPA AND FEDERAL ARTS PROJECT   The Works Progress Administration (WPA) under the Federal Arts Project, officially established in 1935 by the United States government, employed out-of-work artists in many capacities. The program was essentially devised to help artists survive during the Depression, but it also had the idealistic goals of enhancing and dignifying American culture. Many painters and sculptors were given their first opportunity to work intensely during those years, and to experience a kind of professional solidarity. A mural division, an easel-painting division, and a sculpture division were active by 1935. Most of the artists who became the best-known and most distinguished Abstract Expressionists in the post-war period were employed by the WPA. This communal experience is often credited with having established American artists as legitimate and contributing members of American society.

ZERO GROUP   Formed in Düsseldorf in 1957 by Heinz Mack, Günther Uecker, and Otto Piene to put forward their work and views. The Zero Group was interested in kinetic principles and dematerialized art composed with light.

SOURCE LIST

ADAMI, VALERIO   "It takes more than a key . . .": Exhibition catalogue, B. Mammaton, Paris, 1968.
"Drawing is . . .": Letter to author, 1983. Copyright © Valerio Adami.
AGAM, YAACOV   "From my very first experiments . . .": *Lumière et Mouvement* (exhibition catalogue), Musée de la Ville de Paris, 1967.
ALBERS, JOSEF   "They are juxtaposed . . ." / "Despite an even . . ." / "Such action, reaction, interaction . . ." / "Such color deceptions . . ." / "All this will make . . .": "The Color in My Painting," in exhibition catalogue, North Carolina Museum, February 13–May 11, 1962.
ALECHINSKY, PIERRE   "COBRA was my school . . ." / "When I paint . . ." / "A man may be so affected . . ." / "Ensor wrote repeatedly . . .": Interview with

Jacques Putnam in *L'Oeil* (Paris), no. 82. Reprinted in exhibition catalogue, Lefebre Gallery, New York, April 13–May 8, 1965.

L'Esprit des Chutes. 1978. Private collection. Photograph courtesy of Lefebre Gallery, New York.

ANDRE, CARL   "There is no symbolic content . . ." / "The art of association . . ." / "My works are in . . ." / "I think it is futile . . ." / "Place is a pedestal . . .": From symposium at Windham College, Putney, Vermont, April 30, 1968. Copyright © Carl André.

ARDON, MORDECAI   "Pictures are exhibited . . .": Exhibition catalogue, Marlborough Gallery, London, 1973.

ARIKHA, AVIGDOR   "All that's visible . . .": Statement in exhibition catalogue, Marlborough Gallery, New York, 1971.

ARP, JEAN (HANS)   "We don't want to copy nature . . .": Jean Arp, "On Concrete Art," in Jean Arp, *Arp on Arp,* ed. Marcel Jean, trans. Joachim Neugroschel (New York: Viking, 1972). Copyright © 1969, 1972 by the Viking Press, Inc. Reprinted by permission of Viking Penguin Inc.

AUERBACH, FRANK   "What I'm not hoping . . ." / "The problem of painting . . ." / "I mean, to put down . . .": Catherine Lampert, "A Conversation with Frank Auerbach," in *Frank Auerbach* (London: Arts Council of Great Britain, 1978).

Head of E.O.W. 1961. Private collection on loan to the Tate Gallery, London. Photograph courtesy of Marlborough Gallery, New York.

BACON, FRANCIS   "I would like to make images . . ." / "Any work that I like . . ." / "Death is the only absolute . . ." / "There are two sides to me . . ." / "Painting is in a peculiar stage . . .": "Remarks from an Interview with Peter Beard," in Henry Geldzahler, ed., *Francis Bacon: Recent Paintings, 1968–74* (New York: Metropolitan Museum of Art, 1975).

Man with Dog. 1953. Albright-Knox Art Gallery, Buffalo, N.Y.; gift of Seymour H. Knox, 1955.

BAERTLING, OLLE   "Art for me . . .": Exhibition catalogue, Galerie Denise René, Paris, 1974.

BALLA, GIACOMO   "With the perfecting of photography . . .": *Fu Balla-Balla Futurista* (exhibition catalogue), Rome, December 1915. Reprinted in Umbro Apollonio, ed., *Futurist Manifestoes,* trans. Robert Brain, R. W. Flint, J. C. Higgitt, Caroline Tisdall (New York: Viking, 1973). English translation copyright © 1973 by Thames & Hudson, Ltd., London. Reprinted by permission of Viking Penguin Inc.

"Any store in a modern town . . .": *Futurballa* (exhibition catalogue), Rome, 1918. Reprinted in Apollonio, *op. cit.* Reprinted by permission of Viking Penguin Inc.

Automobile Dynamics. 1913. Whereabouts unknown.

BARLACH, ERNST   "Just like a dramatist . . .": From a 1906 notebook, in Victor Meisel, *Voices of German Expressionism* (Englewood Cliffs, N.J.: Prentice-Hall, 1970).

Head (detail, *War Monument,* Gustrow Cathedral), 1927. Collection, the Museum of Modern Art, New York; gift of Edward M. M. Warburg.

BAZIOTES, WILLIAM   "Inspiration comes to me . . .": "The Creative Process" (symposium), *Art Digest* 28, no. 8 (January 15, 1954).

BEARDEN, ROMARE   "I did the new work . . .": Exhibition catalogue, State University of New York at Albany, November 25–December 22, 1968.

"I think a quality . . .": Statement in *Leonardo* (Elmsford, N.Y.) 2 (1969).

Evening, 9:10, 461 Lenox Avenue. 1964. Davidson College Art Gallery, Davidson, N.C. Photograph courtesy of Cordier & Ekstrom, Inc., New York.

BERLEWI, HENRYK "The technical means . . .": Henryk Berlewi, "Mechano-Faktur," in *Constructivism in Poland, 1923–1936* (exhibition catalogue), Essen, 1976.

BEUYS, JOSEPH "My objects are to be seen . . .": Joseph Beuys, "Introduction," in Caroline Tisdall, *Joseph Beuys* (London: Thames & Hudson, 1979). Copyright © 1979 The Solomon Guggenheim Foundation, New York.

BIEDERMAN, CHARLES JOSEPH "The new art I pursue . . .": Charles Joseph Biederman, *Letters on the New Art* (self-published, 1951).

BILL, MAX "I am convinced . . .": "The Mathematical Approach in Contemporary Art" (1948), translated by Morton Shand, in *Arts and Architecture*, no. 8 (1954).

BISSIER, JULIUS "Some forms in nature . . .": From his journals (1942–1949), in exhibition catalogue, San Francisco Museum of Art and Guggenheim Museum, New York, 1968. © 1968 San Francisco Museum of Art and Julius Bissier. *6 July 1959*. 1959. Collection, the Museum of Modern Art, New York; Gertrud A. Mellon Fund.

BLUME, PETER "Since I am concerned . . .": Lee Nordness, ed., *Art:USA:Now* (New York: Viking, 1963). Copyright 1963 in all countries of the International Copyright Union. Reprinted by permission of Viking Penguin Inc.

BOLOTOWSKY, ILYA "In the early forties . . .": Interview with Louise Averill Svendson in exhibition catalogue, Guggenheim Museum, New York, 1974.

BOMBERG, DAVID "We gladly make known . . .": Statement (July 1953). Reprinted in William Lipke, *David Bomberg* (Cranbury, N.J.: A. S. Barnes, 1968).

BONEVARDI, MARCELO "If my dreams . . .": Note in exhibition catalogue, Galeria Bonino, New York, 1965. Copyright © Marcelo Bonevardi.

BORDUAS, PAUL-ÉMILE "Magic booty, magically wrested . . ." / "It is naïve and misleading . . .": "Refus Globale" ("Global Refusal"), Montreal, 1948.

BOURGEOIS, LOUISE "Several years ago . . .": Exhibition catalogue, Museum of Modern Art, New York, 1983. *Blind Man's Buff*. 1984. Robert Miller Gallery, New York.

BRANCUSI, CONSTANTIN "After Michelangelo, sculptors wanted . . .": Carola Giedeon-Welcker, *Constantin Brancusi* (Stuttgart: Benno Schwabe Verlag, 1958). *View of the Artist's Studio*. 1918. Collection, the Museum of Modern Art, New York; the Joan and Lester Avnet Collection.

BRAUNER, VICTOR "My latest pictures are without . . .": Statement (December 1940) in *View* 1, no. 7–8 (October–November 1941).

BUREN, DANIEL "I believe we are the only ones . . .": Quoted in Lucy Lippard, *Six Years: The Dematerialization of the Art Object from 1966 to 1972* (New York: Praeger Publishers, 1973). Reprinted by permission of the publisher.

BURRI, ALBERTO "Words are no help . . .": *The New Decade: 22 European Painters and Sculptors* (exhibition catalogue), Museum of Modern Art, New York, 1955.

BURY, POL "When he wishes . . ." / "A circular cutting tool . . .": Statement in Dore Ashton, *Pol Bury* (Paris: Maeght, 1970). Copyright © Maeght.

CALDER, ALEXANDER "The underlying sense of form . . .": "What Abstract Art Means to Me," *Museum of Modern Art Bulletin* 18, no. 3 (Spring 1951). *"Which has influenced you . . ."*: Katherine Kuh, *The Artist's Voice* (New York: Harper & Row, 1960). *The Only Only Bird*. 1952. The Pace Gallery, New York.

CANOGAR, RAFAEL "After passing through . . .": Statement (1962) in archives of Spanish artists, Museum of Modern Art, New York.

CARO, ANTHONY "I think part of the trouble . . .": Interview with Andrew Forge in *Studio International* (London) 171, no. 873 (January 1966).

CHILLIDA, EDUARDO   "A piece of iron is . . .": Pierre Volbout, *Chillida* (New York: Abrams, 1967).
Iru Burni (also titled *Space Modulation IV*). 1966. Hastings Foundation, New York. Photograph courtesy of Galerie Maeght Lelong, Paris.

CHRISTO (CHRISTO JARACHEFF)   "Our perception of art . . .": Interview in Barbaralee Diamondstein, *Inside New York's Art World* (New York: Rizzoli, 1979). Reprinted by permission of Barbaralee Diamondstein.

COLDSTREAM, SIR WILLIAM   "I lived in a room . . .": R. S. Lambert, ed., *Art in England* (London: Pelican, 1938). Reprinted by permission of Penguin Books, Ltd.

COLLA, ETTORE   "Of this only have I . . .": Lawrence Alloway, *Colla* (Rome: Grafica, 1960).
Solar Workshop. 1964. L'Isola Gallery, Rome.

CORNELL, JOSEPH   "Shadow boxes become . . .": Exhibition catalogue, Hugo Gallery, New York, December 1946.
"Impressions intriguingly diverse . . .": Exhibition catalogue, Copley Gallery, Beverly Hills, Calif., September 1948.

DAVIS, STUART   "Modern art rediscovered humanity . . .": Stuart Davis, "The Cube Root," *ARTnews* 15, no. 18 (February 1–14, 1943), pp. 33, 34. Reprinted in Diane Kelder, *Stuart Davis* (New York: Praeger, 1971). Copyright ARTnews Associates, 1943.
Ready to Wear. 1955. The Art Institute of Chicago; Sigmund W. Kunstader Gift and Goodman Foundation.

DEKKERS, AD   "Mondrian and later van Doesburg . . .": *'60–'80 Attitudes, Concepts, and Images* (exhibition catalogue), Stedelijk Museum, Amsterdam, 1982.

DE KOONING, WILLEM   "For the painter to come to . . ." / "Kandinsky understood . . ." / "Spiritually I am . . ." / "The argument often used . . ." / "Personally, I do not need . . .": "What Abstract Art Means to Me" (symposium, Museum of Modern Art, February 15, 1951), *Museum of Modern Art Bulletin* 18, no. 3 (Spring 1951).
Woman, 1950. Weatherspoon Art Gallery, University of North Carolina at Greensboro, Lena Kernodle McDuffie Memorial Gift.

DEMUTH, CHARLES   "Across a Greco . . .": "Across a Greco Is Written," *Creative Art* 5, no. 3 (September 1929).
Incense of a New Church. 1912. Columbus Museum of Art, Ohio; gift of Ferdinand Howald.

DERAIN, ANDRÉ   "Everything comes from nature . . ." / "One must seize nature . . ." / "Style is the constant coming . . .": Georges Hilaire, *Derain* (Geneva: Cailler, 1939).

DIBBETS, JAN   "I thought that the lawn . . ." / "Nature consists of a large number . . .": *To Do with Nature* (exhibition catalogue), Visual Arts Office for Abroad, Amsterdam, 1979.
Forest Piece, 1969. Photograph by Shunk-Kender courtesy of Leo Castelli Gallery, New York.

DIEBENKORN, RICHARD   "All paintings start out . . .": *Modern Painting, Sculpture, and Drawing Collected by Louise and Joseph Pulitzer, Jr.* (catalogue for Pulitzer Collection, St. Louis) (Cambridge, Mass.: Harvard College, 1958).
Ocean Park #117. 1979. Collection Mr. and Mrs. Oscar Kolin. Photograph courtesy of M. Knoedler & Co., Inc., New York.

DILLER, BURGOYNE "The work presented . . .": "Pages from Diller's Notebook" (1961; collection of Dr. and Mrs. Arthur Lejwa, New York), in exhibition catalogue, Walker Art Center, Minneapolis, December 1971–January 1972.

DINE, JIM *What is your attitude . . ."* / *"Who are you . . ."*: Statement in Michael Compton, *Pop Art* (London: Hamlyn, 1970).

DI SUVERO, MARK "Steel is very direct . . ." / "I think we are deeply influenced . . ." / "We have seen sculpture grow . . ." / "I have worked for about . . ." / "I've finally arrived . . ." / "It is the re-formation . . .": Interview with Dean Fleming in *Ocular* (Spring 1981).

DIX, OTTO "You know, if one paints . . .": Fritz Loffler, *Otto Dix: Leben und Werk* (Dresden, 1967).

DOESBURG, THEO VAN "1. I speak here for . . ." / "The artist speaks from within . . .": *Grundbegriffe der neuen Kunst* (The Bauhaus, 1925). Reproduced from Theo van Doesburg, *Principles of Neo-Plastic Art*, trans. Janet Seligman (London: Lund Humphries, 1969).
Composition (The Cow). 1916–1917. Collection, the Museum of Modern Art, New York; purchase.

DORAZIO, PIERO "Nonobjective painting . . .": "Note on the Art of Painting" (1961), *Tracks* 1, no. 2 (Spring 1975).

DOVE, ARTHUR GARFIELD "At the age of nine I painted . . .": Letter to Sam Kootz in Kootz, *Modern American Painters* (New York: Brewer & Warren, 1930).

DUBUFFET, JEAN "Many people, having made up . . .": From "Apercevoir," as reprinted in *Prospectus et Tous Écrites Suivants*, vol. 2 (Paris: Gallimard, 1967). Copyright Jean Dubuffet.
"It is true that . . .": "L'Auteur Répond à Quelques Objections." Preface to *Miro-bulus, Macadam & Cie* (exhibition catalogue) as reprinted in *Prospectus et Tous Écrites Suivants*, vol. 2 (Paris: Gallimard, 1967). Copyright Jean Dubuffet.
"And now what happens . . .": "Anti-Cultural Positions," from a lecture at the Arts Club of Chicago, December 20, 1951. Copyright Jean Dubuffet.

DUCHAMP, MARCEL "In 1913 I had the happy idea . . .": Talk at Museum of Modern Art, October 19, 1961. Reprinted in Michel Sanouillet, ed., *Salt Seller* (New York: Oxford University Press, 1973).

ERNST, MAX "The procedure of *frottage* . . .": *Beyond Painting* (New York: Wittenborn & Schultz, 1948). Reprinted by permission of Wittenborn Art Books, Inc. The first three footnotes are Ernst's.

EVERGOOD, PHILIP "Diverse emotions stir . . ." / "I feel the search . . .": *Evergood, Twenty Years* (exhibition catalogue), ACA Gallery, New York, 1946.

FAHLSTRÖM, ÖYVIND "**Art.** Consider art . . ." / "**Games.** Seen either . . ." / "**Multiples.** Painting, sculpture . . ." / "**Risk reforms.** Attitude to society . . .": "Take Care of the World" (statement, 1966) in exhibition catalogue, Guggenheim Museum, New York, 1982.

FAUTRIER, JEAN "The unreality . . .": "To Each His Reality," *XXe Siècle* (Paris), no. 9 (1957).

FLAVIN, DAN "In time, I came to these conclusions . . .": Dan Flavin, "Dan Flavin: An Autobiographical Sketch, ' . . . daylight, or cool white,' " *Artforum* 4, no. 4 (December 1965), pp. 20–24. Copyright © Artforum International Magazine.

FONTANA, LUCIO 'It is necessary . . .": From "Spazialismo" (manifesto), 1946.

FORGE, ANDREW "To recapture the studio monologue . . .": Letter to author, March 1984.

FRANCIS, SAM "What we want is . . .": *The New American Painting* (exhibition catalogue), Museum of Modern Art, New York, 1959.

"I live in a paradise of . . .": Letter to Yoshiaki Tono in Peter Selz, *Sam Francis* (New York: Abrams, 1975).

Untitled (Blue Over Yellow). 1963. Edition of twenty. Tamarind Collection, University of New Mexico Art Museum, Albuquerque.

GABO, NAUM   "I would say that . . .": Interview with Ibram Lassaw and Ilya Bolotowsky in Herbert Read and Leslie Martin, *Naum Gabo, Introductory Essays* (London: Lund Humphries, 1957).

GERZSO, GUNTHER   "In painting . . .": "Gerzso on Gerzso," in *Gunther Gerzso: Paintings and Graphics Reviewed* (exhibition catalogue), The University of Texas at Austin, April–May 1976.

Morada Antigua. 1964. Private collection. Photograph courtesy of Mary-Ann Martin/Fine Art, New York.

GHIKA, NIKOLAS   *"Are you aware . . ."*: Interview with Bryan Robertson in exhibition catalogue, Whitechapel Gallery, London, July–August 1968.

GIACOMETTI, ALBERTO   "One day when I was drawing . . .": *Alberto Giacometti* (exhibition catalogue), Galerie Engelberts, Geneva, 1967.

"If one sets one's heart . . ." / "One could not express in words . . .": Interview with André Parinaud in *Arts* (Paris), no. 873 (June 1962).

"It might be supposed that realism . . .": Quoted by David Sylvester in exhibition catalogue, Tate Gallery, London, July–August 1965.

The Artist's Mother. 1937. Collection Pierre Matisse, New York.

GOERITZ, MATHIAS   "In the El Eco experiment . . .": "Manifesto of Emotional Architecture," Mexico City, 1953.

GOLUB, LEON   "My recent paintings . . .": *New Images of Man* (exhibition catalogue; Peter Selz, ed.), Museum of Modern Art, New York, 1959.

GONCHAROVA, NATALIA SERGEEVNA   "I am convinced that . . .": Preface to exhibition, 1913. Reprinted in John Bowlt, ed. and trans., *Russian Art of the Avant-Garde: Theory and Criticism 1902–1934* (New York: Viking, 1976). Copyright © 1976 by John Bowlt. Reprinted by permission of Viking Penguin Inc.

La Femme au Chapeau. 1912. Musée National d'Art Moderne, Centre Georges Pompidou, Paris.

GONZÁLEZ, JULIO   "The age of iron began . . .": Unpublished notes in Andrew C. Ritchie, *Sculpture of the Twentieth Century* (New York: Museum of Modern Art, 1952).

"To project and design . . ." / "The synthetic deformities . . .": "Réponse à Enquête sur l'Art Actuel," *Cahiers d'Art* (Paris) 10, no. 7–10 (1935), p. 242.

GORKY, ARSHILE   "My dearest ones . . ." / "Beloveds, the stuff of thought . . .": Letters to Vartoosh (1939), translated from the Armenian by Karlen Mooradian, in Mooradian, *Arshile Gorky Adoian* (Chicago: Gilgamesh Press Ltd., 1978). Copyright © 1978 by Karlen Mooradian.

"I like the heat . . .": Statement (1942), Museum of Modern Art files.

"Surrealism is academic art . . .": Letter to Vartoosh (1947), translated from the Armenian by Karlen Mooradian, in Mooradian, *op. cit.* Copyright © 1978 by Karlen Mooradian.

Portrait of Vartoosh. Mid-1930s. Hirshhorn Museum and Sculpture Garden, Smithsonian Institution, Washington, D.C.

GOTTLIEB, ADOLPH   "I would start . . ." / "There's a tremendous difference . . .": Interview with Jeanne Siegel, WBAI Radio, New York, May 1967 (copy in Museum of Modern Art Library).

GRIS, JUAN   "I work with the elements . . .": Statement in *L'Esprit Nouveau* (Paris), no. 5 (1921). Reprinted in D. H. Kahnweiler, *Juan Gris, His Life and Work* (New York: Valentia, 1947).

GROSZ, GEORGE   "The artistic revolutions . . .": George Grosz, "On My Next Paintings," in Victor Meisel, *Voices of German Expressionism* (Englewood Cliffs, N.J.: Prentice-Hall, 1970). Reprinted by permission of the Estate of George Grosz, Princeton, New Jersey.
A German at Home (illustration from Daudet). Private collection. Photograph courtesy of Associated American Artists Galleries, New York, reproduced by permission of the Estate of George Grosz.

GUSTON, PHILIP   "In my experience . . ." / "The strange and the familiar . . ." / "Of the two writers . . ." / "I think that probably . . ." / "I think in my studies . . .": "Philip Guston Talking," lecture at the University of Minnesota, March 1978.
The Magnet. 1975. The Saatchi Collection, London. Photograph courtesy of David McKee, Inc., New York.

HAACKE, HANS   "What is considered beautiful . . .": Interview with Margaret Sheffield (Oxford: Museum of Modern Art, 1978). Copyright © Hans Haacke.
Seurat's "Les Poseuses" (Small Version) 1888–1975. 1975. An edition of three. Photograph courtesy of John Weber Gallery, New York.

HAMILTON, RICHARD   "It Seems to me . . ." / "In much the same way . . ." / "Futurism has ebbed . . .": Richard Hamilton, *Richard Hamilton, Collected Words 1953–1982* (London: Thames & Hudson, 1982). Reprinted by permission of Edition Hansjörg Mayer, Stuttgart. Copyright © Richard Hamilton.

HARE, DAVID   "I believe that . . .": *Fourteen Americans* (exhibition catalogue), Museum of Modern Art, New York, 1946.

HARTUNG, HANS   "I could very well . . .": Heidi Burklin, "Conversation with Hans Hartung," *Cimaise* (Paris) (September–December 1974). Copyright © J. R. Arnaud.

HELD, AL   "I fundamentally believe . . ." / "I think one characteristic . . .": Interview with Mark C. Morris in exhibition catalogue, Donald Morris Gallery, Detroit, 1983.

HÉLION, JEAN   "I am not preoccupied . . ." / "I understand abstract art . . .": Myfanwy Evans, ed., *The Painter's Object* (London: Gerald Howe, 1937).
"My pictorial course . . .": Statement (August 1973) in exhibition catalogue, Karl Flinker Gallery, Paris, May 1975.

HEPWORTH, DAME BARBARA   "Being a carver . . ." / "I think it would be true . . .": Warren Forma, *Five British Sculptors* (New York: Grossman, 1964).
Solitary Eye. 1972. Barbara Hepworth Museum (Tate Gallery), London.

HERBIN, AUGUSTE   "Having renounced the representation . . ." / "[The painter] begins . . ." / "The deterioration of the idea . . ." / "the idea *object* . . .": Auguste Herbin, *L'Art Non-Figuratif* (Paris: Editions Lydia Conti, 1948).

HESSE, EVA   "irregular, edges, six to seven feet . . .": *Art in Process IV* (exhibition catalogue), Finch College, New York, Fall 1969.

HILTON, ROGER   "All my thinking . . ." / "The combination artist-picture . . ." / "The painter today . . ." / "At heart everyone knows . . ." / "I see art . . ." / "It may be thought . . ." / "Abstraction in itself . . ." / "Now that we have conquered . . .": Exhibition catalogue (Alan Bowness, ed.), Galerie Charles Lienhard, Zurich, 1961.

HOCKNEY, DAVID   "I can say that . . .": Commune of Milan and British Council, *English Art Today* (2 vols.) (New York: Rizzoli, 1976). Reprinted by permission of Electa Editrice, Milan, Italy.

HODLER, FERDINAND   "Color exists simultaneously . . .": Exhibition catalogue (Peter Selz, ed.), University Art Museum, Berkeley, Calif., 1973.

HOFER, CARL   "We stand today . . .": Exhibition catalogue, George Walter Vincent Smith Art Gallery, Springfield, Mass., 1941. Copyright George Walter Vincent Smith Art Museum.

HOFMANN, HANS   "Basically I hate . . .": Katherine Kuh, *The Artist's Voice* (New York: Harper & Row, 1960).

IRWIN, ROBERT   "I started out with . . .": Exhibition catalogue (text by Ira Licht), Museum of Modern Art, New York, November 8, 1975–January 4, 1976.

JOHNS, JASPER   "Sometimes I see it . . .": *Sixteen Americans* (exhibition catalogue), Museum of Modern Art, New York, 1959.
0 Through 9. 1961. Private collection. Photograph courtesy of Leo Castelli Gallery, New York.

JORN, ASGER   "People often ask . . .": / "The painter's relation to literature . . ." / "Anything really *new* . . ." / "A creative train of thought . . ." / "In every real experiment . . ." / "Even the most faithful copy . . .": Guy Atkins, *Asger Jorn* (London: Methuen, 1964).
Painting. Photograph courtesy of Lefebre Gallery, New York.

JUDD, DONALD   "In earlier art . . .": "Specific Objects," in *Arts Yearbook* (New York: Arts Magazine, 1965).

KANTOR, TADEUSZ   "In artistic development . . .": "Emballages," in exhibition catalogue, Warsaw, 1963. Translated by Piotr Graff.

KAPROW, ALLAN   "A Happening is . . .": Allan Kaprow, *Some Recent Happenings* (New York: Something Else Press, 1966).
"I was interested . . .": Interview with B. Bermon in exhibition catalogue, Pasadena Museum, September 15–October 22, 1967. Reprinted by permission of Norton Simon Museum of Art, Pasadena, Calif.
"An Environment is . . .": Letters to B. Bermon in *ibid*. Reprinted by permission of Norton Simon Museum of Art, Pasadena, Calif.

KELLY, ELLSWORTH   "When I was younger . . ." / "I'm not interested in edges . . ." / "I like to work from things . . .": Interview with Henry Geldzahler in exhibition catalogue, Washington (D.C.) Gallery of Art, December 11, 1963–January 26, 1964.

KIENHOLZ, ED   "I mostly think of my work . . ." / "I really begin to understand . . .": *Volksemfängers* (exhibition catalogue), Nationalgalerie, Berlin, 1977.
Barney's Beanery. 1965. Stedelijk, Amsterdam. Photograph by Ad Petersen, Amsterdam.

KIESLER, FREDERICK   "The artist creator has always been . . .": Frederick Kiesler, "The Endless Search," in Kiesler, *Inside the Endless House* (New York: Simon & Schuster, 1964). Copyright © 1964 by Frederick J. Kiesler. Reprinted by permission of Simon & Schuster.

KING, PHILLIP   "Why the preoccupation . . .": Commune of Milan and British Council, *English Art Today* (2 vols.) (New York: Rizzoli, 1976). Reprinted by permission of Electa Editrice, Milan, Italy.

KIRCHNER, ERNST LUDWIG   "Years went by as I continued . . .": Letter to Botho Graef (Jena, September 21, 1916) in Victor Meisel, *Voices of German Expressionism*

(Englewood Cliffs, N.J.: Prentice-Hall, 1970). Copyright by Dr. Wolfgang and Ingeborg Henze, Campione d'Italia.

"What *you* write about art . . .": Letter to Dr. Eberhard Grisebach (Kreuzlinger, December 1, 1917) in *ibid.*

Artillerymen. 1915. Collection, the Museum of Modern Art, New York; gift of Mr. and Mrs. Morten D. May.

KITAJ, R. B.   "To my way of thinking . . ." / "Whatever looms in the offing . . ." / "In an epoch . . .": Exhibition catalogue, University Art Museum, Berkeley, Calif., October 7–November 12, 1967. Copyright © 1967 by the Regents of the University of California.

KLINE, FRANZ   "Somebody will say . . .": Frank O'Hara, "Franz Kline Talking," *Evergreen Review* 2, no. 6, pp. 58–68.

Ink Drawing. 1959. Formerly collection of the Estate of Franz Kline. Photograph reproduced by permission of Mrs. E. Ross Zogbaum.

KOKOSCHKA, OSKAR   "How do I define . . ." / " 'Man know thyself,' the device . . .": Heinz Spielmann, ed., *Das Schriftliche Werk* (Hamburg: Hans Christian Verlag). Translated by P. S. Falla for an exhibition catalogue, Marlborough Gallery, London, 1981.

"I myself see no cause . . .": Letter to James Plant (1948) in exhibition catalogue, Marlborough Gallery, London, 1981.

"The difference between experience . . ." / "Let us be clear to begin . . .": Spielmann, *op. cit.*

KOLÁŘ, JIŘÍ   "Art has nothing . . .": *Jiří Kolář* (Cologne: Dumont Schonberg, 1968).

"I believe that . . .": Exhibition catalogue, Guggenheim Museum, New York, 1975.

"If we take the term . . .": Exhibition catalogue, Albright-Knox Gallery, Buffalo, N.Y., 1978.

Reverence to Columbus. 1969. The Solomon R. Guggenheim Museum, New York.

KOLLWITZ, KÄTHE   "On All Souls' Day . . .": Victor Meisel, *Voices of German Expressionism* (Englewood Cliffs, N.J.: Prentice-Hall, 1970).

KUPKA, FRANTIŠEK   "Creation—the basic problem in painting": "La Vie des Lettres" (July 1921). Reprinted in Ludmila Vachtová, *Kupka* (New York: McGraw-Hill, 1968).

LAM, WIFREDO   "I was born in Cuba . . .": Interview with Gerard Xuriguera in Xuriguera, *Lam* (Paris: Filipacchi, E.P.I. Editions, 1974).

"I decided that . . .": Max-Pol Fouchet, *Wifredo Lam* (Barcelona: Ediciones Poligrafa, 1977).

The Jungle. 1943. Collection, the Museum of Modern Art, New York; Inter-American Fund.

LARIONOV, MIKHAIL FEDOROVICH   "Every form exists objectively . . .": "Pictorial Rayonism," *Montjoie!* (Paris), no. 4–6 (April–June 1914). Reprinted in John Bowlt, ed. and trans., *Russian Art of the Avant-Garde: Theory and Criticism 1902–1934* (New York: Viking, 1976). Copyright © 1976 by John Bowlt. Reprinted by permission of Viking Penguin Inc.

LÉGER, FERNAND   "The feat of superbly imitating . . .": Statement (1950) in Fernand Léger, *Functions of Painting*, ed. Edward F. Fry, trans. Alexandra Anderson (New York: Viking, 1973). English translation © 1973 by the Viking Press, Inc. Reprinted by permission of Viking Penguin Inc.

LEWIS, PERCY WYNDHAM   "Long Live the Vortex!": *BLAST*, no. 1. Reprinted in

Walter Michel and C. J. Fox, eds., *Wyndham Lewis on Art* (New York: Funk & Wagnalls, 1969).

LeWITT, SOL   ". . . I will refer to . . .": Sol LeWitt, "Paragraphs on Conceptual Art," *Artform* 5, no. 10 (June 1967), pp. 79–83. Copyright © Artforum International Magazine.
Serial Project No. 1 (ABCD). 1966. Collection, the Museum of Modern Art, New York; purchase and exchange.

LICHTENSTEIN, ROY   *"What is Pop Art . . ."*: Interview in G. R. Swenson, *ARTnews* 62, no. 7 (November 1963), p. 25. Copyright ARTnews Associates, 1963.

LICINI, OSVALDO   "Art for us . . .": Exhibition catalogue, Galleria Lorenzelli, Milan, 1961.
Ritmo. 1956. L'Isola Gallery, Rome.

LINDNER, RICHARD   "Subject matter for me . . .": Interview with John Gruen in *ARTnews* 77 (Summer 1978), pp. 74–77.

LIPCHITZ, JACQUES   "There is one thing I would like . . .": Jacques Lipchitz and H. H. Arnason, *My Life in Sculpture* (New York: Viking, 1972). Copyright © 1972 by Jacques Lipchitz and H. H. Arnason. Reprinted by permission of Viking Penguin Inc.

LISSITZKY, EL   "I cannot define absolutely . . .": *ABC-Beitrage zum Bauen* (Basel, 1925). Reprinted in Sophie Lissitzky-Kuppers, *Lissitzky*, trans. Helene Aldwinckle and Mary Whittall (London: Thames & Hudson, 1968).
The Gravediggers, from *Figurines, Plastic Representation of the Electromechanical Production "Victory Over the Sun."* 1923. Collection, the Museum of Modern Art, New York.

LONG, RICHARD   "My art is . . .": Exhibition catalogue, Anthony D'Offay Gallery, London, September 1980.

LUCEBERT   "I think that art *can* speak . . .": *Dutch Art and Architecture Today* (Amsterdam), no. 4 (November 1978).

MACK, HEINZ   "The dynamic structure . . .": *Mack, Piene, Uecker* (exhibition catalogue), Kestner Gesellschaft, Hanover, 1950.

MAGNELLI, ALBERTO   "If you consider . . .": Alberto Magnelli, "Temoignages pour l'art abstract," in *Art d'Aujourd'hui* (Paris, 1952).

MAGRITTE, RENÉ   "To equate my painting . . ." / "The images must be seen . . ." / "The word 'dream'. . ." / "If one is a determinist . . .": Suzi Gablik, *Magritte* (New York: New York Graphic Society, 1970).
The Palace of Curtains, III. 1928–1929. The Sidney and Harriet Janis Collection; gift to the Museum of Modern Art, New York.

MALEVICH, KASIMIR   "My new painting does not belong . . .": Letter to Matyushin (1916) in Larissa Zhdanova, *Malevich* (London: Thames & Hudson, 1982).
"But we will discover . . .": Letter to Matyushin (June 23, 1916) in *ibid.*
"It has become clear to me that new frameworks . . .": Kasimir Malevich, "Non-Objective Creation and Suprematism," in exhibition catalogue for Tenth State Exhibition, Moscow, 1919.
Reprinted in Troels Anderson, ed., *Essays on Art* (Copenhagen: Borgen, 1969).
Suprematist Composition. Undated. Collection, the Museum of Modern Art, New York.

MARINI, MARINO   "I do not think . . .": Exhibition catalogue, Curt Valentin Gallery, New York, October 27–November 21, 1953.

MARTIN, AGNES   "It is all awarness of . . .": "We Are in the Midst of Reality," lecture at Yale University, New Haven, Conn., April 5, 1976. Reprinted in exhibition catalogue, Arts Council of Great Britain, London, 1977.

MARTIN, KENNETH "Construction stems from within . . .": "Construction from Within," *Structure* (Amsterdam) 6, no. 1 (1964).

MASSON, ANDRÉ "It was obvious . . .": Lecture at Mt. Holyoke College, South Hadley, Mass., 1943.
"Fundamentally I am more a sympathizer . . .": "Europeans in America," *Museum of Modern Art Bulletin* 13, no. 4–5 (1946).
Automatic Drawing. 1925. Private collection.

MATHIEU, GEORGES "From the ideal to the real . . .": *Vers une Structuration Nouvelle des Formes* (exhibition catalogue), Bruges, 1958.

MATISSE, HENRI "I can say nothing . . .": Maria Lus, "Temoignages: Henri Matisse," *XXe Siècle,* n.s. 2 (January 1952). Reprinted as "Testimonial" in Jack D. Flam, *Matisse on Art* (Oxford: Phaidon Press, 1978). Copyright 1978.

MATTA ECHAURREN, ROBERTO "When I started painting . . .": Exhibition catalogue, Andrew Crispo Gallery, New York, 1975.

MIRÓ, JOAN "The spectacle of the sky . . ." / "When I began . . ." / "Immobility strikes me . . ." / "What I am seeking . . ." / "I begin my pictures . . ." / "In a picture, it should be possible . . ." / "I feel the need . . .": "I Work Like a Gardener" (sayings collected by Yvon Taillandier), in Joyce Reeves, trans., *Miró* (exhibition catalogue), Tate Gallery, London, 1963.
Femme et Oiseau. (In collaboration with the potter Artigas.) 1962. Pierre Matisse Gallery, New York.

MOHOLY-NAGY, LÁSZLÓ "All technical achievements . . .": László Moholy-Nagy, "From Pigment to Light," in Richard Kostelanetz, ed., *Moholy-Nagy* (New York: Praeger, 1970).
"The Function of the Artist": László Moholy-Nagy, *The New Vision, 1928* (New York: Wittenborn & Schultz, 1949). Reprinted by permission of Wittenborn Art Books, Inc.

MONDRIAN, PIET "Not everyone realizes that . . .": Statement (November 1941) in exhibition catalogue, Art of This Century, New York, 1942.
"Reality manifests itself . . .": "Notes," *Tracks* 3, no. 1–2 (1977).

MOORE, HENRY "The human figure . . ." / "My aim in work . . .": Herbert Read, ed., *Unit One* (London, 1934).
"A piece of stone . . .": Myfanwy Evans, ed., *The Painter's Object* (London: Gerald Howe, 1937).
"The most striking quality . . .": Statement in *The Listener* 25, no. 641 (April 24, 1941).

MORANDI, GIORGIO "I have always avoided . . .": Edouard Roditi, *Dialogues on Art* (London: Secker & Warburg, 1960).

MORRIS, ROBERT ". . . the simple regular . . .": Robert Morris, "Robert Morris: Notes on Sculpture," *Artforum* 4, no. 6 (February 1966), pp. 42–44. Copyright © Artforum International Magazine.

MOTHERWELL, ROBERT "I believe that the New York School . . ." / "An odd contradiction . . ." / "That painting and sculpture . . ." / "The ancient Chinese painters . . ." / "Generally, I use . . .": Exhibition catalogue, Städtische Kunsthalle, Düsseldorf, 1976.
Nip and Tuck. 1984. Collection of the artist. Photograph courtesy of M. Knoedler & Co., Inc., New York.

NAKIAN, REUBEN "The [Metropolitan] Museum was . . .": Interview in "Is To-day's Artist with or Against the Past?" *ARTnews* 57, no. 4 (Summer 1958), p. 29. Copyright ARTnews Associates, 1958.

NEVELSON, LOUISE "Another thing about creation . . ." / "Now in the reality . . ." / "I have given shadow . . .": Louise Nevelson, *Dawns and Dusks* (New York: Scribners, 1976).

NEWMAN, BARNETT "If we could describe . . .": Essay (c. 1944) in T. B. Hess, *Barnett Newman* (London: Tate Gallery, 1972).

NICHOLSON, BEN "1. It must be understood . . .": Martin, Nicholson, and Gabo, eds., *Circle* (London: Faber & Faber, 1937). Reprinted by permission of Faber and Faber Ltd.
"About space-construction . . .": In *Horizon* (October 1941).

NOGUCHI, ISAMU "The essence of sculpture . . .": *Fourteen Americans* (exhibition catalogue), Museum of Modern Art, New York, 1946.
The Self. 1957. The Tate Gallery, London.

NOLDE, EMIL "Art is exalted . . .": Notes in Victor Meisel, *Voices of German Expressionism* (Englewood Cliffs, N.J.: Prentice-Hall, 1970).

O'KEEFFE, GEORGIA "It is surprising to me . . .": Georgia O'Keeffe, *Georgia O'Keeffe* (New York: Viking, 1976).
Light Coming on the Plains III. 1917. The Amon Carter Museum, Fort Worth.

OLDENBURG, CLAES ". . . My work makes a great demand . . .": Claes Oldenburg, "Claes Oldenburg: Extracts from the Studio Notes," *Artforum* 4, no. 5 (January 1966), pp. 32–33. Copyright © Artforum International Magazine.
"I use naïve imitation . . .": "Store Days" (1966). Reprinted in Michael Compton, *Pop Art* (London: Hamlyn, 1970).

OPPENHEIM, DENNIS "In 1967, there was . . .": Interview with Alain Parent in exhibition catalogue, Musée d'Art Contemporain, Montreal, 1977.

PAOLOZZI, EDUARDO "Key phrases . . ." / "The multi-evocative image . . ." / "Here is a list . . ." / "At the elbow . . ." / "My preoccupation . . .": "Notes from a Lecture at the Institute of Contemporary Arts, 1958," *Uppercase* (London), no. 1.
Box Headed Figure. 1957. Whereabouts unknown. Photograph published by kind permission of the artist.

PASMORE, VICTOR "In spite of his independence . . .": "Abstract Painting and Sculpture in England," in The American Abstract Artists, ed., *The World of Abstract Art* (New York: Wittenborn, 1957). Reprinted by permission of Wittenborn Art Books, Inc.

PICABIA, FRANCIS "If you want to have clean ideas . . .": "Aphorisms," in exhibition catalogue (text by William H. Camfield), Solomon R. Guggenheim Museum, New York, 1970.
Prenez Garde à la Peinture (Beware of Wet Paint). C. 1916. Moderna Museet, Stockholm.

PICASSO, PABLO "No doubt, it is useful . . ." / "The secret of many . . ." / "I consider a work of art . . ." / "Braque always said . . ." / "Something holy, that's it . . ." / "What I find horrible . . .": Dore Ashton, ed., *Picasso on Art: A Selection of Views* (New York: Viking, 1972). Copyright © 1972 by Dore Ashton. Reprinted by permission of Viking Penguin Inc.
Portrait of Igor Stravinsky. 1920. Musée Picasso, Paris.

PRENDERGAST, MAURICE BRAZIL "Very blue this afternoon . . .": Van Wyck

284 ■

SOURCE LIST

Brooks, "Introduction," exhibition catalogue, Addison Gallery of American Art, Andover, Mass., 1938.

RAUSCHENBERG, ROBERT   "Any incentive to paint . . .": *Sixteen Americans* (exhibition catalogue), Museum of Modern Art, New York, 1959.
Drift. 1956. Private collection. Photograph courtesy of Leo Castelli Gallery, New York.

RAYSSE, MARTIAL   "The unconditioned eye . . .": Statement, 1967.

REINHARDT, AD   "Separation, in the past . . .": *The New Decade: 35 American Painters and Sculptors* (exhibition catalogue), Whitney Museum of American Art, New York, 1955.

REUTERSWÄRD, CARL FREDRIK   "My works and activities . . .": Interview with Per Wästberg in *Dagens Nyheter* (Stockholm), October 9, 1978.

RICHIER, GERMAINE   "The human image . . .": *New Images of Man* (exhibition catalogue; Peter Selz, ed.), Museum of Modern Art, New York, 1959.

RILEY, BRIDGET LOUISE   "My paintings are not . . .": Muriel Emanuel et al., eds., *Contemporary Artists*, 2nd ed. (New York: St. Martin's Press, 1983).

RIOPELLE, JEAN-PAUL   "Since I'm Canadian . . .": Pierre Schneider, *Riopelle* (Paris: Maeght, 1972). Copyright © Maeght.
Lointain. 1962. Yale University Art Gallery. Gift of Susan Morse Hilles.

RIVERS, LARRY   "In relation to the dominant interests . . .": *Twelve Americans* (exhibition catalogue), Museum of Modern Art, New York, 1956.

RODCHENKO, ALEXANDER   "Slogans": "Slogans" (February 1921), in German Karginov, *Rodchenko* (London: Thames & Hudson, 1979).
"It is almost impossible . . .": "On Photography," in *ibid.*

ROSENQUIST, JAMES   "I'm amazed and excited . . ." / "When I use a combination . . .": Statement (1964) in Michael Compton, *Pop Art* (London: Hamlyn, 1970).

ROTHKO, MARK   "Why the most gifted painters . . ." / "The real essence . . ." / "I insist upon . . ." / "I love both . . ." / "Rather be prodigal . . ." / "Pictures must be miraculous . . ." / "If I must place my trust . . .": Dore Ashton, *About Rothko* (New York: Oxford University Press, 1983).

ROZANOVA, OLGA VLADIMIROVNA   "The art of painting . . .": Olga Vladimirovna Rozanova, "The Bases of the New Creation and Reasons Why It Is Misunderstood," in John Bowlt, ed. and trans., *Russian Art of the Avant-Garde: Theory and Criticism 1902–1934* (New York: Viking, 1976). Copyright © 1976 by John Bowlt. Reprinted by permission of Viking Penguin Inc.

SAURA, ANTONIO   "What interests me . . .": *Cuatros Pintores Españoles* (exhibition catalogue), El Paso, Madrid, 1958.

SCHIELE, EGON   "I have become aware . . .": Letter to Dr. Oskar Reichel (September 1911) in Alessandre Comini, *Egon Schiele's Portraits* (Berkeley, Calif.: University of California Press, 1974).
Seated Girl with Clasped Hands. 1918. The Metropolitan Museum of Art, New York; bequest of Scofield Thayer, 1982.

SCHLEMMER, OSKAR   "I view future developments . . ." / " 'Abstract' figures, completely divested . . .": *The Letters and Diaries of Oskar Schlemmer* (Middletown, Conn.: Wesleyan University Press, 1972).
Study for Triadic Ballet. 1922. Collection, the Museum of Modern Art, New York; gift of Lily Auchincloss.

SCHOONHOVEN, JAN   " 'Weltanschauung' is a vague term . . ." / "My drawings have been described . . .": Interview with Gijs van Tuyl (1975) in *Contemporary Art from the Netherlands* (exhibition catalogue), Museum of Contemporary Art, Chicago, 1982.

SCHWITTERS, KURT   "I call small compositions . . .": *Merz 20* (catalogue, c. 1927). Reprinted in exhibition catalogue, University of California, Los Angeles, 1965.

SEGAL, GEORGE   "I introduced a lot . . ." / "I love to watch people . . ." / "Driving home from New York . . .": *George Segal Sculptures* (exhibition catalogue), Walker Art Center, Minneapolis, 1978. Reprinted by permission of Walker Art Center. © Walker Art Center.

SHAHN, BEN   "Generalities and abstractions . . ." / "Yes, one rankles . . .": *The Shape of Content* (Cambridge, Mass.: Harvard University Press, 1957). Copyright © 1957 by the President and Fellows of Harvard College. Reprinted by permission.

SHEMI, YEHIEL   "Cézanne and the early Constructivists . . .": Letter to author, 1984.
New-York I (second wall). 1975. Collection of the artist.

SIQUEIROS, DAVID ALFARO   "Modern Mexican painting . . .": Statement read at the First American Artists' Congress, New York, 1936.
Proletarian Victim. 1933. Collection, the Museum of Modern Art, New York; gift of the Estate of George Gershwin.

SMITH, DAVID   "The artist has been . . .": "Who Is the Artist, How Does He Act?" *Everyday Art Quarterly* (Minneapolis), no. 23 (1952). Picasso quote ("A picture is not thought out . . .") from "Zervos: Conversation with Picasso," *Cahiers d'Art* 10 (1935). Reprinted by permission of Walker Art Center.
"When I begin a sculpture . . ." / "I make no claim . . ." / "Art is a paradox . . ." / "I believe that my time . . .": Cleve Gray, ed., *David Smith by David Smith* (New York: Holt, Rinehart & Winston, 1968).
O Drawing. 1957. Collection of Roger I. Davidson. Photograph courtesy of David Smith.

SMITH, TONY   "I'm interested in the inscrutability . . ." / "I'm not aware . . ." / "We think in two dimensions . . ." / "I view art as something . . .": Samuel Wagstaff, Jr., "Talking to Tony Smith," *Artforum* 5, no. 4 (December 1966), pp. 14–19. Copyright © Artforum International Magazine.
#40, Free Ride. 1962. An edition of three. Photograph courtesy of Xavier Fourcade, Inc., New York.

SMITHSON, ROBERT   "Many architectural concepts . . .": Robert Smithson, "The New Monuments and Entropy," *Artforum* 4, no. 10 (June 1966), pp. 26–31. Copyright © Artforum International Magazine.

SOTO, JESÚS RAFAEL   "*Penetrables,* the new works . . ." / "The immaterial is . . ." / "I separate art and politics . . .": *Lumière et Mouvement* (exhibition catalogue), Musée de la Ville de Paris, 1967. Interview with Claude-Louis Renard (Paris, 1974). Exhibition catalogue, Solomon R. Guggenheim Museum, New York, 1974.

SOULAGES, PIERRE   "Let's be done . . ." / ". . . Black trees . . ." / "A painting is a physical experience . . ." / "Painting is a play . . .": Exhibition catalogue (text by James Johnson Sweeney), Knoedler Gallery, New York, February 1968.

STAEL, NICHOLAS DE   "An eye that rams . . ." / "Never assess space . . ." / "With Rembrandt an Indian turban . . .": Letters (November–December 1949) in Denys Sutton, *Nicholas de Stael,* trans. Rita Barisse (New York: Grove Press, 1955). All Rights Reserved by Grove Press, Inc.

Landscape in Vaucluse No. 2. 1953. Albright-Knox Art Gallery, Buffalo, N.Y.; gift of the Seymour H. Knox Foundation, Inc., 1969.

STAŻEWSKI, HENRYK "To struggle against society . . .": *Henryk Stażewski* (exhibition catalogue; Kazimierz Zolziechowski, trans.), Annely Judah Gallery, London, November–December 1982.

STELLA, FRANK "The painterly problems . . .": Lecture at Pratt Institute, Brooklyn, winter 1959–1960. Reprinted in Robert Rosenblum, *Frank Stella* (Baltimore: Penguin, 1971).

STELLA, JOSEPH "Seen for the first time . . .": "Brooklyn Bridge, a Page of My Life," *Transition* 16 (June 1929).

STILL, CLYFFORD "That pigment on canvas . . .": Letter (1952) in *Fifteen Americans* (exhibition catalogue), Museum of Modern Art, New York, 1952.

STREICHMAN, YEHESKIEL "I do not think . . .": *Art in Israel* (exhibition catalogue), Museum of Modern Art, New York, 1964.

STRZEMINSKI, WŁADYSŁAW "I define art . . .": Statement (1923) in *Constructivism in Poland 1923–1926* (exhibition catalogue), Essen, 1976.

SVANBERG, MAX WALTER "One can only reach . . .": *Dokumentation* (exhibition catalogue), Konsthalle Malmö, Sweden, 1979.

TAL-COAT, PIERRE "Prior to the naming . . .": Statement in Muriel Emanuel et al., eds., *Contemporary Artists*, 2nd ed. (New York: St. Martin's Press, 1983).

TAMAYO, RUFINO "Outside of Orozco . . .": Emily Genauer, *Rufino Tamayo* (New York: Abrams, 1974).

TÀPIES, ANTONI "Then came the time . . .": Roland Penrose, *Tàpies* (New York: Rizzoli, 1979). Reprinted by permission of Rizzoli INT Publications.
"Outworn forms cannot contribute . . .": Alexander Cirici, *Tàpies: Testimony of Silence* (New York: Tudor, 1972).
"The artist will always be . . .": Penrose, *op. cit.* Reprinted by permission of Rizzoli INT Publications.

TATLIN, VLADIMIR "1. The lack of variation . . .": *Art Out into Technology* (exhibition catalogue), Moderna Museet, Stockholm, July–September 1968.

TINGUELY, JEAN "Modern Art: Playing . . .": "Art Is Revolution" (extract from *National Zeitung*, Basel, October 13, 1967). Reprinted in K. G. Pontus Hulten, *Jean Tinguely* (London: Thames & Hudson, 1975).

TOBEY, MARK "Line became dominant . . .": Letter to Katherine Kuh (October 28, 1954) in Kuh, *The Artist's Voice* (New York: Harper & Row, 1960).
New York. 1944. National Gallery of Art, Washington; gift of the Avalon Foundation.

TORRES-GARCÍA, JOAQUÍN "One day [Amédée] Ozenfant said . . .": *Universalismo Constructivo* (Buenos Aires, 1944).
Constructive Composition. 1932. Museum of Art, Rhode Island School of Design; Nancy Sayles Day Collection.

TUCKER, WILLIAM "Sculpture is subject to . . .": William Tucker, *The Condition of Sculpture* (London: Arts Council of Great Britain, 1975).
Rim. 1981. L'Isola Gallery, Rome.

TWORKOV, JACK "Post–World War II painting . . ." / "Above all else, I distinguish . . .": Statement in *Art in America* 61, no. 5 (1973).

UECKER, GÜNTHER "I deliberately call . . .": *Mack, Piene, Uecker* (exhibition catalogue), Kestner Gesellschaft, Hanover, 1950.

VANTONGERLOO, GEORGES "In art there are always . . .": *Paintings, Sculptures,*

Reflections (New York: Wittenborn & Schultz, 1948). Reprinted by permission of Wittenborn Art Books, Inc.

VIEIRA DA SILVA, MARIA ELENA   "We are talked to . . ." / "When I am before my painting . . .": *The New Decade: 22 European Painters and Sculptors* (exhibition catalogue), Museum of Modern Art, New York, 1955.

VISSER, CAREL   "At a given moment . . .": *Dutch Art and Architecture Today* (Amsterdam), no. 7 (June 1980).

VOSTELL, WOLF   "What fascinated me . . .": *Collage to Assemblage* (exhibition catalogue), Institute of Modern Art, Nuremberg, 1968.

WALKER, JOHN   "I didn't want . . .": Interview with Tony Godfrey and Adrian Searle in *Art Log* (Winchester), no. 1, 1978.
Form and Skull I. 1983. Collection of Gerald S. Elliott. Photograph courtesy of M. Knoedler & Co., Inc., New York.

WILMARTH, CHRISTOPHER   "Light gains character . . .": *Nine Clearings for a Standing Man* (exhibition catalogue), Wadsworth Atheneum, Hartford, 1975.
Gnomon's Parade (Late). 1980. The Edward R. Broida Trust, Los Angeles. Photograph courtesy of Hirschl & Adler Modern, New York.

WOLS (ALFRED OTTO WOLFGANG SCHULZE-BATTMANN)   "To believe in nature . . .": Peter Inch, ed., *Aphorisms and Pictures* (Kent, England: Arc, 1971).
Vegetation. 1947. Whereabouts unknown.

WOTRUBA, FRITZ   "The point of working . . ." / "A good piece of sculpture . . ." / "The question arises . . ." / "Technique today . . ." / "I dream of a sculpture . . .": Haakon Chevalier, trans., *From the Private Notebooks*.
Standing Figure. 1958. Photograph courtesy of Marlborough Gallery, New York.

ZARITSKY, YOSSEF   "To be a painter . . ." / "Nobody is painting . . ." / "Art is the one . . ." / "The painter, in my opinion . . .": Interview in *Ha'aretz* (Tel Aviv), March 2, 1984.

INDEX

Page numbers in *italics* refer to illustrations.